IGN\TE
forgiveness

We invite you to enjoy the many other International
best-selling books from the Ignite series

———————

Ignite Your Life for Women

Ignite Your Female Leadership

Ignite Your Parenting

Ignite Your Life for Men

Ignite Your Life for Conscious Leaders

Ignite Your Health and Wellness

Ignite Your Adventurous Spirit

Ignite Female Change Makers

Ignite the Modern Goddess

Ignite Happiness

Ignite Love

Ignite Your Inner Spirit

Ignite the Entrepreneur

Ignite Possibilities

Ignite the Hunger in You

Ignite Your Life for Women (2nd Edition)

Ignite Your Wisdom

IGNITE Forgiveness

A JOURNEY IN FORGIVENESS, PEACE, AND INNER HARMONY

FOREWORD BY

Dame Doria Cordova

Owner of the Excellerated Business
School® and Money and You®

INTRODUCTION BY

Lady JB Owen

Founder and CEO of Ignite Publishing
and JBO Global Inc.

PROJECT LEADERS

Tish Meehan

International best-selling author
Transformational Soul Coach & Spiritual
Mentor, Divine Channel, Healer

MaryAnn Swan

International best-selling author
Founder A Gathering of Hearts,
Transformational Coach

ADDITIONAL FEATURED AUTHORS

ASH BHADANI • CANDACE BLICK-GEURTSEN • CYNTHIA FONTAINE
DIANE LEMIRE • DIANA LOCKETT • DIANNE VENIT • EMILY THIROUX-THREATT
GORAN KARNA • HOLLI SOLLENBARGER • JAYNE POWELL • JEFFREY BENTON
JERRY TUCKER • KAREN WILSON • KATHERINE DAVIDSON • KRISTEN CONNELL
KRISTEN SVETS • MELANIE SUMMERS • MICHELLE MCCLAIN • MORGAN MCNEIL
SHELINA MANEK • SILVIA HLAVENKOVA • TENISHA GRAHAM • WANDA ZAYACHKOWSKI

PUBLISHED BY IGNITE PUBLISHING AND PRINTED BY JBO GLOBAL INC.

Published by Ignie Publishing and Printed by JBO Global Inc.
5569-47ᵗʰ Street Red Deer, AB
Canada, T4N1S1 1-877-677-6115

Editor-in-Chief JB Owen
Book and Cover design by Dania Zafar
Edited by Alex Blake, Michiko Couchman, and Mimi Safiyah

Designed in Canada, Printed in China

ISBN 978-1-7923-8765-4

First edition: Nov 2022

Ordering Information: Quantity sales. Special discounts are available on quantity purchases by corporations, associations, and others. For details, contact the publisher at the above address. Programs, products, or services provided by the authors are found by contacting them directly.

Dedication

This book is dedicated to all those who have forgiven,
and all those who are ready to forgive.

To learn and grow
We must let go
Then we free our soul

When people treat us wrong
Our narrative plays sad songs
And we struggle to move along

The weight we carry today
Can cause our future delay
And lead us to more pain

When we give in and let go
It will allow our minds to grow
We can enter a state of flow

Forgiveness is the key
It's the secret to setting the past free
We can plant the roots to grow our tree

The unforgiving
Will disrupt our living
Until we get a new beginning

It takes strength to face the facts
Our past pain becomes plaque
And becomes the things that hold us back

Take the time to lean in
This is where you begin
It's the first step to your wins

Take the time to work on your past
This will allow the future to last
And turn life into a blast

Written by Jerry Tucker

TESTIMONIALS FROM AUTHORS

After having been a writer for many years, working with Ignite awakened a new passion for me to write differently and more than I have before; everyone at Ignite is bright and kind. This is a wonderful company to work with.

~ Emily Thiroux Threatt

The healing that has occurred as I have written my story and processed it through the amazing editing sessions has been life-changing. Absolutely amazing experience writing with Ignite. From my fellow authors to the editors to the Ignite team, everyone has been so welcoming and supportive.

~ Candace Geurtsen

Ignite gave me a roadmap to my healing journey and facilitated the acceptance of my past with awareness and compassion. They held me accountable with love and sources for my author's journey. Exceptional is the word that helps me to define their team.

~ Ash Bhadani

Once again, I have had the pleasure of contributing to the Ignite series in this beautiful and tender edition about Forgiveness. This is my second time writing for Ignite, and it has been a wonderful experience with the support and encouragement of a great team. Their tried and true systematic and professional approach to drawing out the best from their authors ensures another impactful and inspiring publication with stories that will bring comfort and insight to many. I'm honored to share these pages with such amazing people and gifted writers. Thank you, JB, and your wonderful team!

~ MaryAnn Swan

Writing with Ignite helped me discover my writing style and taught me how to write with ease.

~ Dr. Silvia Hlavenková

I never thought I'd get the chance to write about my journey, but the Universe literally handed this opportunity to a few amazing people and me. The amazing editors shaped my story and helped me in more than one way. I am beyond grateful for this amazing opportunity.

~ Morgan McNeil

Beautifully supportive. Working with JB and the entire team at Ignite has been a transformational healing process. I felt completely cared for, listened to, honored, and gently guided during the writing process. I had been trying to write for many years but found my many stories were too much for one book. Learning how to craft your story so that it makes sense to the reader, having a thread that runs all the way through the story, and understanding how not to leave the reader hanging was a game changer. This was my second writing experience, and it would be impossible to compare the two! Working with Ignite is a dream come true! Best team you will ever work with!

~ Cynthia Fontaine R.SPE.B

I have always had a dream of writing my first book. Like many authors, our first book is the hardest, and like so many, the first book never gets published. By aligning myself with the Ignite Team, I could write my chapter easily, and the process flow was very planned out and awesome. I was initially skeptical and scared due to the price and commitment to writing my Chapter. As I went, I realized I got more value than I spent, and my fears would hold me back until I moved past them. This was the best investment in my life because it was an investment in me and bringing my dream to life. Now that I have my first Collaboration book complete, I can start writing the books that the world needs to see.

~ Jerry Tucker

Writing my Ignite Your Forgiveness story has been transformational in so many ways. By putting pen to paper, I have been able to take the pieces of my life that have been weighing on me and bring them together to create a beautiful healing. The love, compassion, and support that I received from the Ignite team and fellow authors made it easier to tell my story, which has weighed heavy on my heart.

~ Tish Meehan

My experience of writing with Ignite is nothing less than fabulous! What publisher gives you weekly training on how to write to your audience? JB Owen and her team are considerate professionals. JB dedicated her time throughout the process on a weekly call to share her mindset and guide us in becoming successful authors. Her team of editors gave us one-on-one time with them to go over our work and help us make our stories compelling from the readers' point of view. Wow! A great experience! Thank you for helping get my story published!

~ Karen Louise Wilson

Contents

WHAT IS AN IGNITE BOOK?

BY LADY JB OWEN

The very word *Ignite* signifies the intention of our books and describes the goal behind all the stories we share. We see our books as gifts to the world. Every book we publish is created with the desire to inspire, uplift, and *Ignite* the reader toward something greater within themselves. We believe that our books, and the stories inside them, bridge gaps and foster deep connections. Each story that is divinely shared becomes a beacon for what is possible for every person on our planet.

Now, more than ever, we need to find hope and inspiration in one another. We need to know that life, with all its challenges, has more meaning than just day-to-day events. Ignite believes that stories, and the heartfelt sharing of them, is the key not only to bringing people together, but to heal humanity on a global scale. Stories speak directly to the heart of the reader and touch them in a profound way. Honest and authentic stories open the mind and expand compassion, connection, and the understanding that we all desire. The stories in this book have been created to do just that. To awaken the mind, while speaking directly to the heart and instilling a new sense of connection, opportunity, and possibilities.

As you begin reading the upcoming pages, you will find that every story starts with a *Power Quote*. It is a self-affirming, self-empowering statement designed to make you ponder, push you forward, and encourage you to break outside your comfort zone. Power quotes are phrases that offer encouragement, insight, and hope. They are meaningful statements intended to provoke thought, Ignite ideas, spark action, and evoke change. Every power quote is written to Ignite something in you, so you can be all that you desire to be.

Since this book is all about forgiveness, these power quotes are designed to inspire just that. They are written with the hope that whatever you have gone through, or are going through, you can embrace forgiveness and move forward feeling more in harmony.

Below the power quote, you will find each author's personal *Intention*. These are the individual insights and genuine wishes that the author wants to share with you. The power quote is the wisdom behind the reason for writing their story, filled with purpose and meaning. Each author desires to IGNITE something powerful in you, and they share that lovingly in their intention. From the beginning of their chapter, they want you to know what they wish their story will do for you.

After the intention, you will read the author's transformational *Ignite Moment*. It is a genuine account of how the author went through their journey to emerge with a greater expression of themselves. Through their unique experiences and circumstances, the authors explain how their Ignite Moment transformed them, awakened them, and set them on a new trajectory in life. They reveal their honest feelings and share their personal discoveries. They give an insightful account of a precise moment that resulted in deep internal compassion and valuable forgiveness.

We all have Ignite Moments that change us, define us, and set us forth on a wonderful new journey of inner exploration. These stories derive from those moments and are told in the most endearing and heartfelt way. They show us that *life-altering* situations are designed to impact us in a way that inspires us to step into the person we were born to become. Ignite Moments are universal and transcend all barriers. They allow us to be more connected on a deeper level, and in many ways show how we are all One.

Once you have read the story and discovered the author's gems of wisdom, you will find their exciting *Ignite Action Steps*. Each author shares a powerful, doable action that you can use to move yourself toward greater forgiveness and new understandings that will benefit you. Each action step is an idea, process, and practice that has been successful in the author's life. The goal is for you to implement that step into your life and manifest positive change. Each Ignite Action Step is different and unique, *just like you*, and each has proven to have amazing results when done diligently and consistently.

As you sit down to read this book, know that it is not required you read it in the traditional way; by starting at the beginning and reading through to the end. Many readers flip to a page at random and read from there, trusting that the page they landed on holds the exact story they need to read. Others glance over the table of contents, searching for the title that resonates with them. Some readers will go directly to a story recommended by a friend. However you decide to read this book, we trust it will be right for you. We know that you may read it from cover to cover in one single sitting, or you might pick it up and put it down a dozen times. The way you read an Ignite book is as personal as every story in it, so we give you complete permission to enjoy it in whatever way fits you.

We ask that if a story touches you in some way or inspires your heart, you reach out and tell the author. Your words will mean the world to them. Since our book is all about Igniting humanity, we want to foster more of that among all of us. Feel free to share your sentiments with the authors by using their contact information at the end of each chapter. There isn't an Ignite author who wouldn't love to hear from you and know how their story impacted your life. And, if a story speaks to you profoundly, we encourage you to share it with someone special in your life, as that story may just be the exact thing that they need to hear.

We know that the phrase 'Ignite Moments' will now become a part of your vocabulary. You'll begin to think about your own impactful moments and the times in your life that Ignited you in a new way. If sharing your story feels important, or the idea of writing your Ignite Moment is percolating to the surface, please reach out to us. We believe every person has a story, and everyone deserves to be seen, heard, and acknowledged for that story. If your words are longing to come forth, we want to be there for you to make it happen. Our desire is to Ignite a billion lives through a billion words and share seven billion Ignite Moments. We can only do that by publishing Ignite Moments from people like you!

Inside the pages of this book, you will find a part of your story, thoughts, worries, wishes, ideas, and dreams. Somewhere within these pages will be a reflection of *your* journey and the Ignite Moments you have felt. We know this because Ignite stories represent the stories in all of us. It doesn't matter where you live, your skin color, your gender, or how much money you have in your pocket, Ignite stories reflect everyone. They are stories of the human condition; they touch the very essence of what makes us human and our powerful human experience. They bring us together, showing us that our stories do not define us but, instead, refine who we can become.

As you turn the page, we want to welcome you to the Ignite family. We are excited for what is about to happen, because we know the stories in this book will inspire forgiveness in yourself and others. As you dive into the upcoming pages, a million different emotions will fill your heart, and a kindred spirit with our authors will be established. We know that this will be a book that both awakens and inspires, transforms, and motivates.

May you be loved and supported from this page forward, and may all your Ignite Moments be filled with both joyful lessons and heartfelt blessings.

INTRODUCTION

BY LADY JB OWEN

Founder and CEO of Ignite

THE MEANING OF FORGIVENESS

Forgiveness is one of those beautiful yet complicated words. On one hand, it means to pardon and release a wrongdoing or offense. On the other hand, it means to forgive a sin or overlook a transgression. Forgiveness asks you to look beyond the fault of another and allow ease and kindness to filter in. It asks you to move beyond a misdeed and grant more understanding. Offering ease, sympathy, and compassion toward an offense, misdeed, or sin is not always easy to achieve. One can forgive a child for tipping over a glass of milk or look beyond a gardener who trimmed the hedges too low. It is easy to forgive infractions such as a person stepping on your toe, a colleague bumping into you while carrying a cup of coffee, an airline losing your luggage, or a stranger putting a dent in your car. It is when we get into the more difficult, painful, personal violations that we struggle to forgive. Many of us forgive the simple stuff yet harbor and hold back on forgiving for the bigger things for many years, sometimes even decades.

Forgiveness is both taught and learned. It is a process we have witnessed from our parents and observed in the world around us. We learned about it in church, on television, through our teachers, and from our elders. How we were shown forgiveness is often how we administer it. If we saw forgiveness offered freely, we likely learned to do the same. If we seldom saw forgiveness, it is fair to say we probably seldom give it. Forgiveness is not a reaction that comes as easily as others. It requires much more intention and reflective decision-making. We have to consciously decide to forgive. We have to ponder, think, and move from one thought to an opposite thought, from an infraction to absolution. For many, this transition can be difficult. Feeling one way about a certain issue to then feeling the opposite can be challenging. To go from not liking a misdeed to accepting it and moving on can be a difficult shift. Depending on the degree of the infraction and what you were taught, forgiving can be easy, or it can be arduous.

How we received forgiveness also plays a factor. When you made a mistake, how were you treated? Have others graciously forgiven you? Have your transgressions been absolved, or is someone holding on to something and refusing to forgive you? The way others treat you when it comes to forgiving plays an important role in how much forgiveness you will offer in return. We treat others how we are treated. We give what we receive. If you have never felt the love, understanding, compassion, and clemency of forgiveness, you may be unwilling and reluctant to offer someone else the same.

While writing *Ignite Forgiveness,* the many facets around forgiveness were pondered and considered. As publishers and mentors, alongside the authors in the book, we spoke extensively about the complexity of forgiving and where forgiveness is required and warranted. What we came up with after much introspection is that forgiveness is a necessary process; it is not mandatory, but deeply necessary. Not for the infractor of the deed, but for the person who is holding it against them, harboring ill feelings, and is unable to live their life fully because of inner animosity. We unanimously concluded that when we forgive, we free ourselves and others. When forgiveness is offered, something beautiful transpires. It creates new opportunities, awakens further learning, builds stronger connections, and allows love into our lives. The process of forgiving is one of utmost importance, and we all agreed, that to live in our joy and happiness, forgiving is necessary.

Each individual in this book came together to write about forgiveness because they have first-hand experience of how forgiveness has impacted them. Every author in the book had a situation in which forgiveness was both transformative and necessary in their life. They had to move beyond what they had learned, push past what they had received, and decide that the only way to go forward was through forgiveness. It may have been a situation, another person, or even forgiving themself. Somewhere in their journey, something transpired that called them to open up and forgive. Situations unfolded and wrongdoings were done that forced them to consciously choose to forgive and set themselves free.

Each of these authors has shared their forgiveness process in a vulnerable and heartfelt way. All the stories in the book are true and honest accounts of how they began to forgive and how forgiveness became the catalyst for something greater. For many, it was one of the hardest decisions of their life. For some, it took years. For all, it took perseverance, compassion, growth, understanding, and willingness to release themselves of all they carried. They had to make a decision and move from *holding on* to *letting go*. It did not mean that they permitted or condoned the situation; on the contrary, these brave and caring individuals chose to forgive and pardon, to release and liberate, to unburden and empower their own loving souls.

Forgiveness is indeed a complicated concept when we resist its gifts. We believe we are doing the 'right thing' by holding onto our anger, but inside we are robbing ourselves of the blessings forgiveness brings. Within these pages, you will discover the genuine blessings woven within life's lessons and recognize the beauty beyond the hurt. You will see how, despite the many transgressions that occurred, these individuals decided forgiving was the best route. It may have been a rough and rocky process but, in the end, it brought forth a new awareness that did what forgiveness is designed to do; liberate. It released the individual from the burden they were carrying and set them on a new, more joyful path.

I invite you to enjoy the many stories you will find in this book. They run the gambit from heart-wrenching to heartfelt, from painful to peaceful, and from hurt to happiness. They show how you can feel one way and then, over time and through inner work, you can emerge on the other side. Forgiveness allows you to go forward and find gratitude, not for what happened, but for what you learned and who you became. Forgiveness causes a shift and change that ignites something new. It gives you a different perspective and a more open heart. It enables you to write a new narrative and create a more positive result. Through the forgiving process, you find inner contentment and become a better version of yourself.

Although forgiveness can appear complicated, it can be straightforward, immediate, and rewarding. It can be something you welcome into your life, while at the same time letting go of what you no longer need. If something is heavy on your heart and you are ready to forgive, let the stories within this book be the starting point for that process, and the beacon you need to take the first step. Let the lessons each of these authors have gone through be the strength you need to make your own choice. Now is the time. Use what they have shared to forge your own path to forgiveness and forgive entirely. Let the flame of forgiving spark forgiveness in you. What makes forgiveness so necessary is that when you decide to forgive, you give *yourself* the wonderful blessings of love, compassion, and understanding that you deeply deserve.

May forgiveness fill your heart and revitalize your soul. May you let the loveliness of forgiveness permeate your life and release you. Let your forgiveness create a ripple effect outward and foster more forgiveness for you and everyone.

Much love,

JB Owen

WAYS YOU CAN FORGIVE

What we like to do at Ignite is empower people. As the leaders in empowerment publishing, we pride ourselves in making sure our readers get the most out of our books. Along with powerful and captivating stories, designed to inspire and motivate, we are also dedicated to transforming and uplifting your spirit, mind, and heart.

We recognize how difficult forgiveness can be, and we wouldn't be fulfilling our mission if we didn't do our best to give you the tools and strategies you require to help you in your forgiveness journey. There are many different ways to approach forgiveness, and not one way works for everyone. Forgiveness is a process with many layers and a multitude of options that can unfold. For some it takes time, for others it takes restitution. Some need space, others need connection. Sometimes a conversation will spark forgiveness, other times a slow release will need to happen for it to fully transpire.

Whichever way forgiveness unfolds in your life, remember that it is necessary. Necessary for you to regain your power, find renewed strength, and feel complete freedom. When we release the chains that bind us and let go of the burdens we carry, we feel the exhilaration of personal liberation. It may not feel like that right now if you are still unwilling to forgive, but we hope the stories that you read here, and the tips we share, will be the starting point for more forgiveness to unfold.

In conjunction with all the forgiveness stories and Ignite Moments in this book, each of the authors has offered another forgiveness tool. In between the pages of each story is a prayer, poem, or affirmation. We felt these added mantras of support would be wonderful ways for you to begin your healing process. Reading over these special gifts and implementing them into your day will be a fabulous way for you to shift from where you are and get closer to forgiving. Read a poem each night before bedtime, say an affirmation each morning when you wake up, or say one of the prayers out loud, as often as you can, to activate more forgiveness. These added forms of evoking forgiveness are here to awaken a new perspective and welcome in the blessings forgiveness brings.

Many times the most powerful and transformative forgiveness happens within ourselves. We don't need outside confirmation nor anyone else to agree. Our forgiveness isn't about the other person, it is only about how we feel. Forgiving ourselves is a process many of us need. Letting go of the mistakes we made, the things we lost, the words we spoke, or the people we hurt, plagues our minds and prevents us from living our own enjoyment. Lack of forgiveness is like an anchor, dragging along the sea; it pulls down and keeps us from having the joy we intrinsically need.

If you are bobbing on the surface, unsure if you are ready to forgive, I encourage you to open this book to any random page. Just trust, flip the pages, and find the story that will be ideal for you to read. Have faith that the story is the right and perfect story for your healing. See the gifts within it, the hidden gems and golden nuggets forgiveness brings. Discover how that story relates to you and what learning you can gain. Try the action steps at the end, for they might be exactly what you need to help you find your desire to forgive. Taking action consistently and consecutively may be the very thing that brings forgiveness into your life.

As another way to create forgiveness, we have put together some ideas of how you can move closer to forgiving both yourself and others. Often when a difficulty occurs we struggle to forgive the other person, then we regret or blame ourselves for the part we played. Other times an affront is so hurtful that we can't seem to let go of the injustice it made. We become stuck and firm. We lock ourselves into our emotions and suffer the consequences that come when we refuse to forgive. When that happens, we block the blessings and lessons that can help us. We don't see the many gifts that are trying to unfold.

Forgiving is a personal exploration, and, like any voyage into unknown waters, it can feel both worrisome and frightening. The purpose of this book is to give you examples of others who have undergone that process and arrived triumphant on the other side. The affirmations, prayers, and poems are there to remind you how to shift your words and move your emotions into a more peaceful, forgiving place. And for those of you who like steps and processes, please enjoy the following points you can use to keep you grounded, focused, and moving toward forgiving consistently.

Read over the following steps to bring you closer to making forgiveness a part of your daily life.

F- Free Yourself

The state of your heart and mind is paramount. How you feel inside is the barometer of all that you do. When you forgive, you free yourself. You release what is no longer serving you. Forgiving isn't for the other person, it is for you. You deserve to live in peace, feel love, and enjoy contentment. When you forgive you give yourself a gift. You move beyond the confines and you free yourself.

O- Open Your Heart

An open heart is a precious gift. When the heart is full, life is bliss. Good things come to an open heart. More opportunities, possibilities, and experiences arise when the heart is open to receiving them. Heartfelt energy is always laced with love, kindness, and peace. What you feel inside is what you emulate. Let others see the openness in you and feel the gifts your open heart permeates.

R- Release What Doesn't Serve You

Like a pressure valve, you can release what no longer serves you to make room for what does. Two things cannot occupy the same space at the same time. If you release what doesn't serve you, you make room for the things that do. Welcome in newness by removing the old. Allow yourself to release what you have been holding onto so that you have the capacity to enjoy something new.

G- Give to Get

An irrefutable law that always applies, is how we must give to get. We must give first to receive in return. We must give to ourselves, family, friends, co-workers, neighbors, and even strangers. Giving is a commodity we all have and that accumulates. The more you give, the more you get. Give your time and talents, your wisdom and observations. Give your joy and laughter, your acceptance and harmony. Most importantly, give your grace and understanding to yourself. When you give that, all will be given in return.

I- Invite in Peace

Forgiveness creates peace. It shifts the way things were to the way things are meant to be. You must choose to be in a state of peace. You must call peace in. Peace is a decision we create. It comes from intention, deciding to honor it. It grows with desire, choosing to cherish it. It expands with conviction, making it important. It comes when you forgive and commit. If you desire peace, invite it into your life.

V- Visualize Love

Love is the highest vibration. Through love, miracles can happen and change can occur. The greatest step in forgiving is the step toward love. Loving yourself enough to feel free. Loving others enough to forgive their mistakes. Loving the world and knowing that forgiveness and peace will benefit humanity. When we love, we fill ourselves with the highest vibration which attracts love, creates love, and manifests more love in you and everyone around you.

E- Expand Forgiveness to Everyone

You are the catalyst for change. What you do creates a chain reaction in those around you. When you forgive, you move the molecules and shift the energy. People cannot help but feel the difference, and your new state will inspire them. Your forgiveness will spark forgiveness in someone else. Your actions will permeate outward without you even knowing it. Your forgiving will free someone else to do the same. We are all interconnected on many levels and when one forgives it opens the way for more to forgive. Be that person; be the one who starts the chain of forgiveness. Expand your willingness to forgive and know that by forgiving one person, many more will be forgiving in return.

"To forgive is to give, so give it all you got." ~ *JB Owen*

Dame Doria (DC) Cordova

Foreword

by Dame Doria (DC) Cordova

Owner of the Excellerated Business School®
and Money and You®

"The number one tool to self-mastery is forgiveness."

Forgiveness has been a discipline that has taken me through a profoundly transformational journey. At moments, I have witnessed a wondrous result — almost divine! At other times, it has taken me many years to see the blessings and the benefits.

Ultimately, forgiveness has brought me tremendous peace and an understanding of others. You could say that forgiveness has allowed me to 'make things right,' as taught in the sacred *Ho'oponopono* forgiveness process that I have been practicing since November 1984.

There's so much I can say about forgiveness because the practice has changed my life. It has allowed me to constantly elevate my 'deservability' level to create more success and prosperity in my personal and business life.

I am honored to be invited to do the foreword for this powerful book, *Ignite Forgiveness,* and I encourage you to devour every word in every chapter. Each story is a gift from the author that provides us with an opportunity to learn from the experience. Sharing with others what we have learned from our mistakes, corrections, and redemptions can save us from tremendous pain, suffering, and separation from those we love.

Forgiveness is the key to a purpose-driven life. It allows us to speak more lovingly and take actions that are congruent with a life of integrity. That alone will bring you tremendous respect, appreciation, and admiration from others.

One of my greatest experiences of forgiveness takes me back to my early '30s when I embarked on a 5,588-mile trip from Los Angeles, California, to Santiago, Chile, to find the man whom I used to call 'the sperm donor.' When people asked me a question about my father, I used to shock them with my response, "Oh, you mean the sperm donor." Sometimes they would nervously laugh, and it wouldn't take long for me to willingly explain why I was calling this human who had given me life by such a contemptuous name.

And, as many know, the learning experiences that are offered by the Universe can lead us to 'complete' with the precious people in our lives, such as our parents, family members, and business associates — anyone from whom we may have felt dishonored, hurt, taken advantage of, or abused by. Some of those incidents could live in our consciousness forever until cleared. I believe that when the Universe gives us a lesson or a situation to heal through forgiveness, it's wise to see it through.

To give you a little background, I started running a business at the age of twenty-nine that, to this day, I still own. When I think of how young I was, and had it not been that I was surrounded by masters and experts in business who guided me, I may have had tremendously tough learning experiences, which, thank God, I didn't. Through their support, I was (and continue to be) blessed. One of our programs is a live three-and-a-half day event called *Money & You* which in the early '80s was only presented in the USA. Now it is mostly presented in the Asia Pacific region.

It was at one of those events that I had the experience of falling in love within five minutes with a total stranger — a participant in one of my programs. And, he was married.

That was the beginning of the Universe testing me on my understanding of one of the most important principles taught in our programs: *Integrity*. This was my test to see if I was really committed to 'walking the talk' by practicing it in real life.

I am a student of Dr. R. Buckminster (Bucky) Fuller, the great visionary, engineer, inventor, mathematician, philosopher, author, designer, scientist, 'cosmogonist,' and new-world thinker. One of the most profound teachings I learned from him was to live a life of integrity.

I found myself in this love situation while I was running one of the most magnificent entrepreneurial business training companies. For this reason,

I felt that this was a test of my commitment to my work and my integrity.

The fact that I was in a situation where I could be 'the other woman' and be in a relationship with a man whom I loved so deeply tested every part of my being. There was no way that it was acceptable. Growing up in Chile in the '50s, it was common for my family to label the other woman who had relations with my father as a "horrible woman who had taken my father away." There was no way in heaven that I was going to become that hated figure and break up a marriage.

In addition to studying the principles that Bucky Fuller taught us and that our work was based on, I started learning and practicing spiritual principles. I knew that *God makes no mistakes*, so when I walked away from the man that I was so deeply in love with, it was one of the most painful experiences in my young life.

As I was healing, knowing that I had no choice but to choose integrity, I kept asking myself, *What is the lesson I am to learn from this?* It dawned on me that this had to be related to my father, Mario. I realized I needed to find him, speak with him, and share how I felt. I wanted to express that it was one of the toughest experiences of my life. I wanted him to know how resentful and upset I was when he exited my life and became a ghost when I was just three years old. To share my memories of the yearly visits when he would bring me a Danish treat, which still reminds me of him when I see them in special bakeries. And, most importantly, I wanted to share how hurt I was that he had several other families and children with other women and had not been responsible for any of us except possibly the family he had finally settled with. The man was an irresponsible Casanova! *What a loser!* I told myself. This was my belief, and I felt constantly gripped by feelings of resentment.

The miracles began as soon as I decided it was time to find my father.

He lived with his family in my homeland, Santiago, Chile. It took three minutes for the international operator to find his number. I couldn't believe it! Nervously, I called. A young man answered the phone, so I introduced myself, "I'm Mario Cordova's daughter, who now lives in the U.S., and I'm looking for Mario." The voice on the other end suddenly sounded very happy. He said, "I am your little brother. I know exactly who you are. Our father always talks so highly of you. He misses you so much. He will be so happy to know that you are looking for him!"

I was blown away by his loving voice and the realization that I had just spoken with my half-brother whom I had never met! Out of the ten of us children born to four different women, I had only met my eldest half-brother. I vaguely recalled having played with other children who were my half-brothers and sisters at our grandmother Lola's home, but I didn't really remember them.

The miracles continued to unfold. He shared with me that they had moved out of that house a week earlier, but had left cans of paint inside, and he had come in for only one minute to pick them up when the phone rang. And just so you understand the amazing timing of this call, in Chile in the '80s it would take years to get phones installed in homes. Once you moved and your phone was disconnected, the number wasn't transferred. It may have taken years for me to have found him! It was meant to be...

My desire to forgive had started creating miracles.

We made plans for my father to return to that empty house the next day at the same time so that I'd have the chance to speak to him. It went so much better than we had planned. We spoke; we both cried. I shared that I was willing to fly to Santiago to visit with him and get to know him now that I was an adult. I had much to share and wanted to create a father-daughter relationship. The last time I saw him was when I was fifteen years old. Seventeen years had passed.

The healing had begun. From the moment that I landed in Santiago five months later, I began to experience the loveliness of my homeland. I was very emotional while I was in line to go through customs. As I began to cry, several women approached me to ask if I was okay. I found out that in Chile at that time you didn't get to cry alone, it was everybody's business to ensure you were okay. When I shared with those hugging me that I had not seen my father for seventeen years and that I was going to meet my brothers, sisters, and their children for the first time, they were so happy! Just like in a movie, they started telling everyone around us why I was crying. There was a sense of celebration! They were all shaking their heads with approval and were joyous that this family reunion was about to occur. It was truly a beautiful experience. I felt loved and supported by total strangers.

I found out that I just wanted to know my father, and that I had missed him so deeply. Not until his passing in 2001 did my 'search for Mario' end. As a child, I looked for him everywhere. Though, I had an *adopted* father, my Papito Pedro, whom I knew as my 'daddy-next-door.' He was a wonderful neighbor who had fallen in love with me as an eighteen-month-old when we first moved to my childhood neighborhood. He treated me as his own daughter and we loved each other deeply, especially after his eleven-year-old passed away from diphtheria. I became a permanent fixture next to him. Even then, I still longed for my real father.

There are many facets to share about that visit; it was beyond my dreams. I spent a couple of hours every day walking alone with my father and asked him about the many things I had been curious about. There was only one question he wouldn't answer. He wouldn't tell me where he went every afternoon. He said, "It's none of your business." I honored his response.

After those daily walks, learning about each other, and sharing my judgments with him, including the sperm donor title that I had given him out of unresolved resentments, my relationships with my male business partners and associates, as well as my personal relationships, changed for the better. I became much more present, and I didn't feel abandoned. I never again fell in love with a married man. The healing affected every area of my life.

This was a process of forgiveness in action, and it changed my life. I experienced forgiveness at the core of my being. Plus, some other beautiful things came out of that first trip: I got a new extended family. My brothers and sisters were so beautiful, their children were fun and smart, and they loved me, their new auntie. All the Cordova's have the same 'Mario eyes.' It was so fun for me, as an only child until fourteen years old, to now have more brothers and sisters. I have a beautiful half-sister on Mama's side, whom I adore.

The intention to heal with my father worked. It was divine to have the experience of a relationship with my real dad, as opposed to one that I had made up and formed beliefs about; my inner child was content.

I took another trip to see my father and new family years later; our oldest brother and I invited the family to go to the seashore and spend a few days together. It was extraordinary.

Forgiveness had worked its magic!

Years later, I met an additional family, one more brother and another sister. I am yet to meet one last brother. When we sat down to share about our lives and the experiences of our father, I learned much more about him. There was no judgment in my consciousness; I just wanted to know all about him.

Mario was a man of his time. I once had a conversation with my mother when I first started working on my mother and father issues. She was wondering why I wanted to go back and see him someday, why I wanted to get to know him. She said, "Why are you so resentful of him? I am not. That's the way things were in the '40s and '50s. We accepted it, so why don't you?" Now that I look back to that conversation, I realize that if Mama had forgiven him, why not me? I should have traveled to get to know my father earlier in my life!

I forgive myself for that. I forgive myself for how mean-spirited I acted toward others when I didn't understand the power of forgiveness. I was so hurt from the loss of my beloved at the young age of eighteen years old and the later miscarriage of our baby. I was so hurt and angry with God when, on top of losing my fiance and baby, I lost an additional thirteen friends in just three years. I didn't understand that life has its ups and downs. I didn't know how to handle loss, and I certainly didn't know that the healing had to happen from within.

Thank God for the human potential movement that I stepped into in 1976. A movement that I was there to witness the start of, and I became a leader in through entrepreneurial education. My destiny was to bring consciousness to business — and in the process, I had to start forgiving.

First, I started with others — that was easier. When it came to forgiving myself, that was a whole other story. It took patience, studying, and learning. Ultimately, it wasn't until I learned the *Ho'oponopono* prayer from the great Kahuna (keeper of the secrets) Lapa'au (the priest who heals with words) Morrnah Simeona that I truly began to understand the power of forgiveness. To this day, I still do the prayer often and share it with my global network.

I have forgiven many others now. Several who unintentionally hurt me, disrespected me, and even tried to hinder the beautiful work that I have been privileged to bring to the world. Now that I understand myself so deeply, I can understand them too.

Now my heart is peaceful. When upsets and resentments come to the surface, I can do the work. I know that not forgiving others affects me much more than it does them. And believe me when I tell you, it's not easy at times.

Forgiveness is my number one tool for self-mastery. The precessional (ripple) effect of forgiveness is timeless. It's eternal. It's wonderful. It's magical. I highly recommend it!

Devour this book and learn from these inspiring human beings. Allow yourself the gift of forgiveness and watch your life expand into more love, success, prosperity, and peace. Let forgiveness *Ignite* your life and guide you to become the human being you were meant to be.

Let the power of forgiveness take you to your dreams, encourage you to reach your goals, and inspire you to be healthy, vibrant, and loving. To create wealth, to make a difference to others, to have a positive impact on the world, and who knows, maybe you were meant to solve a huge problem, or you will simply empower others to empower themselves.

Just go for it… you have nothing to lose when forgiveness drives your heart, mind, and soul… May the force of forgiveness be with you!

Aloha Nui Loa,

Dame Doria (DC) Cordova
CEO/Owner Excellerated Business Schools®/Money & You®
www.MeetDoria.com

IGN TE
Forgiveness

Lady JB Owen

LADY JB OWEN

"To forgive is to give to yourself, so give it all you got."

My intention with my story is to speak to all those who struggle with forgiving themselves. This story is for those who harbor negative feelings and hold themself to the flame of guilt and fault. I want my story to share with you the freedom and liberation that comes when you decide to forgive yourself and realize the job you did and the effort you gave was more than enough. Recognize that the decisions and the actions you chose unfolded exactly as they should have. You took the steps and made the choices to get you right here in this moment, with this book in your hand, on the brink of learning how you can forgive and liberate yourself.

BEYOND MOMMY GUILT

It was a beautiful sunny morning as I stepped off the plane and scurried through the airport. There was a certain glee in my step and an eagerness in my breath as I quickly made my way through the baggage claim, purposefully not bringing any luggage. My carry-on would get me there faster and outside sooner, so I could be standing in the pickup lane waiting for my son. I had not seen my son in almost three months. Three important months, as he had just moved to a new city after graduating high school. He was only seventeen and had traveled 1,600 kilometers away to start his new 'adult' life. Finally, I was getting to see him after what seemed like forever.

Dodging loaded baggage carts, a stroller carrying twins, and a couple holding hands, I maneuver my way through the crowd to quickly find his car. He had followed in my footsteps, moving away from home right after high school ended. He wanted his independence, his freedom. He was enthusiastic to 'make' something of himself and had started working right away. I was nervous, to say the least. He was my oldest child, but still my baby in my heart. This was the first time we had been apart this long, and I felt 'out of tune' with his every move compared to how I had been 'in tune' with his entire life over the last seventeen years. Not knowing where he went, whether he was home in bed at night, or who he was hanging out with had me worrying constantly. I knew he was responsible, but his new independence and this lengthy separation made me both anxious and excited to see him.

As I waited for him to arrive, I felt my heart racing. I couldn't wait to hug him and see how much he had grown. There was so much to catch up on, and I wanted to hear everything he'd been doing. As the traffic moved at a crawl and arriving passengers filled the sidewalk with friendly greetings, I waited as if it was Christmas and he was the biggest present about to be delivered by Santa Claus.

As each car passed and I scanned the windshields to see if it was him, I thought about all the times he had waited for me. I felt a pang of guilt knowing I was a busy mom, and when he was young, he often had to wait for *my* arrival. But he always did so with joy on his face and delight in his step. He would light up the minute I showed up, and all the waiting he had done was immediately forgiven. I remember when he was three years old, and I came home from the hospital with his little sister; his hug was so big and exuberant that it knocked me over as I knelt down to greet him. We both lovingly tumbled to the ground laughing and locked in a tight embrace. I cried tears of happiness as I kissed his bright and beaming face. The love he showed me that day, and so many days after, has been the greatest love I have ever experienced and it always moves my heart.

Now, it was me who couldn't wait to 'knock him over' in my tight embrace. I could feel tears of happiness stinging the back of my eyes as all the feelings I had for him flooded to the surface. Of course, now the roles were reversed. His day was filled, his calendar overflowing, and I was the one waiting for him to come and collect me.

As I texted to ask how far away he was, I reminisced about all the ways he had been there to support me and his precious little sister. When I left his father, he did the best a five-year-old could to take care of us. He decided in his heart he would be the brave and strong one. I knew it was a burden for him at such a young age, and I worried about the impact that would have on him in the future. I knew he was being saddled with responsibilities that he didn't deserve. But through it all he was so caring, constantly checking in to see if I was okay, if I needed anything, and if somehow he could make me laugh. When he asked me why his dad was gone, all I could say was that Mommy and Daddy needed a 'time out.' I hated myself for not having the courage to be honest with him, and I deeply regret leaving his young mind wondering, wishing, and wanting to see if his dad would ever come back.

Luckily, his loving nature spilled over to his sister and they both did their best to support me through the new life I was trying to create after my divorce. His sister was the sweet one, the 'good' one who swallowed her problems so as not to upset me. She gave everything she could with her forgiving heart, megawatt cuddles, and endless promises that she loved me more than anyone else. She took on the 'good' role as he took on the 'tough' role. She had fun emulating me, how I dressed, laughed, and spoke. She was my salvation and gave me all the freedom I needed to play, dress up, craft, create, cook, and bring acting and theater into our often stress-filled life. I relied on her joyful demeanor a lot, maybe too much. She was forever trying to keep me happy as the three of us waded through our lives as best we could. Being the one to always lighten the mood was a burden she should not have had to carry. I often felt guilty that she, too, was being burdened with more than her fair share.

Being a single mom was hard, and although I gave the kids as much as I could, my son sometimes got the worst of it, the brunt of it, and the parts of me that weren't my best. I'll admit I put a lot of heavy weight on both of my children as I navigated life by myself, yet, in many ways, he got the worst of it. His mischievous nature had him doing all kinds of silliness that young boys do; pizza boxes under the bed, the water sprinkler rigged up over the trampoline. I often lost my patience with his antics and took my lonely life out on him. When my anger hit the boiling point, I turned to my daughter, using her sweet innocence to quelch my rage. She would smile, sing a song, rub my back, pet my hair, and soothe my frazzled nerves. Although she was my reprieve, she carried the weight of helping me through my struggles and growing up faster than she should have. There were times when I knew I was relying on her too much, and inside I struggled with the worry that she might grow to resent having to take care of me.

Along with the mental and emotional struggles, I had financial and personal challenges also. The kids were often late for school, or I'd forget their lunch. Sometimes I'd be working late and get a phone call from the school to come and pick them up because I had lost track of time. I couldn't always afford the extracurricular activities their friends did, like golfing on the weekends and skiing trips during the holidays. I had to buy second-hand from time to time and be on a budget when they needed to take gifts to classmates at their birthday parties. I felt tremendous guilt over not being able to give them more. I started avoiding school events and making up excuses to hide the shame I felt inside.

Some days I could be the parent they needed and I would listen to them share about a score they had reached on their video game or a certain toy they were keen on collecting. Some days the negative noise in my own head was so loud I couldn't even hear them. Recriminations like *how I had failed, why I left their dad, how I could have given up such a good life, and whether I was making a huge mistake* played over in my head. I would lie in bed, paralyzed by my fears and questioning my decisions. My son would always come and share his next big idea to amuse me. My daughter would climb under the covers and squeeze me tight with her endless hugs. We forged through it all, the challenges and hardships. We budgeted our groceries, planned our spending, and when we had to, we hunkered down to weather out life's storms. And, inside, my thoughts were churning, my guilt was growing, and my mind was racing with all the ways I was failing them.

In my loneliness, I met a man who I thought would be a great partner, but soon enough, his addictive nature and hostile attitude plagued our home. I wanted so much to make it work that I let him return repeatedly. He was in our life one day, then gone the next, and it became both confusing and daunting for the children. One week we were laughing like a family, the next, we were stoic and alone. One day he was promising a future, the next things were flying, threats were made, and words were said that cut right to the bone. I did my best to shelter the kids, but I am not sure if it worked. My daughter would flush with sweat when he walked into the room. My son would grit his teeth. Eventually, they began to ask me *why*? "Why did you let him come back? How could you forgive him all those times? Why did you not see what he was doing, the fights, the drinking, the chaos that he caused? Why didn't you keep him away from us? Why didn't you see how horrible he was?"

Those questions haunt my very soul and I have asked myself a million times, *why did I?*

Why didn't I stop the madness and force him to go? Why didn't I see that the fighting in the bathroom, thinking the kids couldn't hear us, wasn't true? They could see the redness in my eyes after a night of crying, and sense the falseness in my voice when I pretended everything was okay. I didn't want to fail again and in that desire, I made some bad decisions. Ones I know cost my kids. Hurt them. Frightened them and made them feel unsafe. I sunk lower and packed on an even heavier burden of more guilt and remorse.

I am not proud of the fact that I tried so hard to believe the deception of an addict. My own innocence and naivety had me thinking I could fix his problems. Until, eventually, the threats turned into an assault, an arrest, him going to jail, and me picking up all the shattered pieces of his wrath. I crumbled, and yet again, my two kids were there to look after me. They sheltered so much of the pain and did their best to put Mommy back together. The stress had taken its toll on me, and for months I suffered from debilitating back pain. I couldn't get out of bed without my son helping me. My daughter was using her pink barbie camper to stand on so she could help make dinner, cooking meals at just eight years old. The two of them carried the load as they did everything they could to help me.

Eventually the pain, the suffering, and the fears of his retaliation became too much and I took my kids out of school and left the country; I had to get away. I needed a reset, a reprieve. I knew I had exposed them to so much hurt and if I was living in that much pain so were they. I had a colossal amount of guilt for bringing that man into their life. I was riddled with regrets and the shame was debilitating. I felt paralyzed by my guilt and vowed to do everything possible to make it up to them. Work was not important, earning money meant little to me. The only thing I wanted was to win back their trust, see their carefree smiles, and ensure that no matter what, they had a future filled with happiness.

For twelve months the children and I traveled, healed, and rediscovered ourselves while doing charity work. We each needed to recover and find peace and giving to others helped to facilitate that. I did my best to nurture away their sadness, and show them a new way to be. We started laughing again, smiling, playing games, and sharing more. Slowly I returned. I could once again see their efforts and hear their needs. The fog that I had been living in lifted and I began to find myself amidst their playful questions and accepting eyes. They were like a lighthouse showing me the way. For a while, I felt I needed them more than they needed me. I pushed aside the guilt and buried away the ways I had let them down. I knew what happened had left some scars but I wanted to deal with those later.

Guilt has a funny way of laying dormant for as long as it needs. Willing to wait out the long journey it takes to forgive oneself. It's able to sit idle, like a hawk watching its prey, striking only when it needs to and coming to the surface like a burning lava field when you least expect it. Every time I saw my children wince or pull back I felt it was my fault. A frown here or a comment there brought forth a barrage of guilt. If they argued, I thought it was because of him. If they clammed up and retreated, I thought it was because of me. I did everything I could to repair what I had broken.

The best thing about healing, growing, and searching for a better life is that it shows up when you least expect it. As we were traveling, I met another man; he was an honest, kind, and caring single dad. He was such a benevolent father, partner, and friend. For almost half a year we got to know each other only casually. His two kids became best friends with my two kids and I could see them all opening up. His gentle way was so inviting, and his endless patience was almost mystifying. I had never met another person like him, genuine and considerate, giving and accepting. He adored my kids and was so endearing with them. I watched him carefully making sure he would never hurt them. I was cautious and particular, making sure not to repeat my mistakes.

Slowly, over time, a deep love grew between us all and before we knew it, the six of us were moving in together. We became an instant family. Suddenly there were a lot more lunches to make and more pickup times to remember, attitudes to adjust to, and habits to work out. My new stepdaughter had to move to a different school and her heart was broken to leave her friends. She wasn't adjusting easily to the change and she wasn't happy with me. My stepson was even more upset, as it was his graduating year and he would be finishing school with strangers, missing out on his graduation ceremony back home. My guilt clamored to the surface, and I felt horrible that two more children were suffering because of me. I tiptoed around them and offered more leeway than I should have. I wasn't parenting my new stepkids, they were parenting me.

With four children in my care, I had to make some serious decisions. I could let the guilt I was feeling control me, or I could get control of it. I didn't want to feel like I was failing at being a parent and that the guilt I felt inside took precedence over the mom they needed me to be. I wanted my children to know that I cared, I was present, and I loved them very much. I wanted to build strong relationships with all of the kids. I knew I needed to devote time to each of them, separately and consistently. I had to find new ways to connect with them and show them who I was at my core, and my intentions for us all to be a happy family. Feeling guilty would accomplish nothing and the only way to support them fully was to move through what I was feeling and to start forgiving myself.

It took a while to find my way, but eventually I began to look at all I had been through. I recognized the role I played and the parts that were there to teach me more about myself. I saw not the woman who was broken, but the woman who picked herself back up. I saw the single mom who persevered, and yes, she needed her kids, but we all need someone. We can't do it alone, and I was blessed to have two children with huge hearts and forgiving dispositions. They didn't hold onto the past the way I was, and they certainly were not keeping score. I began to honor the parent I had been, genuine and open. I saw how my vulnerability enhanced their vulnerability. They weren't diminished by my weaknesses, they were empowered to become stronger. They fostered compassion and grew empathy. They welcomed the qualities we all need and became great people with truly loving hearts. Our past was part of us and I let go of feeling as if it was shameful and began to see how getting through it was hopeful, prideful, and grateful.

When it came to my stepkids, I eased off on all the expectations and worked on being a friend. I didn't let the small things become big things and I stopped coloring every situation with the massive brushstroke of guilt. As soon as I stopped feeling guilty, things-to-be-guilty-for stopped happening. Life became easier. Communication improved. Love grew, hearts opened and we found our way together on a level playing field. Being guilty was preventing me from being my authentic self. When I stopped blaming myself for every single issue and forgave myself for things outside my control, things blossomed. Getting rid of guilt made room for joy and harmony to bloom. My filtered lens of guilt and shame was fine-tuned to what was truly happening, we were all grateful and happy with being in a new family.

As the years passed we all grew, each and every one of us. I found my joy in parenting and only focused on the good. Guilt had become a useless emotion that did nothing for me or my kids. They needed me to be present, not locked in the past. I focused on building new memories, creating new connections around healthy interactions, and having beneficial conversations. I vowed to always be honest with them and share in a way that served them, not only myself. I took the time to unburden them and let them be kids again. again. We took trips to Disneyland™, the beach, the ski hill, the skating rink, and everything in between. Meals became our time to connect, cooking was a family affair, cleaning had music playing in the background, and all those pickup times were turned into a game. We found healing fun and unpacking our past a part of forging new connections with each other. I put my guilt in a proverbial bottle and let it float out to sea.

A honk from a nearby horn pulls me out of my reminiscing and I see my son driving up in the car we bought for him as his graduation present. Unable to contain myself, I run to greet him as he exits the car with his 6' 2" frame. There is that smile, that caring look, and I squeal with excitement, causing those around me to casually stare. I don't care what anyone thinks, he is my son and I am happy to see him. After much fussing and checking out his new appearance, we settle back in the car and he starts driving. He is instantly animated and full of new stories, details, and ideas about his future. He is proficient, yet relaxed, and confident despite the hectic traffic around us. He weaves his way through the city and onto the busy highway. We have a four-hour drive ahead of us, and I listen with contentment and joy to how his new life is unfolding.

I am amazed at how much he has grown, not just in stature but in his new outlook on life. He shares about his new job, his devoted work ethic, his commitment to going to the gym. He confesses a few, "You were right Mom, when you told me what life would be like living on my own." Yet, he also shares about the new books he is reading on personal growth and the podcasts he is listening to on growing a business, improving your mindset, and what it takes to become a good man. I can tell he is happy, excited, and carefree. All my mommy senses are delighted to see how confident and courageous he is, how bold and committed he is. I ease into my seat knowing that all that he has been through has made him the man he is destined to become.

I then get a text from my daughter, a loving checkup to see how long we will be attached with lots of heart emojis and a picture of her eating ice cream with my beautiful stepdaughter. She has grown into a stunning and kind young woman. Her demeanor is one of calm and caring. At fourteen, she is already the kind of person you can rely on. I sometimes see the budding therapist or counselor in her. She is always supportive and encouraging. Her childhood has shaped her into being one of the most genuine people I have ever known. I can also see the love she has for her stepsister who has bravely made the transition from not liking her new home to now loving it. She has integrated herself into the family and the community. She has honors at school, marches in the city showband, volunteers to manage the high school basketball team, walks dogs in the neighborhood, works part-time, and gives all of herself to her dreams. I love her like my own, and see how much she loves me in return. All the kids are doing amazing and I know it is because when I moved out of feeling guilty and decided to feel great about myself, it gave them permission to feel great about themselves in return.

I respond to the text with a few emojis of my own and tell them we will be there soon. Her and her stepsister are driving with my husband-to-be from the other direction to meet us at the venue where we will get married! It's been five years and it's time to make it official. We know without a shadow of a doubt that our lives, our kids, and our futures are meant to be united. The kids are gleeful, and excited that their mom and dad are becoming more than just parents, friends, and confidants. We are exchanging vows and becoming man and wife.

Before you know it I am walking down the aisle on the arm of my son, holding onto him tightly. I can feel his strength along with his care. He has been there beside me for so many years, and today I feel both his pride and confidence. All my guilt has vanished for he has truly become a loving caring individual despite those early years. At the end of the aisle I see my two beam-ing beauties in their matching bridesmaid dresses, their eyes sparkle and their smiles are infectious. Just looking at them I see their happiness. I am overtaken with joy and hold back the tears of happiness I feel inside. To see them all, my kids, so bright and so full of life, a parent couldn't be happier.

Next to them is my groom, a shining example of the most adoring man a woman could find. He has been our rock, our pillar of strength, and it is through him I found full forgiveness for myself and my past. He showed me my strength and character, not just as a parent, but as a woman and a mother. He allowed me to find my way and become who I could be. Our love has created more love and dissolved any guilt I was harboring. His journey as a single dad for six years revealed that we all do the best that we can. Parenting is not a perfect science and no one has it all figured out. He admits he made his own mistakes, but feeling guilty for them serves no purpose. Through him I was able to see the gifts that my journey took me on, and that everything that happened was part of a grander plan. Those moments of hardship brought me to this moment, surrounded by so much love.

As my husband and I say our vows, we also involve the children. Each of them stands with us at the altar as the minister takes a large ribbon and gently binds our hands together in a symbol of devoted unity. She shares how each of us have a role in the family, and precious gifts to give one another. She also explains how the ribbon is a commitment to one another and a promise to hold strong to our bond. I take a moment to look at each of their faces and run through all the memories of the past, rewriting each one as a milestone and cornerstone to bring us to this very moment in time. Everything had to happen as it did for all of us to be here, and now all the sadness and pain has been replaced with new feelings and new memories.

Forgiving myself was easy when I saw who my kids had become. Their past did not define them, it refined them into amazing human beings. As I forgave myself, I saw how everything that occurred had happened for a reason; I saw the blessings all around. I had forgiven myself completely and they too had forgiven me. The act of forgiving had freed us. All of our lives were better and the future ahead looked about as bright as bright could be.

That night after the wedding, when all the fun and joy was over, I took a moment to thank God for all the gifts he had given me. Back when I was hurting, I would pray for a better life. I would ask God to show me the way, give me the strength, and deliver me toward the salvation He had created for me. I now knew that He was listening. I knew that He held my hand through my son's hand. He comforted me through my daughter's caring embrace. He gave me new love through my new step kids and came to me through them. They were His angels and His gifts to hold me when I needed support. I had nothing to feel guilty about, God gave me these lessons, but He also provided me with my children as masterful supportive gifts that he knew I would need on this journey. He blessed me with their strength and showered me with their playful energy. Everything made perfect sense and I smiled with deep reverence knowing all of that led to this. I felt immensely grateful and deeply thankful. I forgave Him for all the times I thought He wasn't listening and knew without a shadow of a doubt that He heard me and has been with me all along. When I let go and trusted, forgave and welcomed, overcame and surrendered, I found all the divine happiness I was meant to receive.

I know many parents suffer from feelings of guilt and shame. We wish things were different, we worry about our kids and we get down on ourselves for not being perfect. As I am writing this story, I can hear my daughter getting ready for school, singing gaily in the bathroom. Her carefree willingness to sing shows how free she is. She had a really hard time growing up, but she has overcome it. Kids are resilient, brave, adaptable and they never hold grudges if you show up being authentically you. You can be the real you if you choose to forgive yourself. Let go of what you didn't do and focus on what you *did* do. Start right now, with loving more and let the past be in the past. Push through old guilt that doesn't serve you and forgive yourself. Know that everything that happened, happened perfectly.

Forgiveness can be the gateway to a bigger and brighter future. Often, when we hang on to negative emotions and live in guilt, we block off all the joy and magnificence that is trying to make its way in. Those unenjoyable feelings can get stuck, and stagnant, and keep us swirling in more of what we don't want, instead of enjoying what we do want. I like to think that forgiveness can be like a light switch, one day you decide to turn it on, and from there you let it shine the way for more forgiveness, acceptance, and understanding. Forgiving yourself is a magical transformation in your life. It is like a kaleidoscope of possibilities bursting forth. When you forgive, you open the way for all that you dream of to come in. Forgiveness is like a beacon for good to arrive and more happiness to blossom.

Start by forgiving yourself. There may have been many transgressions in your life, but forgiving yourself is the most important first step. Become your *own* hero and triumph in your life. You set the tone and declare the future you want. Forgiveness not only frees you, it becomes the playground for all that you want. Walk down the aisle of your life with the people you love, surrounded by the feelings you know are possible. Hold hands with others who care about you and give that same love in return. Bind yourself in a promise to take care of your needs and use your gifts and talents to support those around you who need you. Walk free of burdens and cast off old doubts. You've got this, you deserve this, and all that you envision is just waiting to happen for you.

The greatest gift you can receive is the gifts you give yourself. ~ JB Owen

IGNITE ACTION STEPS

It takes time for guilt to dissipate. Forgiveness is a key ingredient in that process and can help you to move from feeling guilty to feeling happy and carefree.

When you feel an excess amount of guilt, decide to sit down with it and make a conscious effort to move through it. Visualization can help with this, as guilt is an energy that needs transmuting to be released.

Sit down and 'imagine' your guilt filling up a water pitcher. Hold that guilt-filled pitcher in one hand and a similar empty pitcher in the other hand. Give your guilt a color and a texture. It might be muddy, black, and thick like molasses. It could be sparkling blue like fish scales and move like icy slush. Whatever your guilt looks like, imagine it filling one of the pitchers.

Close your eyes and then physically put your two hands out in front of you as if you are holding out both pitchers. This may feel odd because it is imaginary, but physically doing it is important to move the energy and begin to eliminate the guilt. With your eyes closed, move your hands to pour the guilt back and forth between each of the two pitchers. As you do this, envision the guilt reducing and diminishing each time you pour it from one pitcher to the next. Feel yourself forgiving the guilt itself and letting it go; disappearing into the air. Do this for as long as you need to until the guilt is removed and gone. Visualizing this process and physically doing it with your hands will begin to shift the energy around the guilt and layer in the forgiveness process. It will shift the energy and make room for all the happiness you want to welcome in.

Lady JB Owen—Canada
Founder and CEO of Ignite Publishing, Ignite Moments Media
JBO Global Inc and Lotus Liners | Award Winning Humanitarian Winner
Knighted Lady | 22x International Best-Selling Author | Publisher
Speaker | Philanthropist | Executive Producer
www.jbowen.website | www.igniteyou.life | www.lotusliners.com
ThePinkBillionaire
JB.Owen.herself
ThePinkBillionaire
JB_Owen

Through forgiveness we find peace

Through forgiving we find joy

Through forgiving fully we feel compassion

Through forgiveness we know

Through forgiveness we accept

Through forgiving we let go

Through forgiving we find ourselves

Through forgiveness we know.

Through forgiveness, we grow

Through forgiving our hearts expand

Through forgiving our life is full

Through forgiveness we know

Tish Meehan

Tish Meehan

"The journey to freedom is led by three wise teachers—
compassion, forgiveness, and love."

The pathway to forgiveness isn't always an easy one to embark upon, whether the forgiveness is for another, for a situation, or for yourself. It can actually feel like a loss of control to offer forgiveness because so often, we hold onto the pain that is created because it offers an understanding of something that is incomprehensible. It is my intention that you will discover forgiveness is a state of being that invites a release of resistance, pain, and suffering and allows movement toward personal peace and freedom.

Love is a Battlefield

The words escaped my lips, and my breath caught in my lungs as I told my husband the truth that was laying heavy in my heart. "We need to separate. I am not happy anymore, and I can't live like this."

We sat in the dining room, my hands tracing the lines in the wood of our harvest table. Hot tears ran down my face. I felt the words lay between us, disbelief on his face as he struggled to comprehend what I was saying. I stared at my hands resting on the cold, hard surface, my eyes averted from the pain I knew I was creating.

I loved that table. It always made me think of my family and holidays, making memories. I sat there at our family's gathering place, wishing I could be anywhere else. I could hear the squeals of our three kids outside, bouncing happily on the trampoline, and a wave of sadness and guilt washed over me. I was ending things because I was unhappy. *How could I do that to my family? How could I be so selfish?* These things rang through my head, but I held steady to the knowing that was clawing in my stomach. I wasn't just unhappy, I was miserable… a shell of the person I wanted to be and could be, invisible and lost in a sea of depression, anxiety, and unfulfilled dreams.

From the outside, our family looked perfect: three healthy kids, a big, beautiful home in the country, good jobs, more than most people have. I know that for those looking at us, we had it all, yet I felt a hollowness inside. There was a lot of love, laughter, and joy throughout the twelve years of marriage. I believe that most marriages start out that way, but without consistent effort, open communication, and sharing of hopes, dreams, and feelings, the spark can fade. I saw that happening, but I clung to the foundation we had created because I needed it. I needed the safety and security of my marriage, our home, and the family we had built. I had fought back the rage and resentment that had been growing inside me year after year, but a feeling of brokenness prevailed.

The day I ended my marriage, I thought I was regaining control of my life, reclaiming my identity. It was as if I was standing there, holding a grenade in my hand. I felt courage pulse through my body, a wave of adrenaline that pushed away the fear and guilt that was waiting on the sidelines for me to pick up. I pulled the pin, tossed the grenade over my shoulder, and walked away from my husband, up the stairs, and into our bedroom. I had blown the foundation of my family apart by choice. I was taking away everything my kids ever knew, and their lives would be forever changed. I knew this, and when the adrenaline faded, I was left with the devastation of what was to come and what I had to do. I had dreamt of this life for so long, where I was free to be me, to think, speak, travel, spend, and work in any way I wanted. But wave after wave of guilt, shame, sadness, and anxiety moved through me in the days, weeks, and months after I had taken that first step to move toward a life that I longed for.

An inner battle began, and the self-hatred won over every single time. I wouldn't allow my husband to take any of the blame for how things had gone sideways between us. He had suffered from anxiety and fear around money and his job, but he always came home at the end of the day and helped with the kids and the house. He didn't drink or get angry; a really great dad. But he wasn't a strong communicator. We couldn't talk about any issues, and he deflected any opportunity to engage in sharing what was truly on our minds. I felt like my words and needs weren't valid; the emotional breakdowns I was having at work were less important than the stability that my teaching career provided for him. I felt like I didn't matter. I couldn't lean on him, but I also couldn't blame him, as he chose not to reveal his feelings and pain to me despite having difficulties in his own life.

The day I moved my things out of our home was one of the hardest days of my life. It was a hot afternoon in June when I packed up the few belongings that I was taking with me to the little townhouse I had rented. I was going there alone to prepare the home for my three kids and me to live in whenever I had custody. It had been a long year filled with so much pain, heartbreak, and guilt as I dismantled my family unit in order to build a new one that I thought would be so much happier and easier. I went into the old house, through the garage, leaving the doors and trunk of my white Volkswagen open so that I could quickly put the things in that I needed. The kids were at school, and my husband was at work. I had planned it this way so I could avoid seeing them and remove my stuff without them having to watch — my clothes from the closet, my favorite lamps, and a few dishes from the kitchen that he had left out for me. I don't remember what else I took. I only remember that with every load that I hurriedly put in the car, the worse I felt. My heart ached with pain; tears mixed with sweat as I rushed to finish before the kids got home from school.

I was almost successful. I had just gotten in my car when the bus pulled up. My kids ran up the driveway, happy to see me as it had been several days since I had officially stopped living in our home. We hugged so close, the four of us, on the driveway. I felt their little arms around me, squeezing me as tightly as they could. Shame and guilt washed over me for what seemed like the millionth time since I had thrown that grenade. I looked into three sets of eyes — the lightest blue of my beautiful, soulful daughter, the tear-rimmed gray eyes of my oldest son, who stood bravely beside his siblings as if he would do anything and everything to protect them, and finally down to the deepest blue eyes of my sweet and innocent six-year-old. "I have to go now, my beautiful babies. I have to go and get our house ready for you to come to stay in a few days." Another punch to my heart as I said these words to them, the pit in my stomach heavy with angst and fear. *Am I doing the right thing?* I asked myself as we all stood on the asphalt, not knowing what to do next. I got into my car, loaded to the brim, and drove away down our long driveway, watching the kids watch me, tears streaming down my face as I smiled and waved goodbye to them, our family, and our home.

That was when I truly felt my heart shatter. I hated myself so much at that moment that I promised I would do anything and everything to make this easier on them and their father. The looks on their faces are forever etched in my heart and are my crux to bear. It was at that point that I began to beat myself up for destroying their lives. It was as though they had been collateral damage, hit by the debris from the grenade I had thrown into my marriage.

Kids are resilient, though, and mine showed signs of healing faster than I could have realized. They were getting more settled with the new routine, even with obvious hiccups as we figured out this new world we were all living in. But I was still very entrenched in the guilt of what I had put them through. I remember talking to my father about my kids shortly after I had moved into my own place, and he shared information from a radio program he had been listening to. It was about the children of divorce and how detrimental the experience was to their mental health and well-being. Then he said something to me that I will never forget. He looked me in the eyes and said, "Divorce is harder on kids than losing a parent. It's easier if one parent dies." I felt a heat rise inside of me, tears burning my eyes, yet I said nothing. That statement sunk deep into my heart, and the shame and guilt I felt grew stronger; its hold on me grew tighter. *How could he say that?* He knew the devastation we had been through when my mom died. He knew how the grief still permeated my life almost thirty years later.

When I was fourteen, my mom died of a massive heart attack. One moment she was here; the next she was gone. The bomb that had detonated when my mom died spread shrapnel through all areas of my life. She had been the center of my family, and without her, I was completely lost and emotionally fragile. I became a victim to my pain and suffering; my pathway forward seemed pointless and empty. I felt as though I was walking through a minefield, and one wrong step would blow another part of my life to smithereens. My two sisters and I were trauma bonded, and my dad was doing his best, but I fell further into the pit of an emotional wasteland. I hid behind a fake smile and became a yes person because it felt safer. When I met the man that I would eventually marry, it felt as though those gaps in my foundation were finally being filled, and I gave myself over to him to protect, stabilize, and show me the way.

That worked for a while, at least I thought it did because the pain I felt inside was diminished, yet as the years went by, the facade that I had created began to crumble, and underneath was my unstable, unhealthy base that I had built my life on. I didn't know who I was anymore. I felt angry, resentful, and powerless, the victim once again. I found myself edging closer to my forties, with three kids, a husband who didn't listen to me, and a job that was stealing my joy. I knew I had to take back control of myself, my life, and find the way forward, somehow knowing that this was becoming a *need*, not a want. I held on for as long as I could, probably longer than I should have.

As the months passed after my husband and I split up and I moved into my own place, we got into a new rhythm and routine. I bought all new furniture for my home, leaving the house I had shared with them as undisturbed as possible. I asked for very little from him because I felt I didn't deserve any financial support or money from our home. When I would try to discuss things about our separation or the kids, it was always met with resistance or a lack of response from him. But to keep things good between us, I wouldn't push, speak up, or ask for what I needed. I would tell myself to 'suck it up,' that this was the price that I had to pay. The kids struggled with drop-offs and pickups, but I always managed to plaster a smile on my face. When he would make comments about my new home or what he felt were things I needed to do better, I would grin and take it. The guilt I felt was all-consuming, so I allowed his commentary, believing it was what I deserved.

Instead of finding the freedom and possibility to begin building my new foundation, I found myself in another sort of mental and emotional prison. I felt trapped in an inner war zone, and I was my own worst enemy. I tried to make peace and find happiness in new friendships and a new romantic relationship, but the worry and shame would always take over, and I would eventually sabotage any joy that I could find. I was suffering from anxiety attacks at work, overwhelmed with the demands of my job as a teacher. I had very little energy for my kids as a darkness moved into me, and I was unable to find any light. I was miserable, lost, angry, scared, and I couldn't control it anymore. Depression and anxiety shrouded my clarity, the medication numbing the gnawing feeling in my stomach. No matter what I did to get over that battle that was raging inside of me, I still kept myself as a prisoner. I had been the judge, jury, and executioner of my choices, and the more I held tight to that, the more stuck I became. Yet there was part of me waving a white flag and a feeling of desperation that was starting to grow inside of me. *There has to be more than this.* This was the beginning of my self-realization and path to forgiveness and self-love.

Over the next year, I began to find some inner peace. The antidepressants helped me to compartmentalize everything that I had been through, and I could finally begin to process things. I spent my time going to therapy, working with coaches and spiritual mentors, and embarking on a path of growth, learning, and self-discovery. As the fog began to clear in my head and my emotions settled, I finally saw a glimmer of hope. One night my kids and I were sitting at our new dinner table, white and glossy, and we were laughing. We were talking about funny things that had happened at school, smiling about a new memory they made with their dad, and just enjoying this space we shared. As I took my first truly deep breath in ages, I began to feel a slow, steady peace wash over me, like a rising sun's warming rays. I could see that my children were settled. They were happy and thriving. I reflected on how they would come to me when they were struggling, and we were learning how to share our feelings and emotions with each other. A glimmer of hope washed over me after all the devastation.

I had to slow down and learn to be in the present moment in order to see what was right in front of my eyes. Yes, my choices had impacted their lives, and they struggled with sadness, grief, and stress from the separation. Yet, they were still happy... genuinely happy. And they saw it reflected in me, also. I remember the day when one of my children told me how much happier their dad and I both seemed now that we weren't together. They felt that we gave them more time and attention than we had when we were living together.

That was a turning point for me, even though I didn't believe it at first, thinking they were reassuring me to make me feel better. But over time, I began to see it and trust it. Their father and I could laugh and spend time together on holidays and birthdays, which we did for our kids. I was learning to stand up for myself when the old habit of saying nothing and feeling bitter and angry would start to seep back in. I was learning to heal those old patterns and my conditioning by facing them head-on — no more avoiding. I leaned into my spirituality that was growing from a hobby into a career, taking the teachings and wisdom I had learned and allowing myself to see my life through that lens, free of judgment.

I had to forgive the parts of my marriage that needed to be healed: the lack of connection, presence, and emotional support from my husband, and move toward empathy and compassion. I learned to feel the guilt and shame as it showed up and face it rather than hiding in it so that I could forgive myself. Today, I speak my truth confidently. I feel my emotions as they arise and be as authentic as I can be for my children and for myself. I haven't found the end of this path yet, but with each step, I am getting closer. I am walking off the battlefield, white flag in hand toward my own personal freedom. And the future is bright.

Walking the path of self-forgiveness requires a lot of courage and determination to live the life that is waiting for you. Give yourself permission to heal from your mistakes and the grace to see the beauty in the destruction. It doesn't always feel good, but walking through the rubble allows the deepest healing to occur and true forgiveness to emerge. You get to choose when you walk off the battlefield toward your own internal peace and joy. You get to build your life the way you want. You are the sovereign leader and have the power to liberate yourself, to rise and reclaim your divine power. To reach your highest glory of happiness and freedom.

IGNITE ACTION STEPS

The pathway to self-love and self-forgiveness is ripe with so many opportunities to grow, learn and receive.

L- Look honestly at your needs, and ask yourself these questions: Am I speaking up when I need to or staying quiet? If you are staying silent, ask yourself why and if it is serving you.

O- Stay open and present in the moment each day so you do not get lost in 'imagined' suffering. When you feel overwhelmed, pause and look around the room. Then say three things out loud that you see that are good, and acknowledge them as signs of happiness existing around you.

V- Allow yourself to experience true openhearted vulnerability by sharing all parts of yourself, the shadow and the light. Find your tribe and allow yourself to experience the love and support that emerges when you can touch the most vulnerable, raw parts of yourself.

E- Evaluate what you need in order to stay on your path to forgiveness and advocate for yourself by taking the required steps, such as going for counseling, meditating, self-reflection, positive affirmations, mirror work, and other modalities that will support you in forgiving yourself wholeheartedly and embodying your true light; your authentic self.

Tish Meehan—Canada
Transformational Soul Coach & Spiritual Mentor, Divine Channel, Healer
www.tishmeehan.com
tishmeehanspiritualhealer
iamtishmeehan

IGNITE
Forgiveness

*Sacred Light, please show me the way today, for
I am struggling to find my way forward.*

*Healing Light, please show me what is mine,
and expel what is not.*

*Help me to transcend and heal my pain with
ease and grace.*

*Loving Light, show me my own goodness,
strength, and heart.*

*Help me find the courage to stay firmly rooted
in my truth.*

*May I be grounded in your loving embrace,
now and always.*

© *Tish Meehan*

MaryAnn Swan

MARYANN SWAN

"Forgiveness is easier when you tell the truth."

I hope that as you read my words here, you'll have a new way of looking at the people in your life who you think have harmed you. May you realize what seemed to be an attack, a transgression, or a trigger was simply a nudge for you to pause, reflect, course correct, and choose your own growth. We all meander, and through my meanderings, I've come to know that my experiences are for my evolution—leading me to better versions of myself with new relationships and opportunities. This is my wish for you; that you'll come to see the beauty of your hard times and how they have contributed to the magnificent person you are today.

FORGIVENESS: AN ACT OF SELF-LOVE

Forgive us our trespasses as we forgive those who trespass against us. This line from my Catholic upbringing, the Lord's Prayer, gets me wondering. Who have I hurt? Who has hurt me?

Certainly, I've had instances where I didn't treat someone well and many, less than stellar moments that I'm not proud of in my life. As a child, there would be the typical schoolyard transgressions: speaking mean words to kids who teased me, fighting (usually in defense of my younger sister), or teasing other children just to go along with the crowd and fit in. I recall that whenever I was rude or mean to people, I would get a sick, heavy feeling in the pit of my stomach, and I could feel the adrenaline running through me. I knew it wasn't right. It wasn't my true nature to be in conflict with others. However, upon repeated taunting behaviors from bullies and in the spirit of standing up for myself, or my siblings, I would lash out verbally or with fists.

My love for my siblings was at the core of my hatred for a particular class-mate. When I was eight years old, my eleven-year-old brother passed away from complications of pneumonia. Our Catholic community rallied around my parents for his funeral, and because the school I went to was right next to the cathedral, my sister's and my classes, grades two and three, respectively, attended. I remember sitting cuddled into my mother, smelling a mixture of her Chanel N°5 and the acrid smell of incense that the priest spread over the front of the room. His booming voice recited the Latin incantations over the small white coffin draped in white lilies at the front of the aisle. My mother was so still, a tear trickling down her face, which was veiled with the lacy black shroud covering her head, and her crumpled hanky was clutched in her hand. I recall looking over at my class sitting in the overflow pews to the right of the altar. *Why were they here?* I felt like we were on display. A bunch of eight-year-olds, solemn and bewildered, glancing over at me with curious and uncomfortable expressions. *Why was my friend avoiding my gaze?* Then I noticed Connie, typically a loud and boisterous girl, catch my eye and begin giggling! I was outraged and vowed from that day forward to ignore her. I hated her for years after for her insensitivity.

Fortunately, I didn't have to stay around her much longer. We moved around a lot when I was young due to my Dad's rising career in the Canadian mining industry. September 1971, I remember walking into my fifth-grade class on the first day, having to stand at the front while the teacher introduced me. She then ushered me to my seat, and I suddenly heard "Look at her ears!" from one of the boys. The teacher's quick reprimand silenced the class's giggles, but the damage was done. In humiliation, I took my seat at the empty desk in front of him. He continued to whisper "Elephant Ears," "Dumbo," and "Radar" when the teacher wasn't looking. Intense hatred welled up inside of me, and I swore never to forgive him for that. I was born with ears that stuck out 90 degrees from my head, and I was very self-conscious about this. It didn't help that my hair was thin and stringy and didn't hide my oversized appendages. Thankfully, my parents were attuned to my distress about this and allowed me to have plastic surgery when I was twelve to make my ears lie flat. No more snide comments were made behind my back, and I have since rocked a pixie haircut for most of my adult life.

Not every situation that would test my ability to forgive involved other children. My parents were old school, having strict Scottish upbringings. We were conditioned to be polite, docile, and well-behaved. When we weren't, we'd get hit, a smack across the back of the head, a skelp across the legs, or worse, chased around the kitchen or living room by Mum brandishing her slipper or the wooden spoon. My siblings and I laugh about it now, but it was traumatizing then. The last time my mum hit me with a belt across my legs, I was sixteen. She was angry that I continued to sneak out and meet a boy my parents had decided would not be good for me. I still remember the sting of the leather on my skin and the utter shock that she had gone that far. It caused a rift between us for years. I was polite and docile toward her as I had been conditioned to be, but I no longer shared my heart with her.

Of course, in time, I was able to forgive these childhood transgressions. My adult self understood life better, my conditioning, and the cultural norms I grew up in. I also accepted that other people act from their own conditioning and perceptions about life. With this awareness, I could forgive the awkward child who laughed at my brother's funeral. I could forgive and forget about the boy who teased me and acted out to get attention as the class clown. I forgave my parents for their punitive disciplinary style, And I forgave my Mum for what she did out of what must have been fear. I was able to move through it. After long periods of silence in those tumultuous teen years, and over time, she and I found our way back to each other and shared many great years of adventure, friendship, and closeness until she passed the year I turned fifty-five.

There were some transgressions; however, that would prove much more challenging to forgive. The biggest of them all, the thing many in my immediate family still cannot forgive, is the betrayal that was the catalyst for the end of my marriage. One mild and sunny Friday morning, I woke up feeling something was off. I remember showering and getting dressed. My husband of twenty-one years—my friend, my partner, the salt of the earth, and the one who always had my back — was up before me and downstairs getting breakfast for our then seventeen-year-old twin boys.

He came to the bedroom to get something, and I don't know why, but I said, "What's up with us? I feel like something is off." He replied, matter-of-factly, with a brutal sort of calm, that our marriage was over.

I blurted out, "What? Can't we work through this?"

Our eyes locked in a deafening, frozen silence.

Then it hit me… "Is there someone else?" He nodded yes. He told me he had struck up a romantic relationship with a woman half our age: we were fifty, she was twenty-five! At that moment, my world fell apart. Time stood still. I was immediately aware of my heart pounding as nausea and light-headedness set in. The shockwave overtook me. *How could this be happening?* "Who are you?!" I blurted out, stunned by his confession. He continued to stare back at me, and for the first time in two decades, I did not recognize the person in front of me. "Who does this? What about our family? What about our wedding vows?" I could not wrap my head around this new reality. I knew our relationship was under stress and figured I had loads of time to set things right. But the fact that he had already taken up with another left me with no recourse to save us. It was over. He was leaving. This stunning, tragic news arrived seemingly out of the blue, given who I thought my husband was and who I thought we were together.

Over the next few weeks, I hurled ugly tirades at him and experienced paralyzing moments of terror, panic, anxiety, and despair. To cope, I isolated myself from family and well-meaning friends, numbing my shame and guilt with too many bottles of wine and getting lost in other people's dramas by binge-watching useless television. Forgiveness was the furthest thing from my mind in those days, but as my healing journey progressed and my worthiness returned, I began to release myself from the demoralizing pain.

As I looked within, I came to forgive him because I could see my part in the erosion of our love. I could see how I hadn't been communicative enough, how our interests diverged and I neglected to insist we work through our issues sooner. Forgiving him was supposed to free me, but I blamed myself for many years and allowed the guilt to consume me until I reclaimed my sense of worthiness and learned a better way.

It was a slow, effortful process, especially when it came to forgiving *her*. They met during his involvement in one of our local political campaigns. She came to the house several times for dinner before they would go off to their meetings. Because of her age, I didn't think anything of it. I couldn't fathom how this young 'cupcake' (as I referred to her in the early days) thought it was okay to take up with a married man. All my old playground instincts wanted to kick in as I imagined what I would say and do to her. I felt she ruined my marriage.

I had to find a way to discover greater peace if I was ever going to forgive her and move forward. It took seven years and happened while I was completing my yoga teacher training. The teaching philosophy was tantric and reinforced the idea of life happening *for* me; *for* my evolution. The teacher taught the classes on a theme, and one particular weekend, the theme was about forgiveness. My teacher stressed the importance of letting go of trespasses more for *my* own benefit than the benefit of others. Truth be told, my husband and his new wife weren't giving me a second thought. They had completely moved on, leaving me mired in my drama. My resentment toward the 'cupcake' was keeping me hostage, in a spiral of negative thinking and feelings of unworthiness. In that class, I was encouraged to focus on the gifts of *the present* and recognize that life is happening for me; that challenges arise to wake me up to the truth of who I really am. All my perceived struggles ignited my resilience, my courage, and elevated me to become my next best self.

While on the mat, relaxing in the final savasana, we were cued to bring to mind that person who wronged us and to let them go — and it hit me!! I saw the image of a photo my sons had shared with me of their two little half-brothers. What I now know to be my intuitive, higher self spoke to me that day, *"Your boys have two beautiful brothers. Those babies would not exist had your marriage not ended."* My husband's choices birthed these little beings into the world. He chose to stay with the 'cupcake' and build a life. Because of the end of my marriage, these two innocent, sweet little boys now walk the planet. Who knows what awaits them and the gifts they will bring into the world? Thinking of their mother in that context is what has allowed me to forgive her. She and my ex were meant to continue together, and my destiny was to spend an extended period of my life alone. I know this to be right and true because that's what happened; everything happens as it should.

In these ten years since my marriage ended, I've done much of my inner work, growing in my spiritual understanding and healing past wounds. Forgiveness has been a key practice in my growth, especially early on. Now, I typically don't feel the need to forgive others. I'm not often triggered by another's actions, and when I am, I choose to be reflective about it. For me, feeling triggered is a sign to look more closely at myself. What am I resisting when I have a strong internal reaction to something I'm seeing in another? Feeling triggered is an opportunity for me to look at my wounds and perceptions and to choose differently. I'm very practiced at seeing the other person's side, and I can find compassion for what they might be going through. I recognize that everyone is doing their best given their particular perceptions of the world and how their upbringing and environment have conditioned them. Forgiveness has been an act of self-love for me. When I forgive, I no longer suffer; I can move on more peacefully and extend love to those triggering thoughts when they arise. I've learned that my experiences are for my evolution—leading me to better versions of myself with new relationships and opportunities. When I can let go of a perceived hurt, there's a relaxation and peace that transpires.

I see how my journey would not have the blessings it does if my marriage hadn't ended. Recently, I met my 'match' on a popular dating site. He's the conscious, generous, loving partner I've been dreaming of for over a decade. I put my wish out to the Universe and said, "this or better" — he's definitely "or better." I found the blessing in my marriage ending in such a *no-going-back* kind of way. It gave me a beautiful new trajectory of discovering a deeper self-love that has set me free.

When I think I've done or said something to hurt another, I typically feel the 'ouch' of it and that same old sick feeling in my stomach even as the words fly out of my mouth. I'll see the effect of my words on the face of the other or in their retort back to me, and I know I have offended. In these instances, I'm pretty forthcoming in coming clean and trying to make amends. The phrase, "Tell the truth faster," has always stuck in my mind from a personal development workshop I attended years ago. I am certainly not perfectly practiced, sometimes getting frustrated by a perceived lack of progress within myself. I think about the distractions I allow to rule, poor habits, or inconsistent efforts that keep me stuck, doubting myself, or feeling unmotivated. When I get bogged down in these thoughts, I find forgiving myself becomes the most important thing I can do.

One of the most impactful ideas that helped me to soften and forgive myself more easily came from Matt Kahn— *"In order for you to become who you were meant to become, Life couldn't have happened any other way."*

Knowing this, I can forgive myself for the trajectory of my life thus far and have no regrets. I'm learning that all the meandering I've done has been for my evolution. I was supposed to start and stop things, lose interest, choose differently and try new opportunities because it has given me the backdrop from which to have my 'Awakening.' I've had such amazing adventures, and through the wonderful teachers and mentors I've met along the way, I have woken up to the *Love* that I am. I know how to sense it, feel it in my body, and express it to others from this expanded awareness.

When I embrace this expanded view of myself and see it in others, I realize that the essence of me can't be hurt. Which begs the question: is there truly anything to forgive if everything is divinely orchestrated? Everything is a thought. I am the one that gives meaning to my thoughts. I can change the meaning anytime and give myself a new understanding of those thoughts. Forgiveness is simply a change of thought, a lowering of resistance to the actions of the other or myself. The essence of true forgiveness is knowing *you can't really be hurt*, and *no one has the power to hurt you unless you let them.* The 'hurts' while felt in the moment, are transcended when you know who you really are and embrace the divine unfolding of all life's synchronicities. Once you see the breadcrumbs of your life as right and perfect for your evolution and embark on a healing journey empowered with insights about your perceptions, and the perceptions of others, you realize there's *nothing* to forgive.

Forgiveness is easier when you embrace your inner *Truth*.

IGNITE ACTION STEPS

Tell the Truth Faster—When you know you've said or done something unintentionally that hurts another, come clean to the person as soon as possible. Stay present and listen, have open, honest communication and take 100 percent responsibility for your part in any situation. This will help you stay in integrity and keep your relationships free of toxicity.

Continue Your Growth Journey—Learn from the teachers whose messages you resonate with; who can support you in working through your past hurts. As you understand yourself better by implementing the teachings and practices that feel right to you, you won't find others' actions as triggering. Everyone is doing their best, given their particular lens of their world. If you're not triggered by others, there's nothing to forgive them for.

Have An Ongoing Gratitude Practice—Upon waking, think of or list five things you are grateful for. Remind yourself daily, even several times a day, of what is working, going well, and your many blessings. It calms your inner critic and helps you step into your observer role. In the observer role, when a perceived hurt or trigger appears, you can catch yourself before reacting in a hurtful way. Give yourself time and space to choose a different, more compassionate response.

MaryAnn Swan—Canada
Author, Founder of A Gathering of Hearts, Transformational Coach
www.maryannswan.com
 maryann.swan
 agatheringofhearts

IGNITE
Forgiveness

Forgiveness is Death to...

Betrayal and Hatred

Disappointment and Regret

Resistance and Closure

Pain and Frustration

Suffering and Trauma

...FEAR

Forgiveness is Birth to...

Inner Truth – Yours and Theirs

Allowing and Flowing

Relaxation and Peace

Open Heartedness and Acceptance

Connection and Community

...HOPE

Forgiveness Transcends into...

...LOVE

Tenisha Graham

Tenisha Graham

*"Give yourself permission to forgive your past and
leap into a new, improved purpose."*

You have permission to change gears, shift careers, and Ignite your creativity by laying down the heaviness of unforgiveness and focusing on loving others. Don't let worry write your story. Don't let regret and lack of forgiveness drive your day. We are here to create through our vibration, energy, and attitude. It is innate and natural. Forgiveness lets you embrace the creativity that's inside of you as you open new doors and make room for self-love.

The Love I Created

The tears wouldn't stop, pooling onto the hardwood floor of the dance studio I'd worked endlessly to build. Since I was a little girl, I had wanted to be a dance teacher. I wanted to create shows, guide kids to become beautiful artists of movement, and build their confidence. I had dedicated almost two decades of my life to running my dance studio. My mother and father sacrificed a great deal to keep me in dance as a child. My mom worked at my dance school, doing what she could to earn my access to classes. She was there for all of the shows that I danced in and directed. We had just finished our 33rd show together, seventeen of which I had created myself. I was living my dream.

Dreams, though, don't pay the bills. They don't give you back the count-less dinners missed with your husband and children. I had become a master at penny-pinching and keeping the business 'afloat,' but the truth was, I was exhausted and didn't even feel creative anymore. I was not great at balancing the many hats one must wear as a business owner. I had the service part down. I showed up and did it all, but I wasn't passionate about the things outside my genius: bookkeeping, ordering costumes, marketing, raising enrollments, and damage control with upset clients. I stressed more days than I enjoyed. It felt as if I thought about bills and money every ten minutes, which left no room in my mind for beauty, art, creativity, or… well… joy. Our entire life savings was poured into this studio. Time with my babies had been exchanged for countless rehearsals with my dancers, and now it was all coming to a close.

We had spent all day moving our things out of the dance studio. The walls were empty; the pictures were all taken down. But the giant mirrors on the wall remained mirrors whose purpose changed in an instant. They were once used to correct ballet dancers as they perfected their form, or as a tool for me to see if my competition teams were precisely on point. But as I walked into the studio for the last time, I looked at myself in the mirror and saw failure. My passion and reality were having a big, 'grown-up fight,' and I didn't want to be a part of it. The burden the studio put on me, and my family, affected my health, as I had learned to live in chaos and stress like it was my destiny. I believed that was as good as it was going to get. The mirror that once was correcting beautiful dancers was just a reflection of me in an empty room. There were no tutus hanging on the ballet barre awaiting a fitting. There were no coffee cups on the counter by the stereo. No music, no life, no artistry, just four walls. I sat and cried for an hour for all the dancers I loved who had once filled that room with beautiful energy, laughter, creativity, and grace. I prayed, "God, why did you let this dream die? Am I supposed to do something else with my life?"

I spent many years prior to the closure in a negative frame of mind, and everything around me followed suit. I know it must have been hard to be near me during those years; I complained, cried, and whined to anyone who would listen. I repeatedly spoke of how broke and tired I was, and felt as though I was losing my dream.

After about two years of reflecting, praying, and learning, I started to have a paradigm shift. I read many books, studied personal development, listened to Les Brown every morning on YouTube®, and dove into energy healing and the power of mindset. I eventually started to see the light at the end of the tunnel. Occasionally, I would ask my husband Jamie what he thought I should do, and his answer was annoyingly always the same. He said, "Tenisha, you need to be a school teacher." I thought, "Um, why give up on my big dreams and settle on teaching school? I think not." Jamie was a teacher and coach, and he loved it, but I wasn't sure a school teacher job could anchor my heart. What I really needed to do was CREATE.

I tried a few jobs here and there, selling enough face cream to earn a Lexus. I wrote a dozen home studies for Child Protective Services until I couldn't read another affidavit about a neglected and abused child. I was a ghostwriter for a book on a subject that I knew nothing about when I started. I volunteered at the Children's Home and mentored three girls there. I started a non-profit organization that helped provide scholarships in the arts for foster children... but still, I was not fulfilled. I didn't feel like I did when teaching dance. I wasn't creating my heart's desire.

During that time, I was very set on 'fixing' a problem, a problem that required healing and redirection to repair. It was hard for me to see the solution when I was living it. I needed to lean into the change, embrace it, and forgive myself for walking away from the business, losing time with my three young boys, and missing out on connecting with my husband because I had to work. I had to give myself permission to build a *new* dream and forgive myself for using all our life savings, sacrificing family time, and giving to a business that was now gone.

Unexpectedly, I got a phone call from a friend trying to find a home for a foreign exchange student from Brazil. There was no way I could possibly take a student in, but I called up my friends, thinking most of them 'had it together' enough to house a young teen. Sadly, no one was open to a seventeen-year-old, nor to having a foreigner living with them.

Interestingly enough, I had been begging my husband to adopt or foster a child for about seven years, but every time he answered with this: "I teach hundreds of kids every day with problems or difficult home lives. I coach them, teach them, love them, and in some way am like a father to them. There is no way I am bringing one of those kids home." "Blah Blah Blah" is what I heard, so I kept asking year after year, hoping he might change his mind.

God had completely taken over my common sense and logic as I could not let go of the compelling idea of having a daughter, some feminine energy in my life. I suppose that is what prompted the deep breath I took that led into the question I asked Jamie: "What do you think about hosting a foreign exchange student?"

I think the pause was about 435 long seconds, and then he finally said, "But we don't have any money." I said, "All we have to do is feed them, it can't be that expensive, right? God had never let *us* go hungry. He has always provided." Then to my disbelief, my husband said, "I guess we can look into it and read some of their profiles. I like that exchange students *want* to study and live here.

They are good kids that aspire to better themselves." I had not even thought of that, but I agreed with him.

The exchange counselor brought the young student my friend had mentioned to our house so we could meet her. She was a beautiful Latino named Jhanna, with long, straight black hair and dark eyes filled with equal parts determination and caution. She sat on my couch saying almost nothing and looked up at me through the top of her eyelids with her chin down. She didn't wear a stitch of makeup and did not need to; she was a natural beauty. "She and I are so different," I thought. I own a treasure trove of makeup designed to accentuate my eyes, but they were still sad and disappointed.

Two weeks after finding out about Jhanna, I had a short dream. I saw a teenage girl with curly hair, mostly brown, with little blonde highlights on the ends. She was facing to the right, and I saw her profile. The wind was in her hair like she was moving on a bicycle as if she was traveling toward me. I sat straight up in bed and felt God whisper to me, "Your exchange student."

I prayed and wondered about my dream and God's message. The girl in my dream looked nothing like Jhanna. Jhanna has straight hair; I was confused. I told Jamie about the dream, and we called the counselor back. Within minutes she sent me a profile of an Italian girl who seemed smart and driven. This girl wanted to attend medical school and already spoke great English. Both of her parents were dentists, like Jamie's father. I thought God had orchestrated that to relate the two of them. After reading her parent's letter, her letter, and her bio, we decided to take her in. Her name was Carla, and she was from Italy. When I saw her picture, I cried. There were the curls from my dream. This was our girl! We later found out that she drove a little moped motorbike in Italy. God had given me a glimpse of her, and now my job was simple: open myself up to receiving her, a blessing, in a new way.

A week passed, and I was excited to get our Italian girl in December after Christmas! However, God started making me think of Jhanna… almost every day. I finally texted the counselor, and she said Jhanna was still looking for a permanent home. My heart fell in my chest. Without another thought, I said, "Ask her if she wants to go to church with us in the morning and hang out tomorrow. Also, give her my cell phone number." Jhanna spent the next day with us, and that same night I got a text from her saying, "Can I ask you a question?… Can I live with you?"

To my astonishment, a week before Thanksgiving, my husband agreed to take in Jhanna as well. On the day before my 37th Birthday, November 27th, Jhanna moved in with us. She and I stayed up talking late and getting to know each other, then just like that, the clock struck midnight, and I instantly felt that The Creator had given me a beautiful daughter, a precious birthday gift. God really does love me; He sees me, and He gave me a wonderful blessing. I opened my heart, and through creating a space of love for Jhanna, I could feel myself forgiving the past and seeing that the best was yet to come.

Did I have an extra room? Not by American standards, in which each child should have their own room. Thankfully, I didn't believe in that. I had extra room as long as all three of my boys (ages eleven, nine, and two) were in one room. That sounded complicated for bedtime, but then both girls could share a room. It felt like a crazy train waiting to happen, but it was possible. We all were eager to make it work, and I was excited to CREATE a bigger family!

It wasn't long before Jhanna was jamming her Portuguese music in her room and bringing her friends to hang out at our house. She danced to One Direction while she washed the dishes (her only chore) and sang aloud with the wrong words and a Brazilian accent. She was adorable, and I fell in love with this playful exchange daughter of mine in no time at all. Then, Carla arrived and was delightful from the instant we met her. With her academic, mature mind, she was the easiest child I have ever partially raised! She studied, understood what was right and appropriate, and was considerate. We loved to have sushi together and enjoy real conversations. I made her laugh in my crazy way. Jhanna and Carla would share a room and eventually become sisters, inseparable, until they both had to return home to their original countries.

Afterward, my exchange coordinator called me many times and asked me if I wanted to host another student. My answer was always the same, "No, I don't think we are ready to host again." Then, one year after Carla and Jhanna went home, our exchange coordinator called me, saying she had a girl who was a perfect fit for us. I blew it off, and then she sent the profile. Just like God always does, he annoyed me to the core with this recurring thought: *Rose... Rose... Rose.* I think I even bought a rose-scented candle. Lo and behold, I found myself reading Jamie a letter written by this girl from Denmark, and he agreed to just one more foreign exchange student. I gave myself a pep talk that I could do this, and we jumped in with both feet and said yes to Røskva, who we instantly nicknamed 'Rose.'

When Rose arrived, she didn't feel like just a daughter, she felt like a close friend. All of my girls taught me things, and I think one of the things Rose taught me was how to live in a happy, positive way. She was a dancer, and I helped direct and choreograph the "Newsies" show we did together. Rose eventually reignited my love for dance and choreography. She sparked in me what I needed to CREATE again. She handed me back a little of myself that I had tried to break off and throw away. Roses symbolize love, and she swept in as a reminder to me that love will always be the best tool to heal. I felt complete, with three boys, three girls, and a new perspective.

Through caring for others, I was starting to heal from the huge disappointment of my dream business failing. Whether I fully realized it or not, I was creating the whole time; I was creating love, creating safe spaces, creating a sense of belonging. My father always said that the world doesn't owe us anything, and I was really putting my energy toward giving instead of receiving. Still, it was time to stop distracting myself with "projects that were people" and dig into the personal healing I still needed. I started studying frequencies and sound and how they could help heal the body, understanding that everything is energy, the things in my life, the thoughts in my mind, my emotions, and my false beliefs about myself. It was time to release that energy.

As I began to dance again, I stumbled upon an amazing solution. I started to pair dancing with intentions, and a remarkable healing took place. I danced and released what no longer served me. I moved toward self-forgiveness. My body started to get stronger as I decoded the emotions and energy trapped inside that were causing pain, mental anguish, and anxiety. I forgave myself for working and missing so much in my children's and husband's lives. I forgave myself for losing my creative steam. It turned out I had been *creating* the whole time. As a ghostwriter, social worker, non-profit organizer, and foreign exchange parent. I had *created* stories, *created* opportunities, *created* safety for those who were hurting, and *created* love for those who needed it. I *created* room in my home and in my heart.

As I got stronger, I started to think about creating a new career that fed my spirit and soul. This time, it would work with my family unit and not take away from it. I am now the Creator of an online dance curriculum called "Maka-Move." This project was designed to build people up and connect the dots of healing and confidence through dance. I speak on many platforms empowering women and building the confidence of women around the world to embrace their gifts in a new way. I am the founder and CEO of "Cue your Creative," where I facilitate the healing for 'up and coming women' and celebrities alike, helping them find their blocks and mindset issues and decode what keeps them stagnant through online courses and coaching. With my proven techniques of releasing energy, my clients have overcome many things, from launching their dream business to getting out of their own way and achieving lifelong goals such as booking roles in movies.

Everything in my journey has been a stepping stone. I didn't need to let my identity die as a dance teacher, I just needed to shift gears, refocus and forgive myself, so I could work with others to do the same. For eighteen years, I guided dancers to find their inner artist, their confidence, and their expression through creative arts, only to meet myself as a beginner student and do the same work internally. The more grace and forgiveness I give myself, the more grace I have to share with the world. I love creating, and the most powerful thing I've created is space for love. By taking the forgiveness journey myself, I found a purpose for my future.

Could *your* calling be on the other side of forgiveness? Could forgiving yourself lead to inner acceptance? Ask yourself what it is you *really* want and *what* is the reason you are not CREATING that dream. If you can imagine it, you can make it happen. Funnel your thoughts and CREATE your wishes; you can manifest anything you set your mind to. Take a leap and dream big. Allow yourself to feel all the exciting possibilities forgiveness can bring to you.

IGNITE ACTION STEPS

- Turn on your favorite empowerment song. Hold your heart, and say out loud that you forgive yourself and anyone that has wronged you. Then, take a deep breath, sway side to side, or dance in your own way to release the energy of that emotion. Let it go and exhale it out.
- Catch your thoughts! If you speak of love and expect blessings, you will attract those things. Your thoughts can transform your world. You can create an energetic pull of wonderful things into your life when you think about what is good, pure, and just. Focus on love and gratitude.
- Speak affirmations out loud daily! We live in a voice-activated world. Choreograph movements to the affirmation and memorize it to a song. Start creating your own reality! These are my morning words of Affirmation: *Speak it and become it! I am successful. I have ideas to create new things. My gifts and talents hold the keys to my dream career.*

Tenisha Graham—United States of America
Certified Emotion Code Practitioner, CEO of Cue Your Creative,
CEO of MakaMOVE
www.cueyourcreative.com | www.MakaMOVE.org | www.TenishaGraham.org
tenisha@cueyourcreative.com
♪ *@tenishagraham* | ⓕ *Tenisha.Graham* | ⓘ *tenishagraham.official*

TO FORGIVE TAKES TIME

If I worry, I am living in a future that doesn't exist yet.

My imagination creates anxiety about goals not yet met.

The future doesn't exist yet.

If I hold on to resentment for myself or others, I am living in the past. The past doesn't exist anymore.

By not forgiving myself and others, I'm letting the waves of past pain shape me like the waves shape the seashore.

I don't want to live in pain anymore.

I choose to forgive myself and others so I can meet myself here in the present.

To live in a time that is real.

There are moments I have missed and people I didn't feel.

*My life can begin because I am now
living in the present time.*

*No more living in the past or future or letting lack of for-
giveness take my time.*

*I've laid my burdens on the beach. No more repeated
waves of anxiety or pretending I'm fine.*

I now live in the moment, this is my time!

Shelina Manek

SHELINA MANEK

"Forgiveness is the key to the flow of life."

Writing this chapter has allowed me to acknowledge that forgiveness is a process. Grieving is also very much a part of that process, and sometimes grief and forgiveness are woven together tighter than we think. When we cannot forgive, it is because we are still grieving the trauma. We are not ready to release the pain that ails us and weighs us down. That pain festers in our hearts and leaves a mark, but forgiveness can be the healing force we need. I invite you to join me as I walk the path of forgiveness hoping it will help you on your own journey forward.

FINDING THE OTHER SIDE OF FORGIVENESS

Today is the day when time stands still: August 19th. It has been exactly six years since my father left us. It has been a difficult journey. A journey where I have come to believe he has only left this plane physically, but that his spirit is still around. I could not sleep last night, and when I finally did, it was only to wake up at the crack of dawn to face the clock as it ticked closer to 9 AM. I called my mom, as I usually do every year, at this exact time since that fateful day six years ago. Nothing has changed; I watch the time, waiting for the minutes to countdown, knowing that was the moment, that was the time of impact, and had I been there, could I have changed things? I relive these moments every year and still feel the pain.

On that fateful morning, I had talked to him just minutes after eight o'clock, and I had asked him if I could go see him. I was happy; I had finally been able to complete a document for him on the computer. He had said, "No, no… I must go for my walk first."

"But I have done what you asked me to do on the computer, and I really want to show you what I have done," I reacted. I was always anxious to show him what I had accomplished, always seeking that seal of approval as a middle daughter. That middle child syndrome is a real thing.

Our conversation had ended and we agreed I would go run my errand while he went for his walk. If he got back first, he was going to call me and if I returned from my errand sooner, I was to call him. Off I went, and within about twenty minutes after my brief side trip, I was returning home. I headed westbound on my street in my neighborhood of forty-five years. One block further west was my dad's street; I would turn there to go and meet him, as he lived very close. But, as I was driving, and before I had even arrived at my block, I could hear them, those sirens. A strange thought passed by my brain, but I could not quite place it. I remember asking myself, *What was that feeling? Why am I feeling this way?*

Just as I was about to get to the lights, a police car blocked my path. That was unusual. I had to turn left on a different street and drive back to my place. I parked my car in my driveway, about six driveways away from a set of flashing red and blue lights. I got out of the car and felt something pulling me. The odd feeling I was having nagged at me, compelling me to march my way toward the lights. A loud voice stopped me in my tracks. A police officer shouted, "Get back! Go back! This area is closed!" His arm was raised, and his hand formed a stop sign to indicate I could walk no further. I stopped, but there was that feeling again. Something washed over me—a wave of worry and fear. I felt a deep knowing in the pit of my stomach that something wasn't right.

I decided to walk around the block to avoid the barricade and approach the area from the opposite side. I scurried as fast as my feet could carry me across the field, then the road, faster and faster as I approached. But there was a barricade on the opposite side also. The scene in front of me frightened me as it hit me that the whole block, typically so busy, was eerily empty. I was in a daze. I stood on a small hill, trying to see what was happening. Across the street, there was another policeman, and it seemed like he was watching me. *Was I becoming a pest?* No other humans were around except for a young boy standing by a truck just on the side of the road. My feet did not allow me to move, and I could not see anything else past the scene before me. Everything was shrouded with a murky haze. I looked to the sky above me; bright blue, dazzling sun. I noticed the clouds moving quickly, yet I felt like time was standing still. Something inside me kept pushing me to look for my father, knowing that this was the route he had walked every day. I needed to see him, to know he was okay.

Finally, after what seemed like an eternity, I had the courage to move, and I headed back to the spot where I had seen the police officer for the first time. While walking, I called my mom and asked her if my father had returned from his walk. I was ever so calm and casual, trying not to worry her as she said, "He probably made a stop somewhere." She did not know what was racing through my head. *Where was he? Why hadn't he returned home yet?*

Between the fluttering in my stomach, the flashing light, and my father's absence, I knew something didn't feel right. *Why was time not ticking by and instead felt so still?* The sun was shining, yet everything felt cloudy. I walked around again, in a daze, back to my original spot by the stoplights in front of my house. I went inside and got my daughter, who was home from university. She was still in her pajamas when I told her I needed her help. She looked at me from her bed with a bowl of cereal in her hands, perplexed. "Your grandfather is missing," I said, the words thick in my throat. She knew she had to come with me. I needed her help and her presence; I was too foggy to think straight.

Together we marched back to the corner where a policeman stood, and I said, "My father is missing… I need to go there," pointing to the road ahead, "But you are stopping me… he went for his morning walk… I need to find him," I shared emphatically. The policeman must have sensed my anxiety and stress. He told us to sit in the backseat of his cruiser, asking for my father's name and a few personal details. It felt odd to be sitting in a police car, my brain trying to make sense of what was happening. We were told to wait as he walked away from us, back towards the scene.

We were there for what seemed to be forever. While the police checks were going on, my daughter held my hand. I would fidget and try to look up the street, but I could not see anything. It was as if my view was clouded. My mum called me saying, "He is not at your uncle's. Where are you? What is going on?" I said very little to her, not wanting to upset her and unsure of what was going on.

The police officer finally came back to my daughter and me, and he said, "They will speak to you now." He escorted us out of his car and told us to follow him. We walked further into the scene. Confusion washed over me as I met a different officer, my daughter still holding my hand. My mom had been calling me constantly, I wasn't picking up, so she sent my uncle to see what was happening. Then my aunt also showed up. I had spoken to her in my worry and told her, "There has been an accident..."

I asked each of them to walk with me, and when the police officer saw us, he directed us to step inside an empty ambulance parked nearby. I hadn't even noticed it. *What? Why are we going inside an ambulance?* My mind began to race, and that *feeling* intensified.

The police officer waited till we were all inside. Then he shut the door. He reached into his pocket, and as he was doing so, he said, "There was an accident this morning." I saw him pull out my dad's keys, his watch, and his phone. The officer asked if we had seen these things before. We all gasped, recognizing every item.

Then all I heard was a distant voice, like I was in a tunnel, as the officer explained. The only sentence that registered in my mind was, "... and he succumbed to his injuries." That officer may have said multiple things, but that one phrase was all I heard!

At that moment, the sky—that bright blue sunny sky—fell.

In the days and weeks that followed, I kept asking myself, why? Why did I not insist on going to see him when I first spoke to him? Why didn't I just show up? Why did I not argue with the policeman who had told me to get back? Why were my feet stuck to the ground like glue on that small hill? I reflected on the incident, replaying every detail in my mind. Little coincidences seemed to line up like dominoes. The fact I'd had to wait an extra few minutes while running my errand; why did that happen? The fact that he had made me wait until he was done with his walk; why did he do that? The fact my daughter had been home to support me; did God arrange that? I wondered and wondered: *What could I have done differently?*

Above all, I was haunted by the feeling that he had been alone in his last moments. I had been trying that morning to see him, and to be with him but had been stopped by circumstances. They had been beyond my control, but I still felt such guilt and questioned whether I could have done more. *Could I have finished my errand faster? Could I have made it in time to stop him from crossing the street?*

In my quest for answers, I walked across the street from my home to the fire department. I was looking for the actual officers who had been on duty that day. They were surprised to see me but allowed me the opportunity to come and ask my questions. The firefighter they finally identified, the man who had been there, was patient and kind. When I asked him what happened about the progression of events, I discovered he was the first one there. As he laid out the details for me, he revealed that my father didn't suffer... that it had been too late. He could see the anguish in my eyes; the inability to accept and come to terms with my horrendous loss. He then turned the conversation in a compassionate direction. He asked me, "What could you have done?"

His question hit my heart, as I replied, "I could have held his hand! He was alone. Why did he have to go like this... alone?"

Then, in the gentlest of ways, the firefighter told me, "Your father was not alone... I was there. I held his hand. He was not alone."

Time stood still again as his words sunk in. Those words brought so much comfort to me. They still do now, to this day.

The path toward healing and forgiveness is the one I am trying to walk, but there are still some sections of it that I struggle with. I cannot easily walk down that busy street anymore, even though it was the same walking route I had done for decades. I have gone twice to that spot where the truck stood that day: once with my son to lay flowers, and once with my cousins who had traveled miles to be with me. I drive by the sacred spot continuously, but walking there is still a process I am working through. Every year, on the same date, at the same time, 9:06 AM and 9:10 AM, I ask myself, *"Could I have done anything differently? Could I have changed anything?"*

Standing on my driveway, on the anniversary of the accident, and looking in that same direction, many things feel the same. The sun is shining in the blue sky, and the clouds are floating just like on that day six years ago. But that morning, there had been that terrifying feeling of doom and that shroud of haze that had kept appearing. I had not been able to see past anything... the police car, the policeman who had stopped me. I will forever remember how I felt so nomadic and felt I could not find my way that morning. But, on this morning, there is no fog, and I begin to see the faint traces of the path before me. It is the path toward forgiveness.

As I wrote this chapter, I revisited those moments in time. Moments that I do not allow myself to think about. But, by doing so, the question came to mind. *What do I have to forgive?* I have been asked, "Have you forgiven the man who took your dad's life?" I don't know if I have fully; time will help. I know that it was an accident; that the man who drove the truck did not know how his day would play out, and he would take a life. I am sure he is on his own forgiveness journey, as I know he had not seen my father crossing the street that day. Forgiveness will be a process for both of us.

What I may spend a lifetime forgiving is a future we will all miss out on. The precious moments, the laughter, being next to him. He was a husband, a father, a father-in-law, a grandfather, a great grandfather-to-be, a brother, an uncle, a friend, a business associate, an elder, a leader, and so much more. He left his mark on so many and his absence is deeply felt amongst us all. Although I will miss him, he would want us all to move on and to live our lives. He was a man of few words, but I know he would tell me, "Forgive and move on."

I came to a realization that I had to forgive myself, and that my dad was not alone. There are many things I wanted to say and do with him. I wanted to spend more time with him. I left home and started my own family when I was quite young. So much unfinished business… He hated the winters and lived away most of his time in warmer climates. He was here for vacation. He loved to travel and had been to so many places. He was an adventurer that I did not know. An enterprising and shrewd business entrepreneur who I admired, along with the hundreds of others who crossed his path. Full of wisdom that I did not get enough of. He was a humble spirit and a simple man, someone I was *lucky* to call 'my dad.'

In life, we are born as part of a family. We come with parents, biological or adopted. And, then, sisters and brothers by blood, or another mother. Neighbors or friends, maybe by coincidence. Everyone that is part of your life is there for a reason. Your family is your community, and community is your family. As my daughter once said, "Our paths are intertwined, and we grow together. We owe it to one another to forgive each other, and that is how it works."

When changes happen and we are not prepared, or when we are shocked to our core or traumatized, the idea of us being forgiving is sometimes questionable. Because to be forgiving means to be good and moral. Sometimes it means being at the mercy of others. At our core, when we get shaken and traumatized, it is that same core that has to be healed and nourished, and filled with love again. That core is part of your divinity that you might not know you have. Forgiveness is not only about the good and divine, but also about letting go. You have to let go of things that are bothering you and forgive. Forgive yourself, forgive your family, forgive your neighbor, forgive the Universe. Let it go, and let it be. When you let go, you allow for beautiful things to happen. You allow yourself to be nourished again.

I know that in time, full forgiveness will come to my spirit. If not, the game of love and blame will just continue. One can only blame everyone or everything else for so long. We ask, "Why me?" until the moment we understand and choose to forgive. In the grand scale of life, when something weighs you down, the scale tips, and something has to give. There may always be hurt. We often get confused when we are hurt and we stumble. But we must keep getting up, keep walking the path. We have to have faith that what is on the other side of forgiveness is beautiful. We need to believe that forgiveness *can* free us. And when we embrace that, even with a trembling hand, we walk the path of love, and love heals us.

IGNITE ACTION STEPS

Of all the human experiences, forgiveness is the hardest to define. My wish is that anyone who is reading this story learns how to embrace forgiveness and the journey that it brings.

When any angry, hurtful feelings keep surfacing about the trauma or pain, work on unpacking them, unraveling them one at a time. Talk to the person involved or a third party. Continue doing this—do not stop until you know you are ready. Stopping, sweeping them under the rug, or thinking they are gone even temporarily doesn't mean they are actually resolved.

Outside of the trauma, find things that will help the inside of you feel good. Whether it is sitting in a quiet spot, reading a book, or listening to music, but things that will give you the space to listen to your heart. Listening to loud things might block what your heart is trying to tell you. So find the time and the space that is quieter so that you can hear your heart.

Letting go is only the beginning. Forgiveness is the goal.

Shelina Manek—Canada
A believer in all things life
Founder of Women's Center for Innovation and Change
Shelinamanek@gmail.com
�f *Shelina Manek*

IGN☤TE
Forgiveness

I allow the process for
FORGIVENESS.

I push out the hate and anger as
IT DOES NOT SERVE ME.

I allow
LOVE TO ENTER.

Melanie Summers

MELANIE SUMMERS

"There is power in choices, and that power belongs to you."

The goal of my story is to prove that when you believe other people's opinions of your life and choices, their opinions will impact you in a way that can alter your whole trajectory, sometimes positively, but many times negatively. However, when you start believing in yourself and all the possibilities in front of you, you claim the power of self-forgiveness. This is necessary because only then will you know how to forgive others.

WALK IN YOUR OWN SHOES

As I ambled through the ancient, 'old town' cemetery, I paused here and there to read the inscriptions and epitaphs on the headstones. I had strolled through this cemetery untold times in my youth when I felt the need to reflect on my life. I noticed many headstones so old that countless rainstorms and winters had erased the name of those who lay there until they were forgotten by time. On a few, I trailed my fingertips over little lambs or butterflies carved over the name of an existence cut short, evidenced by birth and end date, some only a few days or months old. I pondered for the umpteenth time, "What caused the death of so many children?" I wandered on and came to a fenced-in plot with a huge obelisk of polished granite bearing the surname of one of the founding families of my hometown. Smaller headstones for his wife and presumably his progeny, surrounded it, still well-maintained even after so many years.

Moments later, I was surprised when my feet led me to the gravel roadway that snaked through the graveyard. I crossed over it, meandered my way to the top of the hill, and sat down on the grassy knoll overlooking the Ohio River. I noticed the ferryboat in the distance, appearing tiny as it picked up trucks and cars from West Virginia to carry them to Ohio, only to turn around and make the return trip to West Virginia with other vehicles. I cocked my head and focused on bees busy gathering nectar from a nearby honeysuckle bush. Birds flitted or sat in trees, chattering and singing to each other. Big puffy clouds slowly morphed from the shape of a face to an upside-down dog. It was idyllic.

I had first discovered this solemn ground as a child one autumn day while hunting for hickory nuts, which Mom would have baked into cookies or added to penuche fudge for seasonal goodies. Similar to *Alice in Wonderland*, I followed a rabbit through some overgrown brush and found myself in what would become one of my refuges when life had dealt me perceived lemons.

It had been thirty four years since I last visited this spot, and I didn't remember how I wound up there, nor did I know how long I had been there. Though, based on the angle of the sun, I estimated about an hour. I started contemplating all the barbs that had been thrown at me that day by one person or another, beginning at the funeral home and continuing through dinner, feeling sorry for myself one moment and angry the next. Bitter tears began scorching trails down my cheeks.

I had driven there after the traditional family meal that followed my mother's funeral. Mom had been buried several miles away in another graveyard, one nicer and newer than this ancient reminder of days gone by, another reminder of history—*my history*—had been not-so-kindly flung in my face today. There were so many innuendos: assumed reminders of my imperfections and a life of horrible choices that led to well-deserved misery.

There's always a fair amount of excitement and expectation when meeting friends and family after a drought of years with no interaction. Today was no different. I had expected a lot of conversations, catching up with relatives I hadn't seen in forever, and introductions to new folks in the family. Some had gotten married. Some had new additions. Others were in college—they had been in Little League the last time I had seen them!

I had *not* expected they would play darts, with me as the dartboard. My goodness! It appeared to be a competition: who could score the most points with my heart as the bullseye?

First, there was husband number one, who "nobody ever liked," and everyone warned me not to marry. The scorecard said I made a good decision (for once) by divorcing him. Next was my second husband, who "everyone liked" and for whom, according to an older relative, "I should have done more to save our marriage." Another relative added, "We liked your kids' father. He was a keeper!" I silently reflected, thinking, "Well, he's all yours if you want him." But at the same time, I had to be fair. He *was* my children's father, and we had raised two fine young men together. There had been some really good times before everything fell apart. A memory of us at the beach flashed through my brain as I reminisced. I was buried in sand, just my head and feet sticking out while little fingers reached to tickle my toes. I remembered howling and giggling while at the same time desperately trying to get out of my sand bed. I recalled thinking, "My husband is the oldest one of my three boys!" But that was then, and this was now, since "irreconcilable differences" split us apart.

Then there was my third husband, who "everyone thought was a moron." They asked, "What could you have possibly been thinking to have hooked up with him?" He was quite charming when we first met. However, what he wanted and expected and what I wanted and expected were two separate kettles of fish. Rather than continue to make each other miserable, we parted ways. I still think fondly of his four children and treat them like my own. Twelve years later, their kids still call me Grandma.

I had filed for divorce from husband number three the fall before my mother passed away. At around the same time, I filed for bankruptcy.

BANKRUPTCY? I should be hanging my head in shame.

And oh, by the way, "WHY was *he* (my third soon-to-be ex) at Mom's funeral?" I answered under my breath, "I don't know; I didn't invite him."

Another overheard whisper: "I wonder what she did this time to cause her sons to avoid her?" That caught my attention! I thought, *Maybe they just want to catch up with cousins they haven't seen in years?*

Yet another comment, "Her mom and dad must be rolling in their graves!"

Enough was enough! That's when I bailed and ended up in one of my childhood hideaways. Sitting on the knoll, I ran my hand down my face, ending with it cupped around my mouth, my elbow on my drawn-up knee. I sighed.

I had never conformed to *their* way of thinking. I had always gotten in trouble for doing things *my* way. I remembered an overheard conversation between my father and my grandmother when I was just a girl. Grandma said, "Melanie will give you the shirt off her back if you *ask* her for it... but you keep *demanding* her to give it to you! When will you learn that?" His answer: "I do not have to learn anything. *She* has to learn to do what she's told, when she's told. I make the rules."

I mentally gave a nod to my grandmother. I reflected on my decision to become a teacher, where I spent half my paycheck on things my students needed when their parents might not be able to afford them: shoes, school supplies, field trip expenses, and clothes. I had even paid a few lunch bills on occasion. I was the first to volunteer to bake cookies for my own kids' school parties when they were small. I gave weekly to the church contribution. I volunteered at the hospital and the animal rescue. I tutored kids after school for free. Along with husband number two, I even outfitted our home's basement with all sorts of things to entice kids to come to our house after sporting practice—pinball, a pool table, snacks, music, weights, and workout equipment—all, so my children's friends had a drug-free place to hang out. There was dinner for all and a dining room table to do homework with me if they needed it.

However, when I volunteered to bake cookies for my church's Vacation Bible School one summer, my offer was rejected because *they* didn't want a divorced woman to participate in a church function. Feeling chagrined, I found a new church that would accept my so-called contaminated cookies and monetary contributions.

Then I contemplated my life growing up: I remembered some of those same opinionated people used me as their scapegoat of choice to keep themselves out of trouble. I remembered one time in particular when my brother was injured with a broken bike pedal that resulted in a trip to the emergency room and stitches, something our family couldn't easily afford. They said it was *my* fault because I didn't move out of his way when he yelled at me to move. Well, I did move, but not far enough, according to them. I remember Mom shaking her head at me in disappointment when she got home from the emergency room that evening, and I went to bed feeling humiliated but angry, too. Another time, all the kids in the neighborhood were sitting on the fence next to the barn observing a new foal and its mother. They were all being loud and acting in a way that upset Sally, the foal's mama. She charged the fence and bit *me,* leaving me with a bruised and bleeding arm. I ran to the house. My mother's response? "You shouldn't have been yelling around a new mother pony!" I was the only one who stayed quiet, but that was not the story *they* told.

I always worked hard for good grades. It was a given that A's and B's were expected, and I always ensured I delivered. I was on the honor roll every grading cycle. However, it baffled me when they were all bewildered that I received the eighth grade graduation Math Award. I was the only one to score a 100 percent on the one thousand problems required for that award. The whispers in the auditorium that evening were like the 'shot heard round the world' at the beginning of the American Revolution! When I looked around, faces reflected shock and confusion. I remember the pain of seeing a whole room of adults and children who could not feel happy for me. It made me feel like there had been a mistake; I felt compelled to give back the award.

The same was true when I won the Home Economics Award upon graduating high school. Granted, I had only taken that class for the final semester of my senior year, while others had taken four years. They didn't realize I had spent the past ten years taking four-hour projects that required many home economics skills—sewing, cooking, and childcare. *WHAT*? Instead of congratulations, I overheard nasty comments on how I must be "dating" (wink wink) the teacher's son… who I didn't even know.

I began college with several classes awarded to me because of my high ACT scores. As a matter of fact, I received twelve credits between Freshman English and Freshman Math which amounted to a full semester. My parents' response: "Well, that's something we don't have to pay for!" However, I am the one who applied for and received grants and committed to student loans, which I paid back myself after graduation. I was proud when I graduated with several awards and was nominated to several prestigious education associations as a sorority member who graduated Magna Cum Laude in three years, not four. Several professors had even conferenced with me to change my degree preference to their field of study. My art professor went as far as to exhibit several of my works at the entrance of the Fine Arts building, which led to a lot of grumbling from art majors who coveted those spots for themselves. At the time, I had no idea how significant these achievements were or the doors they could open. However, none of my accomplishments were ever noticed—not even in passing—by the ones who should have celebrated: my friends, family, and relatives. Yet, let me do something 'outside the line,' and other people's opinions were quite vociferously and forcefully shoved in my face.

I don't know how long I sat staring at those tombstones, feeling angry one minute and subdued the next. I was *soooo* mentally beat up from the funeral and sore from being the family punching bag yet again. I was adding insult to injury by musing on all my past hurts and injustices.

Suddenly, I sat up! I had an epiphany; actually several. It was like the clouds parted after a violent thunderstorm. What if I looked at all of those situations in my life with a more critical eye; one about choices—my choices—rather than the opinions of others? Were their opinions *my* truth? Did their opinions of my choices define who I was? What if I quit believing that I deserved to be miserable and started believing in myself, owning my choices as hard decisions I had made to move forward in life? What if I began to feel proud of all of my accomplishments instead of being annoyed because others didn't notice them? What if I started to believe in possibilities instead of impossibilities? Finally, I realized I couldn't change others' opinions, but I could change my reactions. I saw the rainbow.

It was at that moment I brushed the tears from my face and shouted to the Universe, "Never again!" I realized that I had never spoken up and voiced my concerns, never corrected falsehoods, and never stood up in defense of myself. Instead of kicking myself more, I could choose to believe in myself, be proud of my accomplishments, and accept my past choices as chances to learn and move on to live in the *now*. I finally understood I could and should forgive myself. I couldn't go back and change history, but I could let go of the negative feelings of inadequacy and doubt and begin imagining all the possibilities I had dreamed of every day since childhood.

Throughout my teaching career, I told countless students that sometimes other people were so miserable that they said things to bring others down because misery loves company. Well, I was *not* misery's company anymore; I shouted that at the top of my voice and then listened to it echo through the hills! I finally recognized that for most of my adult life, I had allowed others to make me the scapegoat for their personal issues. I had allowed them to find comfort in their unfair judgments of my choices. I had allowed others' opinions of my perceived mistakes to steer many of my decisions. I realized at that moment they had never had the epiphanies that I did that day, and may not ever have them. Most of all, I claimed the power of self-forgiveness. Already, I felt a heavy weight had lifted from my heart, and I smiled.

I must admit that the first time I spoke up and confronted one of *them* in the middle of their smirking insult, it was odd. I was not mean-spirited; I simply said, "I'm not sorry for my choices. Perhaps if you had walked in my shoes, you would have made different ones. But then again, you would have to know all the twists and turns of my journey, which you don't know, and never will." And then I walked away. Within a few moments, that person apologized to me for the very first time and I felt as if I had won the million-dollar lottery! "I accept your apology," I said and kept walking.

Since that day that I sat overlooking the Ohio River contemplating life, I have moved mountains by changing the way I think, the way I look at life, and by imagining all the possibilities life has to offer *me*. I choose not to react to *them* anymore. Rather, I have learned to lead by example and walk away with integrity, letting their opinions roll off my back like water off a duck. I laugh more and sing out loud again (and not only in the shower)! You see, I have the power to control myself as well as forgive myself. I have the power to forgive them, also.

There is an old saying: *Forgiveness is for me, not for thee.* To me, that means forgiving yourself first so that you know how to forgive others. The power is in choices, and that power belongs to *you.*

IGNITE ACTION STEPS

1. Establish a meaningful morning routine. I personally recite something I call "My Gratefuls"—which are things I was grateful for yesterday and my expectations for today.
2. Plan your day out, but expect the unexpected.
3. Read from the Scriptures or some other book you hold dear daily and reflect on what you just read. Other books I read are, *Think and Grow Rich* by Napoleon Hill and *The Science of Getting Rich* by Wallace D. Wattles.
4. Do things that make you happy. Think of creating something, such as a vision board. Try a new recipe, color your hair, and try on clothes that look fun. Take a walk and find pictures in the clouds. Paint a picture while you drink a bottle of champagne and listen to music. Sit in the front car of the world's highest, fastest, loopiest roller coaster in the world! Above all, have fun!
5. Think of possibilities rather than impossibilities. Think of the glass as always full, even if you can only see the air that fills the glass.
6. Surround yourself with forward-thinking people. If you are going to listen to the thoughts of others, make sure those people's thoughts align with you. They may not always be the same perspective, but they create positive discussion and genuine reflection.

Melanie Summers—United States of America
Teacher, Certified Health and Wellness Coach, Owner of A Mellie Moment,
International Best Selling Author
www.amelliemoment.com
🇫 *Melanie Summers*
🄾 *mellie_moments*

THE QUEEN

I am the queen of my castle

I am strong

I am brave

I am kind

I am beautiful

I am grateful for you

I am the queen of my castle

I am humble

I am funny

I am soulful

I am loving

I am joyful as I live in my own skin

I am the queen of my castle

I know where I've been

I know where I am

I know where I'm headed

I expect to be surprised!

*But I will always smile as I walk in my own shoes
because –*

I am the queen of my life

Jeff Benton

Jeff Benton

"Forgiveness equals freedom of Self."

My hope is that this story helps you and your loved ones heal and move forward. If we choose to stay stuck in anger or resentment, we cut off access to our higher selves. We must learn to feel our emotions fully, let them pass through us, then release them. Only then can we heal and move beyond them. When we are brave enough to go through the process of forgiveness, we become open to experiencing a deeper kind of love—not only for others but also for ourselves. Forgiveness provides freedom and allows us to access a higher state of consciousness. It awakens us to embody our divinity.

Forgiveness = The Golden Key to Freedom

I was looking out my window at a beautiful, sunny, not-a-cloud-in-the-sky Denver, Colorado day. As I took in the view of the Rocky Mountains on that mid-July afternoon, I was daydreaming about the fun and magnetic lunch date I'd just had with a woman I'd been seeing for the past few weeks. I remember that day so vividly, yet it was almost two decades ago.

Suddenly, my daydream ended as the office phone rang. I answered. My receptionist told me that three police officers were in the lobby, waiting to see me. I started to laugh as we were always playing jokes on each other. But then, in a very direct tone, she said, "Jeff, I'm serious." That brief statement made my heart pound. My mind raced as I searched for an answer to what I could have done to warrant such a visit.

When the officers stepped through the glass door of my office, there was a quiet, almost peaceful energy emitting from them. A tall, athletic-looking officer, who could have been mistaken for a professional football player, was standing in the middle of the other two officers. He took a step toward me, with his head down... for a brief moment... and then... looked up and made eye contact with me. It was at this moment that I truly recognized that something was very wrong. His eyes were sympathetic, and he spoke in a soft but serious tone.

"Mr. Benton, we are deeply sorry to inform you that your mother has taken her life."

My heart dropped, and I became completely numb. In disbelief, I pushed past the officers and sprinted from the office. Immediately, I drove to the house where my mom and stepdad lived. I was driving as fast as I could, but everything around me felt like it was moving in slow motion. It was the most surreal moment of my life. I felt completely out of my body as I tried to absorb the news. I thought this sort of thing only happened to other people, like a tragedy you see in a movie or the shocking loss of a life you hear about in the news. I had just had dinner with my mom eighteen hours earlier, and although her behavior was erratic, this seemed impossible to comprehend.

I called my stepdad to confirm that I was somehow given the wrong information. Instead, he told me that my mother had bought a gun and shot herself in the head. I couldn't grasp her taking her life and even more so in this horrific way. My mom raised me to despise guns and violence. Nothing made sense.

Finally, arriving at my mom's house and seeing my stepdad and uncle crying, I broke down. I was sobbing uncontrollably, gasping for air. When the tears began to recede and the shock settled in, I started to feel the shame and blame of thinking I was responsible. *What could I have done? How could have I helped her?* I knew she was not in a good place but never could have imagined this outcome. *What was life going to look like moving forward?* I was riddled with sadness, guilt, and a barrage of other emotions that suicide brings.

Over the following days, I went into 'Jeff Benton numb-mode,' a skill I had mastered over a lifetime. The first time I remember acquiring this skill was as a very young child. Only later would I come to know that it was a defense mechanism used to tune out my mom's volatility and my former stepdad's abusive and sudden explosions. It was much easier to feel nothing than to accept the intense pain of rejection, shame, and unworthiness.

My strategies for numbing out for most of my life were not to feel my emotions; this included always joking around, distracting myself with technology, never being alone, and working all the time. I was avoiding my emotional pain, yet, I constantly felt this intense physical sensation within my body, almost like electricity zapping through me. It was my emotional pain showing up in a physical way that made me feel as if my bones were hurting. I actually thought my ability to numb myself was a superpower. My motto was, *Take everything away from me, and I will come back stronger.* If I didn't allow myself to feel any pain, no one could hurt me.

My grief and sadness over my mother's death suddenly turned into an eerie state of calm. Everyone around me was falling apart in the aftermath of her passing, while I found myself feeling clear and in control. I considered myself very special for this magic ability to disconnect and move through adversity and challenging times with swift ease. I reached the pinnacle of that feeling during my mom's memorial service. At that moment, everything slowed down. As her only child, I gave my speech honoring her and talked to the grieving community with grace, humor, and clarity. I was the perfect host, demonstrating strength for those around me.

A week later, I returned to the same life I had known before that tragic event—ensuring I stayed busy and numb. I worked around the clock and traveled to New York City for a business trip. On the first night of the trip, I had dinner with a friend. As I walked through Times Square on the way back to my hotel room, I started to feel intense anxiety and pressure in the middle of my chest. My heart began to pound rapidly as my head spun and sweat dripped out of every pore of my body. I lost balance and wasn't sure which way was up or down. I was trying to regain my footing as the lights of the enormous video billboards and the noise of the crowd became unbearable. I was scared to death. All I wanted was to find the way back to my hotel room. This was what I later came to know as my first ever full-blown panic attack.

That night, as I lay in bed, my breathing slowed down and my body began to relax. Then it hit me—the realization that I hadn't processed my mother's death. In fact, I hadn't processed many of my feelings during the thirty-five years that I'd spent on this planet. I still harbored all the anger, shame, sadness, and guilt below the surface that was buried deep within me. I started to recognize how I felt disconnected and lacking in purpose. As I analyzed deeper, I was truly shocked by how long I had managed to hold up this façade that made people think I was doing great.

Feeling the fear and intensity of the panic attack forced me to recognize that I couldn't live that way anymore. I couldn't hold it all in; the bottled-up emotions. I knew I had lost the ability to suppress it all, to force it down and ignore what I was truly feeling. At that moment, I decided to make drastic changes, determined to release the façade and discover the *real me*. I wanted to let go of this image I had created and finally understand who I really was. I made a commitment to myself that going forward I would find the resources, programs, and people that would help me on the journey of finding the more authentic Jeff Benton who believed in himself completely.

My new focus took hold. I wanted to find a way to eliminate the pain within me, but this time by going through it. I began a world tour of transformation by flying anywhere and everywhere I could to practice meditation and participate in retreats and workshops. Self-development and self-awareness became my obsession. Through these programs, I found supportive guides who created safe spaces in which I could be completely raw as I processed my mom's death, my childhood, and how I felt. The vulnerability and openness these guides shared about their own lives allowed me to take deeper risks into feeling my emotions fully. I went deep into my anger, shame, guilt, sadness, and pain. I started to feel and say things that I didn't consciously know existed within me.

The main theme of many of these programs was childhood trauma. My relationship with my mother was the biggest target. I remembered moments of my childhood that I hadn't thought about in years, including memories I had blocked out and stored away in the back of my subconscious memory vault. A week in these programs unlocked a lifetime of trapped feelings. I yelled, screamed, hit pillows, cried uncontrollably, and talked, talked, and talked some more about the injustices of my childhood. I shared all the things my mom had done to hurt me. I uncovered every possible emotion and felt that the direct path to them was to expose my mother for everything I perceived she subjected me to over the years.

Although opening the floodgates of emotions began the healing process, the story about my mom's suicide and my challenging upbringing took over; it became my identity. My life's injustices were the focus of all my conversations. I wore it as a badge of honor as I shared the traumas and adversities of my journey. I became intolerant to small talk and only felt stimulated and alive if each conversation took us to the depths of our souls. I 'felt' more fulfilled, but I wasn't free. When I would tell these dramatic and hurt-filled stories, I received constant validation of how evolved and in touch I was with my feelings. Many admired my newfound vulnerability. Yet, I realized I was too serious and overly focused on my healing versus finding my joy. There was *still* something missing.

As I became aware of the self-centered aspect of my healing approach, it had me yearning to find a way to reconnect to something beyond myself. As a child, I had felt the presence of a Higher Power guiding me through challenging situations. This deeper knowing and sacred connection was something I wanted back in my life.

Through my healing journey around the globe, I was fortunate enough to meet incredibly interesting and accomplished individuals. A few of them felt a deep connection to their spirituality and a Higher Power. These individuals introduced me to the ancient teachings and wisdom of the great mystics and masters. I started to read spiritual books and took classes from experts in a number of different subjects, including Vedanta, Kabbalah, and Buddhism. My heart lit up while reading and learning this material—it felt very familiar to me, and forgiveness was a common theme. Many of the teachings explained how *forgiveness provided the keys to freedom.* I also noticed that the concept of *Oneness*, that we are all interconnected, resonated with me deeply. I loved how science and specifically quantum physics, were able to support these ancient beliefs and teachings.

In the morning and evening, I began to incorporate forgiveness meditation, prayer, rituals, and mantras into my routine. For the first time in my life, it felt as if my mind was actually slowing down and experiencing a more present and quiet way, which was very different from the dissociative state I had known. Finding a deeper level of peace made me feel connected to something far beyond myself. I started to understand what the great Mystics, Avatars, and Seers had been describing for thousands of years. Going beyond the intellectual and emotional level, I experienced a deeper connection to Source, the Quantum Field, and my sense of Divinity within.

When I entered into this state of being, it was impossible to feel anything other than love and gratitude. A warmth grew in my heart, and a world that had for so long seemed adversarial now looked like a peaceful, beautiful place. My body felt no pain, as though a nurturing energy was flowing through it. I was letting go of my anger and letting appreciation take its place.

Feeling this profound connection to Spirit ultimately led to my ability to forgive my mom. I stopped telling the world my painful stories of the past. I realized that the constant sharing and attention I gave these experiences distanced me from feeling the love, compassion, and gratitude that existed deep within me. And, most importantly, I realized that every experience I have had to date, every single one, brought me to exactly where I was meant to be. Without them, I would not have reconnected with the Higher Source and my own Divinity.

Having a new perspective on my life helped me realize and appreciate that my mom had her own journey and challenges. I began to fully understand that she had done the best she could. She was a single mom raising a tiny little baby that she loved more than anything. She was filled with constant fear and did the best she could to help us survive. She was my biggest cheerleader right to the very end. When I fully forgave her, I fully felt her love. Compassion flooded my heart and all I wanted to do was tell her how much I loved her.

Many of the beautiful memories I had of my mom started to come back. I remembered how she played soccer with me every day so I could make the traveling team, and how she gave me motivational books from Norman Vincent Peale to try to uplift me; I realized the effect of these books on my current work today. She laughed at all my jokes. She bought me a car when I was sixteen, even though she didn't have a lot of money. My mother was a powerful force who ultimately helped shape many of my life's great aspects back then and today.

My connection with others in my life reached a new level. I was having more meaningful conversations with friends in one night than in the totality of our friendship. I could feel, relate, and empathize with more presence and fullness than I ever could before. I had stepped out of the darkness and into the light of conscious awareness.

Carl Jung's words resonated more than ever, "There is no coming to consciousness without pain. People will do anything, no matter how absurd, in order to avoid facing their own Souls. One does not become enlightened by imagining figures of light, but by making the darkness conscious." The journey from avoiding pain to now feeling emotions so profoundly was a gift that allowed me to transform in a way I could never have imagined. I realized that trauma wasn't who I truly was. It was simply an important part of my human experience. It was necessary to help me grow and learn the lessons that I couldn't have learned otherwise. And, through this realization, I forgave myself for all the punishment, judgment, and shame I had directed at myself. I truly began to feel what freedom felt like in my body, mind, and soul.

At the highest level, I truly believe that forgiveness is the most powerful force to heal the world. Forgiving myself allowed me to forgive my mom and others, and I started to experience this new-found freedom and a state of gratitude that I never knew existed. And, ultimately, I now experience my true Divinity and the Higher Power within me.

As you go on this journey of forgiveness, know that the lessons and adversities you face will allow you to discover a more authentic, vulnerable, and powerful version of yourself. When you are brave enough to go through the forgiveness process and emerge on the other side, you are more connected to yourself and others. You become an embodiment of love, kindness, and empathy, finding the freedom within that allows you to embody your full divinity. I promise you there are precious gifts and gold when you commit to forgiving fully. Know that your magnificent destiny ahead is part of the beautiful process of forgiving yourself.

IGNITE ACTION STEPS

As you continue on your journey toward embodying forgiveness, I invite you to consider and ask yourself the following:

1. How have the actions of particular individuals shaped you and made you stronger?
2. What gifts have seemingly difficult circumstances cultivated in your life?
3. Can you see how forgiveness creates more freedom in your life?
4. Do you find more strength in yourself when you choose to forgive others?
5. Define the highest version of yourself. What does it look like and how does forgiveness help you reach this highest version?
6. How can forgiveness help you embody more love for yourself and others?
7. Does forgiveness free your soul or Ignite your life in new ways? If so, in what ways?
8. While connecting with respect and love, ask others about their journey toward forgiveness.

Discovering these answers will be the beginning of your inner forgiveness journey.

Jeff Benton—United States of America
Founder & CEO, Paragon Performance Evolution
www.performanceparagon.com
❶ Jeffrey Benton
◎ jeffrey_benton_paragon

ADVICE TO MY YOUNGER SELF:
FORGIVE

So many lessons learned over the years
But one, in particular, is so clear
Our internal state becomes our external lens
No separation of outer and within

As above so below
As below so above
Why did I ever create separation
From myself and eternal love

As I emitted love from within
The world danced and celebrated akin
Why not exist in this state "Amore"
Was it the illusion of not feeling worthy

I now know we all deserve love

Wait, not deserve love, we are love

Let us fully embody what we are

A microcosm of God from afar

And not just afar but ever so close

This deep omnipotent power
blossoming like a rose

As I write these words my heart
continues to expand

God bless this experience on my own Holy Land

Dear child, feel God from within

It is the only thing that truly flows in

Remember this deep truth and
celebrate each day

Then you will free all hearts that
come your way

Candace Geurtsen

CANDACE GEURTSEN

"Forgiveness is the freedom and strength you claim for yourself."

It is my intention to share with you, the reader, that you can survive that which tries to break you. Trauma is a dark place that many of us may visit, but I want you to know that the light can shine again. When others try to take your power and silence your voice, you can take them back through forgiveness. You do not need to forgive the person who hurt you in order to unburden yourself of the weight from the pain. The you that was present for the trauma is the one to forgive: the beliefs that misled you, the knowledge you didn't have. You can embrace the lessons their mistakes taught you and grow stronger as you accept them. The most important person for you to forgive is you!

THE WOMAN WHO COULDN'T KEEP HER MOUTH SHUT

My military uniform is laid out on the bed. The feeling of nausea is overwhelming. The thought of not only putting on the uniform, but also what happens once I do makes me physically sick. After cleaning myself up and lacing my immaculately polished boots, I shudder as I walk out the door.

For three months he puts his hands on me. He brushes my butt, rubs the inside of my thighs, massages my shoulders, and stands too close. He eases past me with hands on my hips when we are both aware that there is more than enough room for him to pass without touching me.

For three months, I endured the sexual comments and questions disguised as interest in my life.

For three months, I've been confused. How can this be happening? He is a superior officer, my Adjutant. He is supposed to look out for me, aid in my training, and be someone I can turn to for help. But instead, he is the man who sexually assaults and harasses me.

I am spiraling into the abyss; shame, guilt, confusion, and the feeling that I've somehow become dirty—these feelings are swallowing me.

I was the first female platoon commander in my infantry reserve unit in London, Ontario; a young woman from a small town wanting to serve her country. I had just returned from summer training when the assaults began. I was caught off guard the first few times, unable to understand why he was doing this to me. I asked him to stop. Nothing. I asked those around me for help: the company commander and a fellow platoon commander. Nothing. One officer I turned to said it wasn't happening to him, therefore, it wasn't his problem to fix. "Figure it out," he said.

Three months later, during a parade night, I was ordered up to my Adjutant's office. I had started to avoid him, so he resorted to ordering me to come to him. Orders from a superior officer cannot be ignored, so I was forced to will my shaking body up the stairs. I was petrified and overwhelmed; my legs gave out on me. My mind disconnected as I sat down as if my body decided on its own to protect me. As I sat there sobbing and trying to figure out what to do, the Operations Officer found me. I told him between sobs what had happened, and he took me to the Commanding Officer; the investigation was launched. I wanted the Adjutant held responsible for what he had done. I felt for the first time that my ordeal may finally be over.

That was not the case. From the moment I came forward, I was ostracized. I was spat on as I walked by groups of men. "Oh, sorry, we didn't see you," they would claim with a smirk. I was given the wrong times for meetings and thewrong coordinates for attacks on exercise. When I sat down at a table in the officers' mess hall, the others who were seated would get up and walk away. I had drinks spilled on me as other officers "tripped." When my dress uniform was hanging in my office, it somehow got muddy bootprints all over it. For all these things I was written up—they were deemed my fault. Those I thought would support and stand by me did not, and that hurt more than anything he had done. The military had chosen who they would rally behind and it was my assailant, not me. He was a "good guy," and I was the "woman who couldn't keep her mouth shut."

Then, for a brief moment, I thought I might be vindicated. My allegations of sexual assault were found to be sustained, and I was so relieved. I truly believed good would triumph and he would be held accountable for the evil he'd done. Yet, to my disgust, I was informed by the Brigade Commander that I should have taken my assailant's reputation and the regiment's reputation into account before opening my mouth. My Adjutant had been personally and professionally embarrassed. He had suffered enough, and despite what I had endured, no further action would be taken against him. I was completely blindsided.

Looking back, I realize how naive I was to think that bad people would be punished for doing bad things, regardless of rank. I was told I should have kept it "in-house," that there was no need for me to make an official complaint, that I should know my place and not speak ill of superior officers. I was repeatedly told that I was the one who had acted in the wrong and was out of line. I was young and naive and believed what they were telling me. It hit me hard! I thought I had found my extended family, that the military was somewhere I could belong. Instead, I had found betrayal.

When I went home and told my mother, she asked me what I had done to encourage him. The shame and guilt of not only being sexually assaulted, but gaslit into believing I was the one at fault sent me spiraling.

I attempted suicide.

I went to a really dark place and went numb to cope with the darkness.

I felt like I was nothing… that I had no future and was unlovable, dirty, and tainted. Who would want to be with someone who had been touched like that by someone else? I had no support.

For years I questioned whether I had encouraged his behavior, believing perhaps I had acted in a way that made me deserving of his actions. Questions rattled in my head: "Could I have done something more to prevent it?" "Why didn't I put a stop to it sooner?" More importantly, "Why did no one believe me?" "Why was no one on my side?"

I felt so small, as though I didn't deserve to be here, and that there was no way out. It took over five years before I searched for help in the form of counseling and even then it took a few therapists before I found one whom I connected with. I wanted to know why I hadn't been good enough for the military; why had they chosen him over me? We slowly started to work through what had happened, and I began to let others in again.

Five years after being released from the military I married my husband, a man I had met on a trip and formed a relationship with over email. It was exactly what I needed, no physical intimacy to get in the way of loving him. I never told him about what I had gone through. I thought if he found out he would leave me, and I couldn't have survived that. He became my rock in only a few years, and I needed his steady presence in my life. He was the one person I could count on to always have my back, as I was still carrying my secret.

We had a daughter four years into our marriage, and that was when everything started to unravel. I had horrible nightmares about men treating my baby girl the way I had been treated. I was panicking. How could I shield her if I couldn't shield myself? I became overprotective, paranoid about the world harming my child. My marriage started to suffer as my husband tried to understand why I was acting so irrationally. I agreed to go back to therapy and made a discovery that would turn my life around.

Eventually, the time came when I had to tell my husband. As I spoke, I couldn't look at him for fear I would see disgust in his eyes. When I finished sharing my painful past, he exploded off the therapist's couch and started pacing. He turned to me, and the look of anger on his face caused me to shrink back. His face turned redder and redder, and it took me a few seconds to realize that his unbelievable rage wasn't directed at me. He was furious that another man would dare to touch me without my consent and that I was shown no support. The tears that came to my eyes as he rose to my defense would be some of the first cleansing tears I had ever cried. The sense of relief and love that came over me as he continued to be my advocate was so uplifting that I became dizzy. I couldn't believe I had married a man who could be so amazingly supportive and love me unconditionally. His devotion helped free me from the shame and guilt I had been harboring. I wasn't dirty. I deserved a love-filled life with a supportive family and his actions made me feel vindicated.

While I was feeling the bliss of my husband's support, my therapist asked me two questions: "If a twenty-one-year-old woman came to you now with the same story, what would you say to her? Would you blame her for what happened or support and believe her?" Sitting on that couch and thinking about these questions forced me to realize how I had been internalizing the continued gaslighting the military had started. I felt a prickling sensation under my skin as the irritation and exasperation swelled. I was incensed as I reflected on what they had done to me and what I had accepted from them. Weightlessness took over as the thick fog of self-resentment began to dissipate, and I could see clearly for the first time. I did not need to forgive my assailant. I did not need to forgive the military. I needed to forgive *myself*.

Upon my therapist's suggestion, I wrote a letter to my twenty-one-year-old self. I was young and naive and I trusted a broken system to work. I knew the military justice system would never give me closure. I needed to forgive myself for believing it would, and for relying on an outside source to help bring me peace. I forgave myself for believing that women in uniform are asking to be assaulted. I let go of accepting the blame and lack of support the military couldn't provide. My assaulter bears the responsibility; he caused the harm. I know that now. Forgiving myself allowed me to move from a victim to a survivor.

I felt so strongly about using my voice for justice and the empowerment of victims of military sexual misconduct that I took part in a class-action lawsuit (CAF-DND Sexual Misconduct Class Action) against the Canadian Government for not protecting the men and women of the Canadian Armed Forces. The government settled for $900 million. I submitted my claim to add my voice to the chorus and was successful. Taking part in the class action was, at times, extremely emotional and triggering, yet, in the end, released many feelings I hadn't realized I was still holding.

I had to open myself up, be vulnerable again, and tell my story to complete strangers so they could judge to what extent I had been harmed. It was at that point I sought a psychologist and received a diagnosis for a specified trauma and stressor-related disorder. Finally being able to put a name to what I felt was a relief, but now the real work of healing was to begin. It is work I still do now, one day at a time. Between my psychologist and my therapist, I am working on overcoming what happened and living with how it has affected me. There are days when I don't think about the assaults at all, and others when I feel so helpless I can't get off the couch. However, the good days outnumber the bad, so I take that as a win.

With the love and support I now enjoy, I have moved from survivor to advocate. I am no longer silent about what happened to me. I did nothing wrong. I have nothing to hide. I now own my past in a way that is freeing. I have a sense of purpose in bringing attention to sexual misconduct in the Canadian Armed Forces. In late 2021, I was part of a panel of people who spoke on the investigative news program W5 on CTV, titled "Military Secrets." The stories that were told by the brave men and women who came forward to speak were all very similar. It was an affirmation that I wasn't alone. Others had suffered as well and we were all, in our way, trying to make it better for those who followed us.

I also look forward to participating in the Restorative Engagement sessions offered to survivors. It will allow them to be heard, responded to, and acknowledged; to contribute to culture change within the forces; to increase awareness and understanding of past experiences of harm and to help restore the relationship of those harmed by the military. I will be able to share my experience of sexual misconduct in uniform with senior defense representatives to contribute to culture change within the military and make it a better place to work. I trust this will foster an opportunity for me to forgive at a deeper level.

I have thought a lot about forgiveness and what it means to me. Could I ever forgive the man who hurt me? I am still working on this. He has done nothing to warrant my forgiveness. He has neither asked for my forgiveness nor atoned for what he did. Forgiving myself is more important and is the part that is within my control. Self-forgiveness empowers me to advocate for those who still need healing and become a role model for my daughter and her generation.

Given the sexual misconduct crisis that has overwhelmed the Canadian Forces, I need to have faith that their ability to change will be successful over time. I have an awakened hope that they will do the right thing and guard their personnel zealously. I hope that civilian oversight and the continued media focus will motivate and inspire them to change for the better. I am on the journey of forgiving the Canadian Armed Forces for the part they played. I know that one day change will occur.

I continue to heal and claim the freedom and strength that is forgiveness for myself. I know then I will inspire my daughter to never let an outside force dictate who she is nor what is acceptable in her life. I share the same sentiment with you. It isn't about them. It's all you! When you release what 'they' did and focus on yourself and the lessons you've received, you begin to become who you fully are. You step into your power and become the *you* that you were meant to be, stronger than ever. Forgiveness is not an outside exercise, it's an inside exploration filled with self-acceptance and inner peace. Find your peace.

IGNITE ACTION STEPS

Discover your own definition of forgiveness. Forgiveness can mean different things to different people. For some, it is an unburdening of the weight of shame and guilt after trauma. For others, it's letting go of what they feel they did wrong at the time of the trauma. Perhaps it's the freeing sensation of letting go of the hate they feel for the one who caused the trauma. There is no one answer to *what is forgiveness?* Find yours as it applies to you.

Talk to someone. Therapy can be a life-altering experience. Find someone to confide in and talk to. Certainly, talking with your friends is a good place to start, but try a professional therapist, too. It may take a few different therapists before you find the one that is right for you, but professional help makes a big difference.

Forgiveness of self. Look in the mirror and forgive the you who underwent the trauma; the you as a child, a teen, or even the you from last year. Forgive who you were when the trauma occurred.

Refuse to accept that which does not belong to you. You were not the cause of your trauma. Refuse to carry someone else's burden. The person who assaulted me is the one who should, and will, carry the burden of their actions. His faults are not mine to carry.

Look internally. Sit and reflect on who you are, how you want to live your life, and what you want to stand for. Then, go out and let nothing stop you from becoming that person.

Candace Geurtsen—Canada
Supervising Nuclear Operator, Veteran, Advocate, Wife, Mother, Badass
Candace Blick-Geurtsen
Candace Blick-Geurtsen

IGNITE
Forgiveness

I am

DESERVING OF FORGIVENESS.

I will open myself to the

FREEDOM FORGIVENESS OFFERS.

I am grateful to learn the

LESSONS FORGIVING MYSELF BESTOWS.

I am ready for

THE PEACE FORGIVENESS BRINGS

or something better.

Michelle A McClain

MICHELLE A MCCLAIN

"Forgiveness = freedom = elevation."

My intention is to support you in elevating you into your greatness, into the next version of you, and for you to receive the lessons from each painful circumstance in your life in order to level up. Life is like a video game, and when you get the lessons, you go to the next level. You have the keys to unlock the freedom and joy in your life already inside of you. I invite you to look for the lessons, forgive the painful circumstances, and allow this to be the new ground you stand on. Until we learn the lesson of self-love, we remain on the same level and our experiences become patterns in our lives that repeat. Forgiving painful circumstances, and acknowledging what they teach us, allows us to transcend. I hope to inspire your transformation through awareness, guidance, and empowerment. You can learn to be resourceful and use the experiences in your life to help you become the highest version of you.

FREE FROM THE CAGE

On my knees in my bedroom, devastated and crying, I asked God: *"HOW? After everything you know I've been through! How am I here now? You know I'm trying to make something of my life. How could you let this happen?"* I had just been fired, losing my main source of income, for drinking on the job. I had been working three jobs, putting myself through school, and doing whatever I could to move forward from the life I grew up with. I'd been running from my childhood, trying to create a beautiful life, and now I felt like I was back in it.

As a child, I remember having spaghetti picnics with my brothers and the neighborhood kids. We would gather on our front lawn and eat a big pot of Mom's famous spaghetti together. It was one of my favorite childhood memories. I also remember taking my little baby doll everywhere I could. My baby watched me make brownies in my Easy Bake Oven® and sneak into my mom's closet to play dress-up in her high heels, bras, and jewelry. I loved playing dress-up, trying on every color, and feeling especially beautiful in pink. I would change outfits about fifteen times a day! My mom would always ask why there were so many clothes everywhere because you could never see my bedroom floor. I had princess jewelry, called Pretty Pretty Princess®, that I would put on and show off my shimmery plastic diamonds, colorful gems, and pearls during my tea parties.

My days were filled with adventure and play, climbing the tree in my back-yard between home-schooling lessons with Mom. But, at around 5 PM every afternoon, everything changed. When my brother and I saw our father's car pull up to the side of the house, our adrenaline shot up and our uncertainty had us walking on eggshells. I learned to stay out of the way and disconnect from reality to avoid ruffling any feathers. I would be quiet, playing games in the corner, entertaining myself to avoid being seen or heard.

When we are in a traumatized state (fight or flight), the brain doesn't hold on to memory well. This is why much of my childhood is blacked out. Our brain protects us from memories that it doesn't believe we can handle. And some parts come to memory only when the soul is ready to heal them.

Certain moments are embedded in my brain and the flashbacks are haunt-ing. Such as the horror of screaming internally as my sweet innocent body got violated in the shower by my father, or my mom hiding me in my closet as I overheard my brother getting beaten. After being violated as a little girl, I cut off the most beautiful, soft parts of myself and became hardened. Building my walls was a catalyst for me to embody as much masculine energy as possible. Terrified, I rejected the creative, delicate, gentle, soft, feminine side of myself, and the walls caged me.

Being sexually abused by my father, the one man who was supposed to pro-tect me from harm's way, convinced me that being vulnerable in my feminine energy would invite pain. That experience had many side effects, including shaping my beliefs around men, myself, and the world. One of my biggest beliefs, that I held for so long, was that *the world was not safe*. Due to that belief, I lived the majority of my life in fight or flight and in fear of the world.

This led me down the unhealthy path of codependency, which I still consciously work on today. When I would allow myself to connect with my feminine side, I would partner it with a cold, rigid, rough, masculine energy in an attempt to intimidate those around me as a protection mechanism. I felt like an injured animal protecting its wounds.

I blamed my dad for everything. From the men I couldn't get it right with, to the trust issues I had, to my fear of intimacy, commitment issues, and sleeping problems. I held him responsible for the fact that I would sit in the back, not wanting to be seen, never speaking up, and would rather let people speak for me. When I struggled to take care of myself, forgetting to brush my teeth or wash my hair for days, it was because I was taught to think I didn't matter. My fear of the dark, my binge eating, my A.D.D., my self-sabotage, self-deprecating behavior, and tendency to pretend things were okay when they weren't... I mean, I really blamed this guy for everything. It felt good to blame him, to throw my pain back onto him and not have to take responsibility for anything that didn't make me feel proud of myself.

After years of mental, physical, and sexual abuse, I sought out numbness, ways to dim the pain I felt. Then I lost my brother in an abrupt accident, which was too much pain to bear. I stopped letting myself feel anything and became more like a robot internally. I would smile, and look okay, but inside I was shut off. Disconnected. Emotionless. Anxious. I wanted to escape the real world and create a fantasy life where everything was fine. I became a professional at avoiding and all I did was drink. It numbed the pain. I stayed busy or was 'four shots deep,' headed to blackout drunk. I look back and think, *wow, there was a lot of pain hidden under the beautiful smile that I showed people.* I kept my invisible walls up because I knew if people got too close, they would see my pain. It wasn't until later that I discovered people could see and feel those walls. I guess I wasn't doing as good of a job at hiding them as I thought. I was embodying the ideas behind my favorite quote by Jim Rohn: "The same walls that keep out pain, keep out joy." And that is exactly what I experienced—a happy smile on the outside, while there was a broken child on the inside, screaming and begging to be free from her cage.

That brought me to that devastating yet fateful day, crying on my bedroom floor. Little did I know that that moment would start the journey of healing that I would embark on; the journey to forgiveness and freedom.

An hour after I called out to God for help, my best friend showed up and found me curled in a fetal position, bawling and clinging to my red comforter. She sat with me, gave me a little pep talk, and suggested we look for a temporary job to pay my rent until we had a resume for me put together. A temp position as a coach was the only one I could apply for without a resume. I was nervous as I filled out the online application. With the charisma and ability to read people that I'd learned (through trauma and needing to read and be aware of the household to stay safe), I was confident that as long as I truly believed in it, I could sell anything.

I requested an interview that night, and twenty-four hours later, I had the job. I could not believe it. It was completely out of my comfort zone, seeing as though I knew nothing about health or nutrition. I was a fast food addict and energy drink junkie. I felt inadequate to be teaching people about living a healthy lifestyle, but I began getting guidance as I guided others. The job consisted of coaching people through a daily nutrition program to help them replace an unhealthy lifestyle with a healthy one. Ironically enough, it was everything I needed to learn for my own lifestyle. Initially, I was just relieved to have a job that would bring me money, but as I started to see the results I was getting for people, and how good they were feeling because of my guidance, I started falling in love with it.

Suddenly, I was being of service in a different way. I went from helping people get drunk at the bar, to helping them save their own lives and see a future for themselves. I wanted people to know what I did. For the first time, I felt proud. I went from being the party girl who was called to pour people shots, to being the trusted coach called to counsel and heal people. My stepdad had tried everything to lose weight, so I asked him if he was interested in letting me coach him, even if it was to support the family. He agreed, and after the first few weeks, he saw results. He cried, and I started feeling emotions again, letting them out of their cage.

Within that job, I got mentorship on how to set goals and visualize my future. Something I had never done before. For the first time, I was being asked what my dream life would look like, what my dream car would look like... questions I didn't even have answers to at the time. I never looked at nice cars because, deep down, I didn't believe I would be able to have one. No one in my family had nice things, so why would I be any different? Now I was learning how to visualize myself five years down the road and I started putting road maps together on how to become that woman.

After reaching small goals, I started to actually believe some of the bigger ones were possible. It felt good to be working on myself in a different way. This wasn't working on my makeup or going to social outings; this was deep diving into my soul and asking what I really wanted to do with my life, the kind of person I wanted to become, and how I wanted to be remembered one day when I'm no longer here. For the first time, I thought about leaving an impact, not just getting a paycheck and living for the weekend.

Then, those dreams started to feel more like reality. The job was doing more than paying my bills; I started being able to pay off my debt! I could now pay bills for my family, take my little brother shopping, and even donate. Not only that, I ended up getting my very first nice car. Things I never in my wildest dreams would have seen as possible for me. I can't tell you how many, "Pinch me. Am I dreaming?" moments I started to have.

Don't get me wrong, it wasn't easy. I was working non-stop and rarely sleeping, but because I was so in love with being in service and receiving not only financial provision but emotional fulfillment. I was happy to work and walk away from partying. I started discovering the talent I had to serve people and how I had a natural gift to coach them toward their greatest selves. I started building an internal confidence in areas I never had before. Most of all, I felt fulfilled in ways I never knew possible. To have people hug me and cry because they had the energy to play with their kids again or could reach past their bellies to tie their shoes... their happy tears gave me more than a paycheck ever could. It became my new addiction. It was such a good addiction, allowing me to go sober. No more wine and Nyquil® to sleep at night; I slept like a baby without them. I realized nothing is accidental and that our Creator always puts us where we need to be for our next steps in life.

In teaching others, I've learned to appreciate and take lessons from all parts of my journey. Even down to being the minority in school, I learned non-judgment. I was often misjudged for my skin color and how I looked; people had a whole story made up in their heads about who I was and what my life was like. How wrong they were. They assumed I had it made at home when, most days, I didn't want to go home. Their assumptions were so far from the truth that they taught me how to be non-judgemental at an early age, to never judge someone based on their outer appearance because you don't know what's going on in their internal world or at home. Pain is still pain, sadness is still sadness regardless of age, gender, or color. Struggles touch us all, and no one is exempt. The outer appearance really means nothing in relation to what's happening internally in your life. I learned to see the soul. To see everyone as a spirit in a human suit, an avatar. I realized that everyone deserves love, compassion, and comfort, and to appreciate the avatar that everyone chooses to show up as in this game of life. This non-judgemental mindset of seeing people for who they are was a game-changer for how my life has turned out;

I couldn't be more grateful for that lesson. If I had not had the childhood I experienced, I would not have seen the true essence of some of my closest friends and business partners. I see people for who they are and, without my walls, I welcome them in.

Getting fired for drinking on the job became my divine intervention, my Ignite Moment. Using my gift of service to others and having them express such joyful appreciation opened my heart again, and I began loving at full capacity. Ever since my brother passed away, I could count the number of times I let myself feel (and they usually included alcohol). Now, I had happy tears that felt like I was cleansing my soul and lighting up my world. I let myself access and acknowledge the pain I had gone through, yet, enjoyed healing myself on a deeper level. I saw the purpose of the walls I'd created. They were a protection mechanism from what I had endured and were the result of fear. I didn't need those walls anymore, they dissolved, and I had found real joy. After traveling through the many stages of grieving, pretending like it didn't happen, I was able to embrace my emotions and have the intelligence around the anger and rage, blaming and resentment, the depression, and sadness, and move through the "why me" victim stage. When I have one of these emotions visit me at any stage in my life, I know how to recognize them and transmute them because I've overcome those 'levels,' and I value the messages they bring. When I think back on that little girl frozen in shock, confusion, and broken-hearted, I lovingly wrap my arms around her and tell her that everything will be okay, and she will write the most amazing life story and become an incredible woman in the world. I assure her that she didn't do anything wrong, that it isn't her fault, and that I will take care of her.

I'm amazed at what the human spirit can truly endure, and how far I've come. Everything I do now, I do for her. For that sweet little girl who wanted nothing but to dance, sing, love, and be loved. I still see her twirling around in her pretty pink dress—It is for her that I do my work now. To serve, give, forgive, create healing and elevation in the world. I live through the heart of that little girl. My journey has given me my purpose in the world, and I believe it is that way for everyone, when we choose to forgive and receive the lesson.

Every single experience is for us and not against us. I believe life is rigged in our favor. And it's simply how we choose to play the cards we are dealt. Through the many stages of healing, I learned to find gratitude in each experience's pain and lessons, and to see the story of my life that I've been gifted to write.

We all have a story to tell, and we each get to be the hero in that story. I decided my story would be one of forgiveness, triumph, overcoming, strength, and inspiration. I invite you to do the same. Start today, from this day forward, writing your story as the victor and hero you are! Watch as you break old cycles and elevate your life.

IGNITE ACTION STEPS

Take some time for your future self by journaling, and use it as a way to welcome in some positive reprogramming:

1. Write. Grab a pen and a journal, find a quiet place to be alone, and write out the painful moments from your past.
2. Identify the beliefs and agreements that were created from those events. What did you decide about life, people, yourself, etc., due to this event?
3. Tell a new truth or belief that benefits your future. For example, replacing the belief, *people are dangerous*, with *I attract people who keep me safe, protect, and love me.*
4. Practice compassion for yourself, and speak in your mind or out loud what you want to be, do, and have, such as *I am proud of myself for doing the work, I am moving through this with ease, The future you is so proud of you right now.*
5. Find purpose from the experience. If life was a video game, what was the lesson from that event? What did it teach you?
6. Visualize the person you see yourself being in five years, or as far in the future as you can see, the healthy, happy, successful version of you. How does that person look, feel, act, treat others, and get treated? Where does that person go, what do they do for fun? What do they do on a daily basis? Then start acting in alignment with that person.

Michelle A McClain—United States of America
Speaker, Author, CEO of BITNESS, Self Mastery & Transformational Coach
TheSoulIntuition.com
MichelleMcClain444@gmail.com
Michelle Mee Shell McClain
DesignYourBody

IGNITE
Forgiveness

Walking through fire

burns away all that no longer serves us,

for the next level.

Walk through the fire,

achieve the metal,

and go to the next level.

"May the hells light up the path to heaven."

"The hells help us burn away the lower version of us.

So the higher version can appear.

And like a snake shedding its skin,

The new will rise again."

"Walk through the fire,

And receive the lesson.

Wrapped in various colors, shapes, and sizes,

the gift of evolution awaits."

"Forgiveness is like the snake shedding skin.

The new will rise again."

Kristen Connell

Kristen Connell

*"Upgrade the output of your life by intentionally curating
the input of everything that surrounds you."*

My hope is for you to discover the signs that are continuously guiding you. Always listen to your internal communication system that provides feedback on the mental, physical, and spiritual environments around you. As you invite those indicators to create internal awareness, you can solve conflict in an authentic and integrated way just by tuning into that guidance and following the highlighted path.

Exposed

We've all been there. An accidental activation of our phone camera in selfie mode from the least flattering angle. Amidst the harsh, fluorescent light in a department store dressing room, it glaringly reveals every dimple and wrinkle. An accidental snapshot from your hand that exposes your double chin. When confronted with an image of ourselves, we often want to look away. *That can't be what I really look like.* When it comes to our lives, it's hard—impossible, sometimes—to see things from an outsider's perspective. And when someone, even someone we trust, tells us a hard truth about ourselves, the same denial kicks in. *This can't be me. And if it is, I don't want to see it.*

Most of us go through life without ever being able to disassociate from our current life patterns to gain perspective.

My journey began during the winter holidays. My husband and I were about to embark on a tour of Peru to celebrate the new year with our dearest friends. As the trip neared, I began having tightness in my chest and struggled to catch my breath. My brain was foggy; I couldn't connect my thoughts or recall simple things. My joints were in pain, and my whole body felt weak. Initially, I dismissed these symptoms as a natural response to the stress of the holidays, the arduous task of packing for a trip, and the guilt of leaving our children behind for ten days.

I had been feeling disconnected and disoriented for several months and had come to the conclusion that it was related to exhaustion from having a baby two years prior, perhaps to a hormonal imbalance or thyroid issues. The list of possible concerns was endless, yet my bloodwork and test results always came back within normal range. Yet, that particular episode prior to our trip was so pronounced that I asked my husband to either cancel or go without me. It was an incredibly unusual request for me to insist on not going, as travel was an integral part of being raised by a family of pilots. My motto was that adventure was just a plane ride away, and I lived that to the core.

My plea for a reprieve from this insurmountable task of going on our luxury vacation was dismissed and minimized. My husband launched immediately into a verbal defense, asking what could possibly be stressing me out when I was a stay-at-home mom of two children, and we all napped for hours every day because I had a full-time caregiver and a housekeeper. I was taken aback by his response, met with blame, shame, and belittlement. I didn't often put my health or needs first, so I acquiesced.

I did what I always did, I pulled myself up by my proverbial bootstraps and bypassed my internal alarm system to ensure I didn't cause any upset or expense to our elaborate vacation plans. My chest was still tight throughout the flight, and it got even worse when I experienced altitude sickness right after arriving at Lake Titicaca, one of the highest points in Peru. I sat in the hotel, breathing from an oxygen tank until my lungs expanded and my head cleared.

As the hours and days passed, I acclimatized to the new environment and found that I actually felt better and even more energized. Peru was a journey that brought me back to reconnect with *Pacha Mama,* Mother Earth, and back to myself. I was feeling a rebirth of sorts. For the first time, I noticed a difference in the environment and the energy in and around me; there was more clarity and purity. Our trip included a lot of time in nature, surrounded by trees and the fresh, mountainous air. The Inca Trail was both a rugged and a beautiful, energetic experience; and we made our way to the Sun's Gate and then to the profoundly captivating Machu Picchu. I was able to see and sense my life through a new lens.

Then we returned back home. Reality hit... HARD. As I walked back into our home, I began to feel all the same symptoms coming back, and quickly. I felt as if I was having a heart attack. I decided to visit a dear friend of ours, an esteemed cardiologist, and explained my concerns and symptoms. He did a comprehensive heart assessment that lasted three full days, forcing me to wear a heart monitor strapped to my side. As I waited for the results I kept thinking, *If only he found something, then I could at least have an answer about why I feel so exhausted, mentally and physically*. I received lab and test results showing I was 'within normal ranges' for all the usual concerns for deteriorating heart conditions. The cardiologist's results from wearing the three-day heart monitor were, again, "normal." But, I did not feel like *my* version of normal.

Then the doctor gave me one small suggestion that changed everything. He recommended I have the rental home, which we have lived in the past nine years, tested for elevated mold and possibly mold. The next day I did exactly that. I had a state-licensed mold assessor come to sample the air quality of our home, along with physically testing various areas in each room that had signs of water intrusion from years past and previous tenants. Those test results came back far from normal. They indicated the mold spore level was hundreds of times higher than the range for safe human exposure, especially in my children's bedrooms. I was shocked, confused, scared, and uneducated, but even with my limited knowledge on the subject of mold, I knew it was not a great diagnosis. I began to look at my children's health history for the past two years: nosebleeds, febrile seizures, headaches, joint pains, trouble sleeping, and extreme emotional outbursts. Their symptoms all came flooding into my present experience, and I had a deep sinking feeling that I had found the source. The only person who wasn't suffering was my husband. He traveled extensively for his job and was home only a few days each week, translating into less time in our covertly toxic environment.

I began researching voraciously through countless websites, ranging from public health sites to building codes and enforcement. I was discovering people with similar challenges who were speaking out and making the public aware of the massive negative impact of living in a toxic environment on personal health. I was literally piecing together a puzzle of titanic importance, realizing with each discovery that this was far bigger of a health threat than just a string of allergic reactions. I was even beginning to wonder if the mold from long-term leaks and water damage in the roof had played a role in the many miscarriages

I had experienced in the nine years we resided in this home. I went to over fifty doctors of varying expertise, only to be told "mold was everywhere," and it was all in my head (then given a prescription for antidepressants). Yet, for me, the reality was becoming clear. My family was suffering silently, in different ways, with different symptoms, all from the same exposure.

It was imperative that we communicate with our landlord about the most recent water intrusion so he could address this ongoing slow leak in the roof. My husband indicated he would handle the logistics of communication and repairs with the owner. We did not realize a small patch in the roof was merely the tip of the iceberg of issues we'd need to resolve. There would end up being many more things that had to be done to clear the air—literally, figuratively, physically and emotionally.

I continued to research ways to mitigate our health concerns. I dove into ways to filter our 'input' with the best air filtration devices, clean out our bodies with healthier food options, and reset with supplements and other modalities for healing the body. We tried salt room sessions and eventually discovered a detox facility that specializes in educating and facilitating recovery for chronic mold exposure. On another front, I set out on a thorough search for other, less toxic options for rental homes in our area. Unfortunately, the prices had doubled for a similar size home as it had been almost ten years since our last search.

My husband constantly rejected each home listing I presented for being too costly for our monthly budget while simultaneously making plans for extravagant social outings, dinners, and vacations. There was a pronounced uptick in the sarcastic jokes he made to our families and social circle about my mental health, as he said my obsession over mold had gone overboard. The toxic assault was coming from all angles inside my home: emotionally from my life partner and physically from the microscopic mold spores. There came a sinking feeling that I would never be given permission to leave this noxious environment and gain the permission to heal, nor the permission to stand up for myself.

As all of those components began to settle into my conscious awareness, I needed to talk it through with someone. I stood in my dining room, staring at our huge, bright-green wall that had once represented freshness, but now only conveyed stagnancy. I called up a friend. I described to her how things had been progressing and relived the conversations I'd had with friends, family, and various practitioners. Then I felt a pit in my stomach, and the floor dropping out from beneath me as an epiphany hit me. I realized that no one in a cape would be swooping in to save me. Not my husband of ten years, not the landlord, not my family nor my friends. No one. I was going to have to be the one to save myself.

It was at that moment I knew that the person I had relied on to be my biggest supporter was actually behaving more like an enemy. It was as if he was working against me on all fronts to discredit and diminish me and my mental health to any other potential allies. He spoke convincingly about how I "looked normal" and how my concerns and fears were all in my head. Much to my surprise, he had been doing that for years, so covertly that he had garnered a full-blown audience of our peers. They engaged in hearing the private details of our saga, and it felt as if he had forayed it into an entertainment platform for those around us.

My life was coming into focus, and I didn't like what I was seeing. I knew I needed out. Out of the house, out of the marriage, and out of the sadness that had grown.

The events that followed were a perfect storm that created the intensity to incite a change. By that, I mean a literal storm system parked right over our home, and the rain fell for what seemed like days. Everything caved in, the roof crashed down, and so did my marriage. The damage was done. It was rotten from all angles. Everything was exposed. The signs were revealing that it was time to move out and time to move on, physically and emotionally. I couldn't save my marriage, but I could save myself.

I began the work of repair and rebuilding after losing everything I owned that had been contaminated. I made it my full-time job to recover and heal structurally and physically. I even began to get calls from people all over the United States who had heard of my story and my struggle from their friends. I did my best to educate them, knowing that each person I spoke to was either at the beginning of their very long journey of awareness, or the end of their very short journey to ignorance. I had wished for ignorance more than once as it seemed the path of least resistance.

As I had more distance from the mold exposure and from the intensity of my dysfunctional partnership, I began to realize that the overflow of unchecked water in our house served as a metaphor for the dysregulated emotional state of myself and my marriage. With time and much work around healing the immense database of traumatic events, I was able to find peace with the role we both played. The distillation of events boiled down to the fact that I had a partner who supported my lifestyle, but not my life. He was a strong provider of all things material, but I felt he was not equipped to go any deeper with me. He was fulfilling the role of husband to the best of his ability, and I had simply evolved. The time had come to process the past, release the emotions, and resolve any residual anger or resentment toward him so I could ultimately find my home within myself and reside in a place of forgiveness.

True forgiveness was an inside job.

Much like the pieces of the puzzle uncovering what was making me feel ill in our home; I had to play investigator to connect the dots on what was beneath all those layers. After all, I had chosen him as a partner, and looking back with a zoomed-out lens I began to see all the ways that he had been consistent from the very beginning. He had always shown me exactly who he was and what his priorities were. I was the one who had dismissed and disregarded those signs all along; I had bypassed myself and my own intuition.

As I owned and forgave my role in the collapse of my relationship, I stepped into my power more and more. I had agency in my life, and the role others played in it changed. I accepted that he could not have done better, and with that realization came a level of peace and forgiveness for him. I came to the *inner*-standing that I had to do better, and set about to do everything in my power to find ways to forgive those who had not been able to see I was suffering: the practitioners who prescribed me anti-depressants, the friends who had been entertained by my husband's claims, and the family who thought I was imagining it all. By extending forgiveness, I was able to get more clarity about what was remaining for me to discover.

I set out to heal all the emotional elements and traumatic events of my story with the same determination I had researching and attaining physical well-being. I went to practitioners that helped educate me on the practices of things as simple as breathwork, meditation, reiki healing, as well as the deeply profound works of family constellation therapy and generational trauma healing. Those practices and countless more revealed a deeper layer of myself that had never been addressed. The subconscious mind and the collective of stored elements and emotions that were in the driver's seat of my so-called life. When I was able to get to this layer, I came to uncover all the events and people I unknowingly energetically attracted throughout my life via my own belief systems. Underneath it *all,* I had been running the mental program and inner belief that I simply was not "worthy." When I got to this foundational piece, dug into the roots, and began to take responsibility, I was able to get to the most important part of forgiveness; forgiving ME!

I am exponentially grateful for the path, the journey to forgiveness, and of all the ways I was exposed.

The beauty of forgiveness is that it allows us to clear the events of the past, along with the old, outdated emotions, and make space for new, more aligned, and conscientious ones. Once we free up the mental resources that have been dedicated to holding onto the past, we can create something different, new, and an increasingly more satisfying future. You can align with who you choose to be, rather than who you have always been. Be your own advocate and discover your power. Design the life you want, and show the world your true capacity for greatness.

IGNITE ACTION STEPS

Curate the information that you allow into your life.
- Write down the top five sources of information that impact you daily via the media, social, business, family, and culture. Rate them on how the information you consume affects you either positively or negatively.
- As you identify how this information you consume daily affects you, you can begin to switch out for more healthy sources that add value.
- Decide to eliminate the extraneous information, the needless things, along with the stuff that has a low vibration and makes you feel bad.
- Choose to replace these information sources with positive, upbeat, and inspiring input. What you consume you become, so only 'take in' what is best for you.

Kristen Connell—United States of America
Founder of The Rewired Mind Method, Speaker, Author
www.theREWIREDmind.com
www.theREWIREDmindmethod.com
Kristen@theREWIREDmind.com
☺ kristenconnellofficial

IGN TE
Forgiveness

FORGIVENESS IS A PROCESS
THAT BEGINS WITH SELF,

yet it takes engaging and committing in close personal relationships to show us what remains for us to explore.

THERE IS ALWAYS ANOTHER LAYER TO UNCOVER

in giving and receiving forgiveness and the emotional mirror of another is the reflection on those fragments of what remains for us to heal.

Morgan McNeil

Morgan McNeil

"Forgiveness means finding peace within you."

My wish for you is to find joy in life and the lessons they bring. To feel your pain but not carry it with you forever. Know that it's okay to put it down to move forward because life is meant to be wonderful. We all deserve to release pain and open ourselves to life's many opportunities. I believe that everything happens for a reason, and when I cannot understand the reason in the moment, I surrender and trust one day I will. Finding forgiveness for self is one of the hardest things to do. I hope that by reading my story, you will find forgiveness within you.

Learning to Dance

Memories are sprites, playful shapeshifters that change with our moods and the phases of the moon. Memories shape our understanding of the world and allow us to predict the best way to handle situations. Yet memories, by nature, can be fickle, vivid, play tricks on us, be elusive, or haunt us for a huge part of our life.

My earliest memories revolve around playing: scavenger hunts, crafting potions from clover, grass, and flowers, and mixing whatever we found outside into concoctions. My sister, Laura, and I would squeeze mud between our fingers as we made mud pies. We would cut shapes into potatoes to stamp them into the paint, making our little artworks for Mom. Mom was the woman who gave us our creative, magical childhood. Mom, Laura, and I would spend most of our time together as Dad worked out of town during the week.

Mom embodied love and patience. When she smiled, she meant it; smiling big, with her gums showing and her lips creasing into her freckles as she laughed her deep, belly laugh. She wore thick, round gold glasses like Harry Potter and always smelled wonderful from the perfume she wore. She was sunshine. But those sunny skies would soon have clouds.

April 1st, 2009—I am eight years old. A breeze cut through the heat, and I swear I could smell the sea despite being miles away in the city of Halifax, Nova Scotia. Today was the day we had been waiting for; the day Mom would get her new heart. You see, Mom had fought and conquered Hodgkin's lymphoma on three separate occasions. What we didn't know is how hard chemotherapy and radiation are on the human body. Mom was experiencing heart failure at thirty-six years old and was pushed to the top of the donor list. We were so excited to get the call from the doctors. My sister and I raced to pack our bags, eager to get to our aunt's house near the hospital while Dad went to be with Mom.

I was playing hopscotch with the neighborhood kids when Dad's black jeep turned down the street. Finally! We can go and see Mom! Excitement took over, and I abandoned my playmates, eagerly running up to Dad. "Can we go see Mommy now?!" Dad looked drained... not excited. The sky and air around me seemed to get thicker. His response to my enthusiastic question held a calm tone, but it also told me something was wrong: "Yes, but I need to talk to you girls first."

We went inside my aunt's house, and Dad sat us down. Mom's heart transplant was a success, but while in recovery she experienced a clot that cut off the blood flow to her brain. Dad explained it to me, using the word "vegetable." *But, carrots grow and are alive, so Mom can just come back, right?* I was confused and not sure what to do.

My father was one of those strong but silent types. You know, the ones who pick you up and brush you off after a fall; the ones who tell you you're okay rather than asking how you're feeling. He loved to sing to us. On weekends when he was home, we would play Singstar™, and he would always choose *Chasing Cars* by Snow Patrol. He always had something playing on the radio. If not music, he was listening to an audiobook.

Only this time, he appeared stark and quiet. He took shallow breaths in, and long, shaky breaths out — and this was the first time I saw my father cry. He stayed kneeling in front of us as my sister's anger took over, and she marched out of the room, throwing her glass of water at the exposed brick wall in the kitchen. Then, things went hazy for me. I remember yelling, crying, and finding myself in a car on the way to the hospital, sitting quietly and holding back my tears.

The glow from the halogen lights set the tone, sterile and serious, making the white tiles look dirty. I know this because I couldn't take my eyes off the floor, aware that looking down was my best bet to keep the tears at bay. We walked into a private hospital room and my grandma was seated in a chair. My desire to be strong evaporated as she opened her arms to me. My tears flowed, drenching her shirt. This was the last time I felt like an eight-year-old. I wanted to be loved, cooed, and comforted, to have someone take care of me. I looked at Mom—my sun. I saw her, but without her big smile—a plastic tube in its place. I didn't hear her belly laugh, just the monitor beeping in a language I didn't understand. I was taken back to the time Mom had a heart attack, and I held her hand until I finally felt her squeezing mine. Surely, this time, if I stayed by her bed, holding her hand, she would wake up again.

She didn't. Instead, a decision was to be made, one that would dictate our new reality. Dad chose to let Laura and I make the call on what would happen next. Our decision was made the instant we were asked. We had been prepped for this. Mom had been on death's door before and told us that it was best to let her go if she couldn't do things for herself—if she couldn't be there in mind, body, and soul. I wanted her to stay, but she wasn't her anymore. We held her hand as we said goodbye, which was easier to do as we sensed she was already gone. We stayed with her as her dim light faded into an empty void. The machine stopped beeping, and the room fell silent. I don't remember anything else from that day. The only thing I do remember about the week following our forever goodbye was selecting a heart-shaped tombstone.

Her funeral was in the same church in which she was married. People filed into the sanctuary until all the seats were full, and overflowed to the sides of the room and balconies. Family and friends came from all over Canada, even my favorite babysitter. We buried Mom in her favorite pink blouse, and we selected her favorite flowers — red roses. I put an angel pin on one of the roses and threw it onto her closed coffin as it was lowered.

Time can be cruel. When tragedy happens, should it not stop, or slow down to pay respect to the world-shattering events? We need a moment of silence and stillness to catch our breaths and comprehend the full brunt of knowing life will never be the same. At eight, I was motherless, with a withdrawn father and an angry older sister. But, time unapologetically went on with business as usual. Days continued at the same pace, and I was told, "people had to return to their lives." All I could think of was *No!* and *How dare they?*

Laura rebelled against the loss and replacement of our mother and having a father who didn't know how to open discussions or listen to us. While the attention was on Laura, I was emotionally left behind. I believed I was responsible for making things a little easier for everyone, so I opted to put my head down and stay quiet while existing in an angry standoff between my dad and Laura. When she moved out at age eighteen, our communication was minimal, and we didn't see each other for five years. As a malleable twelve-year-old, I believed my father's words — that she was a troublemaker and that her depression was for attention.

With Laura out of the picture, I spent most of my time with my nose in books, distracting myself through the words of others. I went incognito, but the Universe had other plans for me. My seventeenth year felt like I'd emerged from a body of water after holding my breath for a long time. I put the books down and went to my first party, connecting with people through dance and music. I was finally living a semi-normal life, like a character from one of my novels. I met a boy with brown hair, blue-green eyes, and a crooked smile. He liked my voice and what I had to say; how I danced, and my dark and twisted humor. I felt truly seen for the first time, and it did not take long for me to fall for him. I could not go back to just existing without being heard, so I started to find my voice. And, I liked it.

Laura moved back to town, and we bonded in a way we never had; she encouraged me to be a teenager: not to worry so much, to love, to party, to dance. It was the push I had been waiting for. But Dad did not favor me growing up, finding my voice, and confiding in a different man. I was getting good grades, but that did not matter. "You can always do better..." It was an impossible standard to live by.

On my eighteenth birthday, Dad returned from a trip south, and in his absence, I was to put a tarp on some furniture that was sitting outside. It had been storming, and despite my best efforts, some items got damaged. When he returned home and realized what had happened, he was furious. He pushed me out the door and slammed it hard in my face. I felt I was a disappointment to him, bringing me to a breaking point. I wanted him to know how hard it is to be his daughter, so for the first time; I contemplated taking my life.

Luckily, my boyfriend and Laura were sending me happy birthday messages, and I thought of my furry best friend, a Chihuahua named Paisley. I could not leave them behind, and miss out on life because I was angry. So with help from my sister, I saw a therapist for the first time. It wasn't a cure-all, but it was a step in the right direction, and with that step, I headed to university. I ended up leaving after I completed my first year, deciding to branch out and try something new. I packed my bags and drove ten hours to Cape Breton, where I stayed with my aunt and uncle. They welcomed me into their home, treated me as if I were their daughter, and accepted me for me, mess and all. I was finally living in a calm environment and found my footing. I went home for Christmas vacation and shared with Dad how happy I was living with my aunt and uncle. "If you like living with them so much, then stay there!" he screamed, red in the face, spit flying out of his mouth.

"Why won't you listen to me? I love you; I don't want to lose the only parent I have left!" I screamed and cried as Dad walked off. Then for the first time in ten years, the clean, airy scent of Red Door by Elizabeth Arden wonderfully wafted over me, and I heard Mom say, "Go!" I left that day.

I became a wanderer, feeling lost as I tried to find the feeling of home. I moved in with my eighty-two-year-old Nanny T., the woman who raised my mom. Spending cool spring mornings drinking tea and eating our usual porridge and brown sugar warmed my heart. Her fall-apart roast beef and veggies wafted a sweet yet savory scent throughout the house, and it tasted just how Mom would make it. These meals didn't just fill my belly; they filled my heart and soul. My time with Nanny was healing, and as the weeks passed, I felt calmer and more connected to Mom, and myself. Mom's grave was a short drive away. Initially, when I would visit, I felt like a stranger. But over time, I felt more connected to her; I could feel her presence as if she was embracing me. Her heart-shaped headstone had a tree above it, keeping her dry from the rain. Every night a sunset cascaded around it, proof she was truly resting in paradise.

I wandered to my friend Lindsay's house next, just for a summer, with Paisley in tow. We were greeted by shiny white floors, a spiral staircase, and the sweetest little corgi named Zoe. While settling into this temporary home, I joined a Wiccan Circle and was introduced to shadow work. I learned to acknowledge my shadow and teach a different response to my inner child. I used tarot cards to get comfortable with my intuition and participated in a past life regression.

After learning about my past lives, my place in the world, and the imprint they created, it was time to pack my bags for another adventure, one without a plan, a home, or a job. Myself, Lindsay, another friend Thomas, and Paisley, crammed into a Chevy Cruze and set off on a 4,500 km drive to the west coast of Canada, each of us trusting and surrendering to our own spiritual journey into the unknown. The Universe was guiding us, and we knew it, and amazing opportunities popped up along the way. We took in the sights of huge mountains defying the earth's gravity and peeking out to the ocean-blue skies. There is something magical about mountains; they contain divine inspiration and spiritual elevation. We danced under the stars, and I felt awe and wonder, the things that make me feel most alive. I was at peace, something I had forgotten. We found the feeling of home amidst those mountains as I settled down in Squamish, British Columbia, after turning twenty years old.

On one of my healing days, I took myself for a walk. I allowed my feet to guide me to the water, sensing something stirring within me. Despite the countless healing experiences I had known in the past decade, I was still holding on to a pain deep inside. There were things I hadn't let go of; things I needed to forgive. Sitting on the cold sand, watching a layer of fog hovering above the river, I decided it was time to write a forgiveness letter to myself.

I'm sorry that you had to grow up and leave part of your inner child behind. I'm sorry that you weren't always shown unconditional love. I'm sorry for forgetting, forgetting my inner child, my past, and my mom.

My tears landed on the paper as I started releasing all the pain I'd carried. Then something divine happened. I was engulfed by the forgotten yet familiar scent of Mom's perfume, and I could feel her near me. Her energy touched my energy; her hand was on my shoulder. I had permission to be free.

Releasing myself from personal guilt, I began to examine what other pain I could be free from. Of all the people who had hurt me, none stuck out more than my dad. Having spent time tuning into my intuition, I had gained empathy, which opened the door to forgiving him. As a child, I looked at my father as a caregiver, who was supposed to protect me, yet I could see that he was struggling, doing the best he could with what he knew and, more importantly, only what he was shown. He is his own child in a grown-up suit. He didn't have all the answers, and how could he? He was dealing with his own grief and pain and that was projected onto me.

I quickly discovered forgiving doesn't mean forgetting or excusing the harm done; instead, it welcomes a kind of peace that helps you let go and go forward. Forgiveness does not happen overnight, and it is something I have to revisit often. I have forgiven Dad but only through forgiving myself. As a people pleaser, it was hard to recognize that forgiveness isn't about the other person; it's about me, no one else.

These have been the most challenging years of my life, yet I am grateful for every lesson and experience I've learned. They have helped me choose to carry myself with love and humility. I wear my newfound forgiveness like a suit of armor, coated with love and valuing my boundaries. I have learned to honor myself and protect my inner child. I have reached a newfound awareness of forgiveness and continue to work on the blessings that forgiveness offers me. Through these lessons, I've realized that we all do our best. I've come to understand more of my purpose; I'm here to help others get through what seems to be the most impossible of times. Help them trust, surrender, and let go of the baggage that holds them down. We can learn to love ourselves despite our past because the past can shift and play with us emotionally, but it can also dance and bring us joy. Forgiveness can mean many things to many people; my wish is that you go inward and remember forgiveness means finding peace within you.

Lewis B. Smedes famously says, *"To forgive is to set a prisoner free and discover that the prisoner was you."*

IGNITE ACTION STEPS

Do something that makes you feel more connected to yourself. Being connected will help you find grace and understanding in all situations.
- Be easy on yourself.
- Hug yourself. Give yourself that squeeze that you need.
- Ask yourself how would your five-year-old self feel? What would a five-year-old do? Reflect on what matters or isn't that important. As you do this, notice what matters and what doesn't.
- Give yourself twenty seconds per day to stop and take in this loving breath. Connect with your body and feel what you need.

Morgan McNeil—Canada
Tarot Reader and Chaneler
🔲 *Morgana's Readings*

IGNITE
Forgiveness

I embrace that

FORGIVENESS IS A
PART OF MY JOURNEY.

Everything I experience brings me

CLOSER TO MY
HIGHEST SELF.

Jerry Tucker

JERRY TUCKER

"When you quit running to see what you are running from, you can decide what you want to run toward."

I want the reader to relate to my past pain and trauma and see that they are not alone in their journey. I have used my past struggles as fuel to set up my future. By finding the courage to forgive those who hurt me, I shifted my focus and took my life in a new direction with intention and confidence. The same is possible for you; when you use forgiveness to guide you, life is filled with gratitude and happiness.

LOST AND FOUND

"Dude, am I gay? Do I have AIDS?" Those were the questions I kept inside my head for six long years between the ages of ten and sixteen.

Before that period of my life, I was a content and normal kid going with the flow. As my father planned his transition out of the military, my parents decided that Aurora, Colorado was where we would live. I never expected that move would be my escape from a molester and an abuser.

On my last night living in North Dakota, I was sexually molested by a neighbor. I was ten years old and had absolutely no framework to understand what had just happened to me. I came to a stop, unable to grow because I suddenly had no idea what growing up was supposed to feel like. At such a young age, I was forced to hide inside my mind. I felt ashamed, embarrassed, and scared. I mostly blamed myself, wondering what I had done to deserve that abuse. At such a pivotal age, I was forced to dig deep and look inward for the answers that I wouldn't find for years. I did not realize that what happened to me that night would affect me so immensely and cause so much pain throughout my life.

Growing up in the eighties, there was no way it would have been okay for me to talk about what happened. That was the height of the HIV/AIDS scare, and the media was portraying it as a disease that came from being gay or homosexual. Since a man had molested me, it was only natural that I thought I was at risk. Thinking that I had AIDS from the age of ten to sixteen was painful, confusing, and impaired much of my mental state. I was scared that I would not survive, but I kept my fears hidden because it was such a taboo. Plus, because I believed I brought it on and was to blame, I did not think I would get support, and I was too ashamed to ask for it.

I grappled with questions about my sexuality because before I knew what masculinity was, mine was shattered. I never thought girls would like me or even be interested in me. I struggled to fit in, and I felt out of place wherever I was. I would try to dress like my peers to avoid any attention from them. Nike Air Max® shoes, Levis® stonewashed jeans, and nice buttoned shirts. I was hiding in plain sight.

I would always escape my demons with my pen. During my teenage years, I would write poems to express my feelings and process my inner pain. I would go to a local diner to eat and write, showing up in crisp jeans, the freshest pair of shoes, a clean button-up shirt, and a matching ballcap. Looking good felt good and helped me write better. The noise and distractions would dissipate as my mind blocked out the outside world, and I went all in on my poetry. I would get a feeling or choose a topic and let the words flow. As I continued to write through the years, I created a talent that defines me to this day, yet it started as an outlet for my childhood pain.

When I was sixteen, all the years of holding in the pain finally caught up to me. I was getting ready to take my finals in my sophomore year of high school. I was not sleeping and started to feel sick, then began throwing up blood. I could sense that my hidden trauma was the reason. My body was telling me to let it all out. I knew I had to break down and talk about my past. I felt the courage to talk to my mom and found the strength to follow through. After telling her about what happened, I felt the burden of six years lifted off my shoulders. I released the heavy weight of fear that I had kept inside. Mom assured me that that was not my fault, and for the first time, I stopped blaming myself. Eventually, I was able to tell other members of my family also.

My older sister was always my biggest support. Growing up, we shared the best times together. We never fought and always got along (our parents fought enough, so we learned that fighting solves nothing). We are very close, but early on I did not feel comfortable sharing my experience with her. I did not want the truth of what had happened to break down the awesome bond we had. But after a few years, I finally opened up to her and realized my internal narrative was 100 degrees off. The closest people around me supported me no matter what hardships my past had caused me. As I worked through the pain over the years, my sister was always there during my lowest downs, and her support kept me above ground. I will always remember my sister would bring me around her friends after our marching band performances at the High School football games. She could have been too cool for school and let me go my own way, but she never turned her back on me.

During these late teen years, I also started seeing a therapist to help me unpack my past. I knew I would not have a future if I did not work on the fears that were consuming me. It became my fuel. Working with a therapist, I slowly started to believe in myself. More importantly, I learned I was not alone. I found out that this has happened to so many people. Over time, I realized people did not judge me for that incident. No one even knew about it till I talked about it. I had spent so many years living under my own limiting lid, feeling like it was easier to hide behind all the distractions than to confront my true feelings. Therapy definitely helped, but it wasn't the only step I took toward healing.

As a young adult, I spent many years in and out of deep and dark depression. I was on medication for years to help balance my mind and find clarity. Along my journey, I discovered that busy hands are happy hands. I started to go all in with my woodworking and metal fabrication. I would get so consumed with projects that I would lose track of time. Working with my hands felt therapeutic, and slowly I realized I had things in common with the male role models in my life that had helped me to see what masculinity is. It felt blissful as I experienced the return of my male energy. I had been hiding alone for so many years until I realized I was the only one who knew my sense of manhood had been rocked. I transitioned from thinking girls may never be into me to being blessed with many meaningful female relationships in my life. Chasing my dream, or my dream girl, no longer felt like a frightening pursuit.

I started to live with clarity. As I let go of the extra pain, I was able to believe in myself, and it gave me the confidence I never knew I had. I slowly worked my way out of the depression that I had fought for many years. I kept writing, working with my hands, and seeking new avenues for healing.

In my late thirties, I started to listen to this crazy Australian skateboarder,

Jason Ellis, on Sirius XM® radio, who was also a survivor of molestation. His radio show and his attitude was wild, carefree, and unique. His confidence was so big after going through something so horrible. I was hooked! I loved his determination so much that I needed to listen without interruptions. I would save shows on my old streaming radio device, and when I wore it out, I started to record his messages using a music software program on my computer. I would convert the show, drop it on my Blackberry World Edition® phone, and listen all night in my shop while I built things. My need to keep listening kept me in the shop for so long that it spurred me to finish each new creation. Ellis would always talk and tell stories from his past in California and Australia, and those stories resonated with me. Listening to him showed me that I was not alone in my past pains and traumas. I will always be grateful to the audio gold he provided me over the years that kept me pushing as the world would push back.

Jason Ellis also started to put on "Ellismania" events at a local boxing gym in Hollywood. These were random comical boxing fights where fans of the show would sign up to participate. I used music software to make audio commercials for his first event, and the producers played them live on his show. I was in my shop bay at the GMC™ dealership and heard my commercial play over the radio; Ellis and his co-hosts talked about how they would close their eyes and let my audio take them to a special place. That was a moment I will always remember, feeling heard and appreciated by someone I admired so much. That taught me that when you find ways to create and have the courage to share your work, it allows others to enjoy your creativity. That commercial led to other rap parodies that I would record and send into the show. It also led to me finding a whole new tribe of like-minded brothers.

One of the defining moments in my journey was at Jason's second Ellismania. I drove to Los Angeles to see the event and was a guest on his radio show. Before the event started, two fighters were not able to show up. So I volunteered to fight. The next morning, I was out getting coffee, and I turned on the footage from the night before. I heard Ellis say, "CrazyJerr, you got rocked!" I watched myself get knocked out. But I also watched myself get back up, refusing to give up. Headgear sideways, I stumbled away from my opponent as the bell rang to end the round. I would have kept fighting, but my corner man looked in my eyes and said, "He is done!" I had to be kept awake to make sure I overcame the concussion. I may have lost the match, but I proved what I was made of, which was more important. Besides, I had already been through much worse.

The community that developed from that show brought many diverse people into a family-like atmosphere. Every year Jason Ellis would put on an event at the Hard Rock Hotel™ in Las Vegas. This would give all of the fans a chance to meet up, party, and laugh at the many concerts and live radio shows hosted throughout the weekend. I met so many kindred spirits there, and I still stay in touch with many of them. The Jason Ellis show and the fans became a second family that gave me a place to fit in and friends to always hang out with. It wasn't just the tribe; it was my place to be my 'crazy' self… CrazyJerr. Where I could let my wild imagination and creativity be free and not judged by an old internal mindset.

That experience, finding so many people like me, gave me the confidence to start looking forward and thinking about the future I wanted to create for myself. During the fall of 2019, I decided to sell a Chevy Malibu to pay for a mentor program with Grant Cardone. It allowed me to join a weekly zoom™ call with Grant and his team. I took notes on new ways to grow our business, ways to adhere to a winning mindset, and how success is an intentional choice. I soon realized that this program would propel my future in a new direction. I stayed in the program until Grant's Growth Conference took me back to Vegas in February, 2020. I learned that your Network is your Net Worth. And, once again, I found another tribe with whom I could connect. The people I met in that group have changed my life forever, in the best of ways. There was something special about getting to be with that group because as soon as the Growth Conference ended, the world shut down for COVID-19, and no one was gathering in groups at all for a long time after.

During the pandemic, I went deeply inward into self-growth as everyone I met in the mentor program started their own courses. So many of my newfound family took the deep dive to become Cardone licensees. As they beta-tested their courses, I was invited into their lessons for free and, in turn, added so much value to myself and my business. Along the way, I realized I have greatness to bring to the world, and it was time to focus on my talents and gifts. Then I saw a video clip of Grant Cardone saying, "You will never fail if you never quit." I noticed the video was filmed at Growth Conference 2020. Seeing my friends on that screen reminded me I was around the right people. I saw the same quote on a meme of Grant Cardone speaking to a crowd, and my business coach, Antonio White, was in the front row of the audience. Aligning myself with him has given my ideas and products direction. This was the first moment where I found the clarity and focus I wanted for my business. The snowball effect of meeting each person gave me increasing confidence that my decisions were good and that I was on the right path toward something amazing. It helped me have the inner peace and strength to move forward and let go of everything that does not serve me.

I started to use my voice and speak about my past and help others to know they are not alone. I was very intentional on the new app, Clubhouse™. I found another tribe of leaders and humanitarians in the '1% Only' rooms where Jay Noland, Scott Harris, and Moe Rock did a marathon room that went for 100 days. It was in those rooms that I uncovered my old gift of writing poems. In the past, my poems were my place to express my feelings. Through my new mindset, I was able to sit in these rooms, take notes and recap the discussion nightly in the form of a poem. When you do something everyday, it becomes a habit. I entertained everyone in the rooms, ensuring I had a poem ready every day. Reading my poems and sharing my life allowed me to help others directly and share with gratitude.

Then, on February 2nd, 2022, at 2:22 pm I made the biggest transition in my life and quit my day job and security of nineteen and a half years at Markley Motors. I loved my job, and the awesome people there built me up to who I am today. It was my time to shift my focus and be very intentional in my life's direction. As I closed one chapter, I opened a new one and made a choice to share my best-kept secret with the world. I decided to use my past pain, trauma, and my voice to inspire others to find their voice because what we tell ourselves leaves a mark. We start to believe our narrative. We become what we say, and we create with unlimited potential that which defines our future.

I have pushed past the taboo and stigma of being molested. I was limited by my pain when I lived most of my early years in fear and in the dark. Now, it's easier to stay in the light after having the courage to face that pain and share it with others. I will always find the courage to talk to anyone that crosses my path. I am proof that you can let the forgiveness of others that did you wrong open up new doors and find the best version of yourself.

As I manifest this next phase of my life, I still use the same tools I learned along the way. You can still find me writing, usually in a diner, and I am still dressed to impress. Everything disappears, and I get lost in my words, but now I know my voice is worth hearing. My Ignite Moment came when I just let go. I found it in my heart to forgive the one that caused me so much suffering in my life. I let everything go that was holding me down. I did not realize the weight I had been carrying for all those years. Everything that brought me down in the world, I let it all go. The weight we carry will always keep us outside our greatness. Finding the ways to let it all go will allow our hearts to live in true authenticity.

I do not have bad days anymore. Because I had so many bad years that I held onto before I found the power of forgiving. Working through everything is important because that's how you start to grow. I used to stay busy and was running from my past, but now I am eager to move toward my future. I have learned that when you quit running, you can see what you are running from and decide what you are going to run toward.

What is your future?

What are you running toward?

What are you ready to set free?

Ignite Action Steps

Action steps you can take to find clarity:

- Align yourself with like-minded people with similar interests; this will allow you to grow into your best self.
- Allow counsel from others that have been through troubles and surround yourself with people that are very intentional and push you to become who you deserve to become by holding you accountable on your path.
- Find your tribe of leaders that bring you value, keeping your heart open to all they can teach you on your journey.

Jerry Tucker—United States of America
Author, Inventor, Business Owner
CrazyJerrCustoms.com
Crazyjerrbooks@yahoo.com
CrazyJerr Tucker
CrazyJerr
CrazyJerr
CrazyJerr
970-825-9675

FORGIVENESS

They say forget and forgive
When we forgive we really live
And drop our limiting lids

Holding on to the past
Will leave ur energy gassed
A solid future will never last

As we learn to let go
We allow our inner growth
And our progress will Show

It may be the hardest thing to do
As we work threw we can feel the blues
Our feelings we will eventually lose
Which will lead us to the future clues

The first step is the one we must take
It aligns us with fate
It allows our growth to not be late

As you take it in strides
You will begin to feel the pride
Before you know it you will not hide
You will let the storms subside

The feeling you get when the pain is gone
These are the moments you become Strong
Your emotions will chip a beautiful Song

As we work on ourselves day-to-day
Doing the work is how we repay
Our changes will come without delay

As we come into this book
We nestled in our favorite nook
We have shared our outlook

Our words on the page
Is what someone needs to read one day
Our words will allow them to release the rage

As we look threw a new lens
Our stories allow us to mend
And we will see the pain end

Threw time we all heal
Our stories are very real
When complete they will seal
This will allow others to feel
Our words complete the deal

Karen L. Wilson

Karen L. Wilson

*"Forgiveness is the doorway to becoming whole
and knowing you are enough!"*

My wish for you is that you take heart from my story and know that you have everything you need inside you to be whole and strong, to accept that you are enough. Know that you only need to forgive those who caused you pain, that they were doing the best they could, and that you *can* let go of whatever you are holding onto from the past. Allow yourself to move into a position of peace and strength, and embrace yourself as perfect just as you are!

The Ten-Ton Boulder

The door closed behind me, and I was left in a huge, empty hospital room. It had cold, metal surfaces, a cold, green, ceramic floor, and a cold, austere side room; its only feature was a shiny drain in the floor. The excruciating labor pains were coming on regularly and I felt alone, helpless, and terrified. Each time I cried out from the pain, no one came. Suddenly, a gush of fluid ran down my legs to the floor. My water had broken! Panicking, I started yelling for help until a nurse arrived. It was just after midnight on May 2nd, 1970. My aunt and uncle dropped me off at the hospital and left me there, barely eighteen years old, to face giving birth with no one there to support me.

In the early morning hours, I gave birth to a beautiful baby boy; a boy I had asked not to see, knowing I was giving him up for adoption. I woke up in a room full of unfamiliar, cast-off pieces of furniture, away from all the other mothers in the delivery ward. I felt like an outcast and more alone and terrified than ever. Something inside told me I had to see my baby after all, but it took me until the next day to get them to bring him to me. He looked at me and knew me as his mother, staring at me with a peaceful, knowing look that I will never forget. I gazed into his eyes, marveling at this instant bond, and held him for just a little while until they came to take him away again.

The next morning, I was told to dress and voluntarily hand him to the adoptive parent who had arrived. I realized I would never see my baby again and couldn't stop crying. My eyes were red and puffy, and I didn't have time to even try to look presentable. I was horror-struck to be giving my baby to a total stranger... until I saw the look on the man's face. He was so eager in his desire for the baby that, in his eyes, I could see I was giving him a priceless gift. I knew then that I did the right thing, even with my heart breaking. At eighteen, I didn't know how to support myself and a baby. I knew it was the best thing I could do for us both; however, I never stopped crying over the loss of my son. I always hoped God would help me find him and bring him back into my life.

In the weeks afterward, I moved from my grandmother's apartment to one across the hall from my aunt. My father arrived with a piece of paper that said I was an "emancipated minor," meaning he was disowning me and no longer responsible for me.

How did I get here?

After my brother was born, when I was three, my parents were focused almost entirely on him. He wasn't well and was constantly being rushed to the hospital in the middle of the night. Often, I would wake up with an empty feeling, calling out, "Mommy, Mommy, where are you?" No answer. I would get up and go to look for them, only to find an empty bed and crib. They had left me all alone with nothing but the scary dark! I would go back to my bed, feeling a lump in my throat and ice in the pit of my stomach. I would curl up and hide, hoping that when I woke up, they would be home again. They didn't care about me. I wasn't important.

My mother dressed me in pretty dresses, flaunting me to the neighbor ladies almost every day. They always said how pretty I looked and what a great mother she was. One day, when I was four, I smudged my yellow sundress. She scolded me that I should be ashamed that I smudged my dress and that she would have to clean it. From then on, I knew it wasn't safe to be anything except perfect! I had to be a good little girl to be accepted, to receive her approval. I also wasn't good enough, an unspoken fact that came through loud and clear. My intimidating father would start yelling suddenly, and his angry outbursts scared me! Starting in first grade, he always expected me to know the answers to all my math homework problems. He was a brilliant, educated man who didn't understand that you can't know algebra without knowing basic math. He was always scowling as I didn't catch on as quickly as he wanted me to. "What's wrong with you?" he would scold disapprovingly. There was no encouragement, and it made me feel worthless.

On the other hand, acceptance was hard to find wearing hand-me-down clothes to school. With my curly red hair and glasses, I didn't look like any of the other kids. I didn't fit in, so none of them tried to be friendly. I was smart, learned to read at three, and by third grade I knew all the answers to the teacher's questions. "Anyone else besides Karen?" the teacher would say. At lunch, the girls wouldn't let me sit with them, always saying that the seat I wanted was taken, being mean, and calling me names. This continued all through elementary school and junior high. I was an outcast and felt completely rejected.

The summer before tenth grade, my youngest brother was born. I would go to school, and my mother would secretly pick me up before school started to take me back home to babysit my brother while she went out to see her boyfriend. I missed so much school, and I was shocked to find out in June that I had flunked tenth grade. My parents were too busy getting divorced to care. We moved to a new town, where I had to repeat tenth grade. At least no one there knew me, and I felt I might fit in.

Then, one day in the summer of my seventeenth year, I was invited to a party at my cousins' house. I met one of their friends, a handsome young man in his twenties, who captured my heart with his mysterious, quiet personality and romantic motorcycle. I said *no* when he wanted to have sex with me, but he promised I wouldn't get pregnant. I wanted so much for someone to like and accept me, so I reluctantly said yes. A month later, my period was late. *Was this really happening to me?* I wished and hoped it would go away, waiting in denial. Finally, after a few months, I faced it: I was pregnant!

I didn't feel well, nauseated with morning sickness, so I finally went to my parents. My mother slapped me in the face and told me to pack my bags and leave. "The baby's father should take responsibility," she said. She neglected to remember that after introducing me to him, she didn't give me any parental guidance. My father offered to take me to England for an abortion. I refused. By that time, in my view, it was a child. My father told me he wouldn't help me either; he washed his hands of me.

My son's father had stopped showing interest in me. Still, I showed up at his apartment with my suitcase and told him that I was pregnant with his child and had been kicked out. He let me stay for a couple of weeks, but subsequently did the same thing, saying he was "sorry" but "it wasn't working out" having me there. He wasn't willing to support us.

It was a late afternoon in November, the last light fading and the chill setting in, when I walked the twenty blocks to my aunt's apartment with my belly bulging, and my pants held closed with a safety pin. I tearfully told her I was pregnant and had nowhere to go.

I spent the next four months sleeping on the couch, a short, ornate antique with carved wooden arms in the shape of swans' necks. It was very uncomfortable having to sleep with my knees curled up against my bulging belly. I had panic attacks almost every day and had to breathe into a paper bag to keep from passing out from terror. *What was going to happen to me?*

I felt truly alone in my predicament, deeply angry with my parents and my son's father. If my parents had paid me any attention instead of letting me run wild, they could have prevented this situation. If my son's father had cared about the child or me, he never showed it. The resentment and anger I felt became an underlying theme for over three decades.

It took me until I was over fifty to find my spiritual path and a mentor to truly help me heal. I had taken some self-help programs and workshops and started peeling the layers of the onion to release the issues underneath. However, I still felt angry. Before an "aha" moment ignited my understanding, I was carrying all the pain of not being accepted, loved, or approved of by my parents; being shunned as an embarrassment to them. I was still looking for acceptance and approval from others.

"You are dragging a ten-ton boulder behind you," my spiritual mentor, Frank, told me. When Frank started helping me with my spiritual growth, I realized that I still needed to forgive my parents and all those who had caused me so much pain. I thought I had already forgiven them. I gasped, knowing I was still in the same place of blaming them after all those years and all that work! I hadn't truly released the resentment, the anger, the weight. I really *was* dragging a ten-ton boulder behind me. It became obvious if I didn't forgive the people who had caused me pain, I would never be free, and I would never be happy!

But how, I wondered? I practiced my spirituality every day and tried to give out love and kindness, but I could feel the anger fastened to me like a big, heavy rock.

I had to begin the long journey of looking in the mirror and working on myself to release those old patterns, forgiving my parents and the man who got me pregnant. It was a very hard struggle to forgive my father for ignoring me, for transferring all his love to my brother after he was born, withdrawing himself from my life, and disowning me when I became pregnant at such a vulnerable age. I had always wanted his approval and acceptance, and what I came to understand was that I didn't accept or approve of myself.

I also had to forgive my mother for not caring about me: for selfishly focusing on her own needs, using me as a babysitter, and abandoning her parental duties because she was incapable due to her own shortcomings. I had to accept that my parents were only capable of being who they were and not the ideal parents I wanted. To me, they were angry, unhappy people, and in their narrow focus on themselves, they couldn't even see me.

I decided to try to rekindle the relationship with my father. I reached out to him, and he rebuffed me. He had kept me at arm's length for most of my life. He accused me of only wanting his money, but I persisted, telling him that I only wanted a relationship before it was too late. At sixty-four, I reached out again, and we chatted for a short time. He was in the hospital dying. And then it happened... he told me, "I love you, Karen," the words I had been waiting for all my life! The boulder cracked, and a big piece fell away. I felt accepted! I felt lighter! A few weeks later, I found out he had passed on, and I was grateful we reconciled just in time.

The path to forgiving my mother was far less smooth. Eight years before my father died, she had to move in with me, as she couldn't support herself and needed a caregiver. We had a very tough time, as it was extremely hard for me to put up with her arrogance. Nothing I did was ever good enough for her. After nine years of taking care of her, she went to a nursing home and died a year after my father. She never showed appreciation or said thank you. It was challenging to forgive her for all the pain she caused me. I was exhausted and sick when she left, and it took me several years to recover my strength and health.

Throughout it all, I never stopped looking for my son. I had signed up for a few adoption websites hoping he would be on one of them. Then, on July 26th of 2018, I heard my inner guidance say to get online and look for just one more adoption website. After putting in the information and running a query, thirty-six names came up, with my son's birthday at the top of the list. I felt excitement and fear running through me as I messaged all thirty-six names, and it dawned on me that I might finally find him!

The next morning, the one at the top of the list responded and asked me my maiden name. He knew the answer before I told him! Once he heard it, he responded "We have a match... we need to talk." I was elated; at sixty-six I had finally found my son! He was forty-eight years old and living in New York. I knew it was divine timing, an absolute miracle!

I could barely sit still, waiting for him to call me. He had been looking for me, had signed up a few years prior, and had forgotten about it when I hadn't responded. As he revealed the truth about his life, there were many moments when I felt regret that I couldn't raise him myself. Self-forgiveness was around the corner, the most vital stage of my forgiveness journey. I had to accept I did my best for him, and as we talked, he accepted it, also. He let go of his anger toward me and embraced me in his life.

I was able to meet him and discovered that not only had my son been returned to me, but I had two beautiful grandchildren! It was a miracle filling the hole I had in my heart! I now had a reason to be grateful for that painful journey of my past.

Shakespeare said, "All the world's a stage, and all the people on it, only players." Everyone comes into life with a part to play. and we all affect each other as we interact and play our parts. We have to take the next step though, and see that we have something to learn from our experiences. If I could incorporate what I learned, it would help me forgive the 'players' from whom I had learned the lessons. I was growing spiritually. I rose above the past and saw it in an entirely different light.

Everything happens for a reason. I now saw my parents' inability to love and accept me differently. I was able to see them as hurt, little children who could only tend to their own needs. All the anger I felt toward them slowly melted away as I realized that, in order to have love in my life, I had to love myself first. I began to rise above the emotional pain and see the whole picture. The triumph came as I finally realized that *I was enough*! I could accept and approve of *myself*! I had wonderful qualities as a woman, with many important gifts to give to others. Through the doorway of forgiveness, I stepped fully into myself as an empowered woman I could like, admire, and respect. The ropes loosened, and my boulder fell away at last.

My gift to the world is helping others step into their greatness using forgiveness. As a trainer, I empower people to discover their emotional wounds and learn how to release them. If you are dragging your own ten-ton boulder behind you, know that you can let go and be free. Forgiveness is a choice. It is easy to forgive when you accept people for who they truly are. That is the best gift you can give them and yourself; the ability to see them with grace so that you can love yourself, know you are enough, and be the real you.

IGNITE ACTION STEPS

Step into forgiving yourself and others with the following practices.

- If the person(s) you want to forgive is still alive, contact them and tell them you would like them to listen to what you have to say. Tell them you forgive them for the pain they caused you. If the person(s) you want to forgive is not alive, imagine them sitting in a chair in front of you and share all your feelings, and then forgive them. Do this step until you feel forgiveness in your heart.
- Forgive yourself for having been hard on yourself, for not having the insights or courage to face this before now. Create a list of everything you are grateful for in your life, your good qualities, health, people who love you, and material things, to help you realize you have a lot going for you, so it is easier to forgive yourself. Do this daily.
- To help you with the courage, self-esteem, and confidence to forgive others and love yourself, stand in front of the mirror in the superwoman/superman pose, say "I love you (your name)" and prize yourself for all your good qualities and accomplishments for two minutes. Do this daily.

Karen L Wilson—United States of America
Author, Trainer, Podcast & TV Show guest
meetkarenwilson.com
🔲 *Karen Wilson*

IGN·TE
Forgiveness

FORGIVENESS
starts with acceptance.

I ACCEPT EVERYONE
as they are and every situation
as a learning experience.

Kristin Svets

KRISTIN SVETS

"Forgiveness is the foundation to the freedom of your soul."

It is my intention that my story inspires forgiveness and shows how it is an evolution, and working through that process involves the body, mind, and soul. People are complicated and layered, with both light and darkness within us. Forgiveness allows us to step towards the light while releasing the darkness. The first step to full forgiveness is to set the other person free. The second step comes when you can tear down the walls you created from the pain while maintaining healthy boundaries, which requires a level of forgiving yourself. That combination of steps is our foundation. This allows freedom and beauty back into our lives and souls, allowing us to receive and evolve so that we can experience our greatest life.

A DELICATE DANCE

On a sunny and warm fall day in Dallas, we somberly walked as a family into my father's church for his funeral. My husband and children had flown in, and we gathered with my mom, siblings, and their relatives. We watched as the parking lot filled up, and people kept coming in. Gorgeous flowers overflowed from the main chapel and spilled out into the hallways, their beautiful scent filling the air. The reception room for the after-service greetings was prepared with a plethora of food and beverages for the large crowd. As I looked at the standing-room-only attendance, one thought kept repeating:

I think I missed something.

Dad was a gifted and dedicated music director and organist for his church, and this community loved him deeply. He was Lutheran, and the rest of our family is Catholic, so we didn't know his congregation very well. Yet, we felt their love for him as several people got up from the packed pews, walked to the pulpit, and shared their stories. I don't even remember what they said. I do remember that it was hard to breathe; that tears streamed down my face. I was humbled and grateful that so many people loved him. I didn't know this version of him.

I must have missed something.

He had unexpectedly passed away from a cardiac arrest at age seventy. He had gone through a similar fainting episode the week before and spent two days in the hospital. He was home for a day and a half between the emergencies. I didn't call him. When he returned to the hospital, he spent eight days on life support. I took a two-hour flight from my home in Chicago to Dallas and didn't leave his side. Even though our relationship was complicated, I loved him very much. It was a little late for the "I forgive you, please forgive me" conversation. Sadly, that was the only option I left for us. And sometimes, I still feel like it was the only option we created.

I think both are valid and true.

Healthy boundaries and forgiveness have always been a complicated, delicate dance for me. I had to ask myself, "When has my healthy boundary gone too far?" "When is it no longer serving me?" "When are my walls too high?" My father's passing revealed that while there were no right answers, I had to live with the decision of the height of the wall that I had built. I had to realize that I held the key to the door in those walls, and I was in control of walking through them whenever I was ready. Yet, I chose not to walk through and realized this had tumbled over into other areas of my life.

I know I'm missing something.

I have found observing reactions and conversations at funerals to be an interesting phenomenon. I listen to beautiful shared stories, and the ones who have passed usually sound like they were saints. This is another delicate dance that comes into play because of course I want to treat people with respect, but I am also aware that the true story is almost always more layered than that. For me, at my father's funeral, my unresolved issues made the stories both harder to hear and more intriguing. When I listened to those stories, I had simultaneous reactions: "Oh, you didn't *really* know him!" and "Wait, did *I* really know him?"

I realize both are valid and true.

As many people are, my father was a very complicated and wounded man.

He had anger management issues and saw himself as the victim in many situations. He also had a few cocktails every night, which exacerbated the conditions where turmoil and discord were always a possibility.

There *were* good parts. One of my favorite memories with my dad includes playing duets on the piano with him, which felt like magic. Our living room always had a baby grand piano and an organ. I remember the carpet beneath our feet, the dog at our side, and the harmony of the music we made together. There was pure laughter and joy that emanated from my dad with the creation of our shared music. He also loved spending summers water-skiing and floating on his oversized raft for hours in the lazy afternoon sun at our family's cottage. He loved watching football and golf every Sunday. He was a great music director; we would go to see his Christmas concert every year. He thanked God for all of his musical gifts, which were plenty. And yet, I find it interesting how the bad outweighs the good. The challenging parts of him defined my relationship with him.

Outside—at work, church, and with friends—it was important to him to be liked. At home, things were different. There was always a sense that turbulence could arise at any moment. When he would pull up in the driveway, my sister and I would run to our shared bedroom and stay there for the rest of the evening, each sitting on our own twin beds, reading books or talking quietly. In the summer, I remember looking out the window at the other kids still playing kick-the-can in the light of the sunset, wishing that I could play with them. But the walls of our room were my safe haven.

I chose to be very reserved all of the time, not wanting to be the cause of his next angry outburst. His nightly intake of gin and tonics fueled the fire of his rage. Most of the time, it was verbal tirades, manipulation, and gaslighting. However, there are core memories of moments I witnessed his physical violence. That time was short-lived, as he seemed to get under control to save his marriage with my mom. But the trauma of those scenes has their own life span in my mind.

The uncertainty and discord of not knowing what would set him off never really went away, either. If one of us turned on the light and the lightbulb blew out, we would be subjected to a loud and scary diatribe of blame: "What is wrong with you? What did you do?" It was terrifying, confusing, shameful, and maddening. This behavior from a parent is a really effective way to teach a child not to trust themselves. As a child in an environment of uncertainty and fear, I did what I could to stay safe. I did what I could to keep the peace.

Don't be seen. Don't make noise. Don't speak.

Stay in my room. Build walls. Very high and dense walls.
Those walls served me well… until they didn't. Often, even after I got married, those walls were still required for some interactions with my dad. Although I probably could have found a kinder balance, I chose to limit his verbal access to me so I didn't have to deal with his commentary. But in the long term, the walls maintained from my lack of forgiveness were primarily boxing *me* in, not him. I was limiting the amount that I evolved. I love a healthy boundary, but without forgiveness, it's just a wall.

I was definitely missing something.
What could forgiveness have looked like if I had explored it in my adult relationship with my dad? Could I have accepted him for his challenges and chosen to see the good? Could I have planned my interactions around things that brought out the best in him? That might have allowed me to see the side of him that I had missed out on. I do wish that this understanding had come to me before he passed away, and I could have acted on it sooner.

Interestingly, distancing myself from him didn't make the pain and fear disappear. I still carried them in my subconscious and my body. Those boundaries that served me well as a child not only limited me from getting to know the good parts of my dad but also sprawled into other areas of my life that didn't need them. Thanks to a dear friend, I would get that message loud and clear in my early thirties.

I was still missing something.
She asked me to lunch and said she needed to talk. We ordered our salads and iced tea as we sat on the patio in the fresh air. She invited me there because she needed to know what I wanted from our friendship. She was confused by my demeanor and interactions with her. From her perspective, she was receiving mixed signals about how deeply I valued our friendship. I was shocked by this conversation because she meant so much to me, and I had no idea that she felt I was pushing her away. The walls I had built to protect me from my dad's anger were limiting my ability to show my friend how much I loved her.

Without the gift of that conversation, I could have missed out on a treasured and endearing friendship. I am so grateful that she had the courage to share, so I could lower my walls enough to cultivate a deeper relationship with her. I started a journey that day; a journey toward opening my heart and freeing my soul.

That evoked some chiseling, tearing down some walls, slowly brick by brick. It began a cascade of new thinking that helped to see that those walls were all self-created and self-imposed. They were blocking out the sunshine and locking out the love. Once I began to remove them, I felt seen, loved more genuinely, and heard more authentically. I could be present, experience the beauty of what life had created for me, and be more intentional with what I could do to make my world a little brighter.

As those walls came down, it unlocked an awareness of my dad's true essence and his gifts. I began to see him in a new light, giving myself permission to appreciate the beauty he brought to the world and what I may have missed. I allowed space for the good in him to be valid and true, which created much more space for my inner peace. The change in perspective was empowering.

I began to see things.

I was able to recognize the correlation between those childhood walls that kept out the bad and the misplaced adult walls that keep me from experiencing the good. It wasn't the little fear of judgment that has been holding me back; it's the big FEAR of not being safe that keeps me stuck. I've been playing it safe within my walls, watching through a self-imposed window while the others play in the light.

This was when the duality of forgiveness became clear to me. Full forgiveness was not only about my dad, what he had done, and how he had made me feel. Full forgiveness was also about me. I had to forgive myself for the missed opportunities and misunderstandings caused by the walls that I had been hiding behind all this time. I had to embody letting go of the pain to liberate myself. I had to choose to create the foundation and step into the freedom of my heart and soul.

I wanted to shine my light.

Deciding to go into business for myself has been where I've had to look at what is truly holding me back. The journey of trying to build my personal brand has been a challenge, as my walls have been up around becoming more visible. The common message in society is: "Use your voice! Show up! Go bigger!" All of these messages are well-intentioned advice that I have wanted to act on, but following through with the action has required some reflection and healing on my end. Several stories play on repeat in my head, such as imposter syndrome and feelings of unworthiness. I appreciate that these are ego stories trying to keep me safe. And yet, I know that fulfillment is on the other side of that wall of fear.

Although I grew up with this discord and disconnection, I intuitively knew there was a better way. My experiences generated a true curiosity and interest in personal growth. I knew that I could create my version of an amazing life. I've stepped into the next chapter with so much gratitude and love. My 20+ year marriage and two teenage boys are my life's greatest pride and joy.

Additionally, the work I get to do through my Life Design and Mindfulness coaching business is fulfilling, helping others create their version of an amazing life. I love sharing tools like meditation, breathwork, and other somatic practices to help release blocks so that lasting transformation can occur, as they have been paramount to my journey. My intention is to serve at an even larger scale through my podcast, my upcoming first solo-written book, and through leading workshops and events. I finally am playing in the light.

My deeper embodiment and expansion into life require this layered approach to forgiveness. Choosing to forgive the person that hurt you is the first step; choosing to believe this and feel it in your heart and soul takes time. It might be a conversation or a letter that you write but never send and maybe even burn. It might require some helpful therapy sessions. It might take prayer, some energy, and spiritual healing. It might be a combination of several things, but above all, it must be a conscious choice.

The next layer of full forgiveness is choosing to forgive yourself for living behind the walls of an old story. You must be willing to release yourself from the burdens you've carried for so long. This requires walking out from behind those walls and choosing to play on the other side. You pull yourself out of the murky waters of unresolved issues and find inner harmony. You dive into the crystal clear waters of liberation and immerse yourself in true fulfillment. Forgiveness then becomes the gift you give yourself so that you can stop missing out. As you let go of that old story and pain, you allow yourself to fully live today and tomorrow from your inner wisdom and heart. This is your foundation and your launchpad. This is the freedom of your soul.

You deserve this freedom. You are truly worthy of creating your version of an amazing life. You hold the key to open the door to the power of forgiveness. You can give yourself the gift of safely breaking down your walls. My wish for you is that you choose to release the pain that no longer serves you and set yourself free. Open up that beautiful heart and soul of yours. Let yourself play in the light.

IGNITE ACTION STEPS

Do you feel like something is still holding you back on your journey of forgiveness? Are you ready to embrace forgiveness on a deeper level because you know that your freedom is on the other side of this evolution? To walk yourself down that path, I highly recommend going within. Approach this inner work with radical loving kindness towards yourself.

- Reflect, journal, and pray about the person you need to forgive. What is the right balance between a healthy boundary and the evolution of who they are and who you are? If this someone is still in your life, how could you create space to allow in the parts you would like to know better and even love?
- Consider what your healthy boundaries have been in the situation and where they might be a disservice to feeling freedom in your life. Has it leaked into areas of your life that you didn't intend? What comes to mind as to how you can operate differently in those areas?
- Reflect on the purpose of still holding on to your pain. Thank your mind and body for protecting you, but let them know that you are ready to release the pain and the story. Tell your brain to stop searching for the pain, as its purpose has long passed. Explore somatic healing practices like breathwork and acupuncture to move stuck energy if that speaks to you.
- Choose forgiveness of yourself as well. If there is resistance to this thought, what happens when you think of forgiveness as a gift to yourself? Set your soul free. Journal about what your heart and soul have to say from that space.

Kristin Svets—United States of America
Life Design & Mindfulness Coach, Author, Podcast Host
www.kristinsvets.com
Kristin Svets Life Design Coaching
kristinsvetscoaching
Podcast: Abundant By Design

TO BE FREE

Hello soul

I hear you

Asking me to choose

To be free

I felt so much pain

Pain is what I know

It's hard to let it go

To be free

My body fears

It tries to plea

For it's safety

My heart hears

Divine guidance

My choice and my destiny

To be free

My eyes finally see

That my mind

Held the key

To be free

To be liberated

To be at peace

To be empowered

To be light

To be love

To be free

Be Free

Dr. Silvia Hlavenková

DR. SILVIA HLAVENKOVÁ

"There's so much fun on the other side of fear."

Dear reader, by writing this story, I would like to Ignite your spark! If you've always been trying to do the 'right thing' and be *perfect* at everything, please permit yourself to follow your heart. Don't let your limiting beliefs, the guilt of being 'selfish,' or your deepest fears dictate the course of your journey. Facing it all can be a freaking rollercoaster, but there's one thing I really want you to know… there's so much fun on the other side of fear!

FROM 'PERFECTION' TO LIBERATION

I'm reading my notes and studying for my last state exam. Thoughts are racing in my mind while I'm fighting against the closing of my heavy eyelids. Thinking about tomorrow makes my heart smile with relief and my stomach dance to a symphony of excitement and fear. If everything goes well tomorrow afternoon, I will officially be a doctor. I look around the room, paying close attention to the *perfect* furniture in my *perfect* apartment, with the *perfect* view. In the eyes of others, *I have it all.* A beautiful home, a supportive and loving family, and a great career ahead. So, why am I not satisfied? *What's wrong with me?* Suddenly, I break into tears; the crying takes over me. I slide down the chair, and before I know it, I'm on my knees on the floor, sobbing. *What will I do after tomorrow?* The exam is the last fixed point awaiting me in my future. My classmates have already signed contracts and know when and where they'll be working. On the other hand, I rejected a job offer as a resident in ophthalmology, the job I had dreamed of for years. And I ask myself again: *What's wrong with me?*

My parents have done everything to build a safe and comfortable life for me and always ensured I wasn't missing anything. Yet, I don't feel complete and content inside. There's so much I haven't seen yet, so many questions without answers. I'm not ready to settle down; stay in my city, living life like my classmates do. Western medicine doesn't give me all the answers. It doesn't satisfy me. It's not enough. I want to intern at a Chinese Medicine Clinic in Italy after graduation. Yet, there's a world pandemic, and internships in foreign countries are on hold. Also, my Italian is terrible.

I hear the question pop up again: *What's wrong with me? Why do I always have to be so different from others? Why is what I already have not enough for me? How will I tell my parents that I need to go explore the world by myself?* I'm so afraid of disappointing them, of making foolish choices that a perfect daughter wouldn't. *What if I'm just spoiled?* Oh yes, now I feel guilt bubbling up in my belly: *I'm horrible. I'm so egocentric and selfish. I don't care about others. I'm so crazy and ungrateful.* I take a deep breath, swallow my sobs, and climb up on the chair again. On the out-breath, I suppress any feelings and calm my mind. I look at the notes on the table in front of me and refocus on the objective: pass the exam. I know exactly how to detach from distractions and become my ambitious success-focused self. I mastered this technique during my six years of studying medicine. I breathe in deeply again, and as I'm breathing out, I take in hand the highlighter and continue re-reading my notes.

Yes, I made it! I am Dr. Silvia Hlavenková. I don't know how I'm feeling. Relieved? Tired? Happy? "Gosh, it's over." I hear the laughter and chatter of my classmates infused with satisfaction while they're opening wine bottles, smiling. It's not right to worry right now. This should be one of the happiest days of my life, so I choose to copy their behavior, forget my troubles, and go with the flow.

Next thing I know, I'm on the tram in the company of these faces I know so well. I look out of the window and listen to their conversations. They're talking about their jobs, what, when, and where. When it's my turn to say what I'm doing next, I start crying. I have no idea what I will do, and I long for clarity so badly! This town that I love so much and know so well, and where I feel so safe, seems so distant now. I observe the familiar buildings, feeling like a stranger in my hometown and wondering *why*. I shake my head to interrupt my thinking and put my famous smile on. I explain to my friends that I'm just exhausted, and make it clear I want to have fun.

After celebrating my success at dinner with my family, I put on some tight jeans, a sexy top, and a checkered shirt, and go to the bar where all of my classmates are. Many young doctors are celebrating graduation, and as the night progresses people keep arriving to share in the festivities. After a year and a half of social distancing, I like seeing so many of my classmates. I smile and join the crowd. Many things happened that night, and I woke up with a broken elbow on my right arm.

The sound of my heartbeat drowns the busy noise of the hospital. Deeply disappointed with myself, I look at my arm covered in a cast from fingers to shoulder resentfully. I didn't know what I would do after my studies, but I certainly wasn't planning on staying home with a lack of mobility for two months. My belly feels like a blender mixing with all kinds of emotions; I'm living my worst nightmare.

Ashamed of my irresponsibility, I dial my dad's phone number. I brace for my parents' anger and disappointment as I tell them. But while they aren't happy, they're still supportive. I wait for them in my apartment. They help me to pack up my things and take me home to my village on the periphery of Bratislava, Slovakia. They love me, and I love my family. Why would I want to go away and travel when I have so much support at home, and it's so comfortable? I smile and decide to see what this broken arm has to teach me. It's been a while since I started working with a mindfulness coach, meditated, and did my inner work; I've learned that there are no coincidences — maybe this is a turning point in my life.

The first days after breaking my arm were hard. I'm used to being independent, but now I have to ask for help doing everything, even asking my dad to wash my hair. My arm hurts. The pain wakes me up every night, but when I get up, I try to be quiet. I don't want to bother anyone. It's my fault I broke my arm, and there's no need to let others know how miserable I am. I feel so guilty for not being able to tell my parents what I'll do after summer. It's time for me to start making money, but I'm no closer to working. I feel like a total loser. The internship should begin in three months, but there's no news about the conditions in Italy, and there's no guarantee the hospitals will open for the trainees before fall. I have no control over my future, just a deep feeling in my heart dragging me to that clinic in Italy.

I'm so frustrated because my efficient and organized, perfectionist self can't approach this thing I desire so much in the way it's used to. There's no other choice than to release it to the Universe to take care of it. If it's meant to be, it will work out. It's so hard and scary to let go of control! I want to have the answers and give my parents a clear answer to what I am doing for the next couple of months. Instead, I keep telling them about my uncertain plan that's *written in the stars*. Even though they didn't disapprove of my decision, I feel I'm asking too much from them. How can I allow myself to be this foolish and just wait? I was triggered. Why? I've always wanted to be close to them, to be like them. Successful at work, having a harmonious family, and a kind heart, thinking their way is the right way. I know they think it would be easier if I had chosen to work in the hospital in Bratislava and stayed at home. And I feel that if I go to Italy, I will stay there longer than just the duration of the internship. But, I choose to ignore this insight because when I think of leaving my family it brings me to tears.

My dad taught me the importance of traveling, but he also explained that one of the biggest mistakes I can make is moving to another country. I will be a foreigner forever. And I'm about to *make* this 'mistake.' A 'mistake,' that's incompatible with me being the perfect human being and daughter I aspire to be. Perfect people don't make mistakes. And, to show how grateful I am for everything my parents have done for me, I should continue building on the perfect life they've made for me and not leave them. There we go. I hear the voice inside my head reminding me how selfish I am. *It's never enough for you; you always have to be something extra.* Those are the sentences I've heard multiple times and have embedded them in my mind. *Am I really that horrible? I just want to be happy, but I don't feel like I will find happiness in Slovakia now… and I hate myself for it.*

After the first week, my arm starts to hurt less, and I begin teaching myself to do many things with my other limbs. I find the fun in opening the door with my feet. I like making everything into a game and having fun; I'm tired of feeling guilty and being afraid.

I decide to treat these months as a retreat with the intention to heal on every level. Asking for guidance, clarity, and help, I spend a lot of time meditating in our garden, which affects me profoundly. Observing the metamorphosis of the vegetation teaches me about the power of presence. There's no rush in nature. Everything works in a harmonious, divinely ordered way. It's us resisting it that creates chaos. I spend a lot of time alone because others have already planned their holidays, and I'm okay with it. Just being there, present with myself, feels good. I've realized I'm enough for myself; I'm complete just by being me. Being alone doesn't mean I'm not loved. On the contrary. During this period, I receive an abundance of support. My dad purchases my favorite food at the grocery store, my sister and her boyfriend come to visit, my mom tries to be with me as much as possible, and as soon as my rehabilitation is over, she takes me on vacation. One friend even works remotely to spend time with me for a few days.

Even though I've changed and understand that I can't control the course of my life events, sometimes I feel my body rocking on needles impatiently, my sleep gets disturbed, and I need to cry alone to release the tension. For the first time in my life, I allow myself to take off my "everything's just fine" mask, be vulnerable, and experience all the colors of my emotions without judgment. Sometimes they're so intense, but I know I need to let them evaporate through the pores of my body. I can't suppress any part of myself anymore. I let the closest people to me meet the desperate, scared, lost, and broken Silvia that I denied for so long. I'm amazed by their reaction. They accept my "crazy" behavior, try to understand me, and just wait for me to return when I'm ready. Seeing how they hold space for me makes me realize that it's mostly me putting myself under pressure. I know now that my family respects and believe in me, and I appreciate them for it; I feel blessed.

At the end of July, I write one more email to the hospital in Italy. If it's possible to do the internship, I'm going; if not, I'll start looking for a job in Slovakia. There's no point in forcing it. Surprisingly it doesn't take long, and I get the answer: I could go to Italy! The hospitals are open for trainees again! This news wakes me up from my zen state, and my executive self activates immediately. I know there's not a lot of time to do all of the paperwork needed, and I see a glimpse of a new opportunity.

Then it's August! In Italy, it's almost a sacred month when everyone stops working. It is hard to get my paperwork because all the offices are closed and reopen at the end of the month. August is a pretty crazy ride, but I somehow managed to make it all work out. On the 18th, we fill up the car with my stuff and drive to Florence. My muscles feel tense, trying to calm down the restless concert in my stomach. Even though I've done a lot of inner work, there's still some guilt inside, and I'm not sure if I'm worthy of so much devotion from my family. I have no idea what I am doing. I'm just taking one step at a time based on my intuition, which freaks me out. All four of us are in the car, my parents, my sister, and me. Observing them soothes my belly with appreciation and warms my heart with love. They truly do support all of my decisions.

When we arrived in Florence, my feelings swirled in circles. I look around, sharpening all of my senses. I hear my heart beat in a rhythm of overwhelm and expectation. It seems unreal that I'm here.

My family stayed for five days, I enjoyed the time with them, and suddenly when I saw them leaving, tears filled my eyes. That's it. Now I'm really on my own. It feels strange, and right at the same time. I take a deep breath, wipe away the tears, and at the end of the outbreath, I smile. *Let's see what this experience has in store for me.*

While writing this story, I sit by the river looking at the scenery of ancient buildings with the tower of Palazzo Vecchio in the middle. I get to observe the sunsets by the sea nearby. And, I get to spend time in my new beautiful home. I've been in Italy for a little more than a year now. It happened only recently that I started allowing myself to fully enjoy my experience and stopped looking at my situation as if I was betraying my family or country. Those thoughts were all an illusion as I had to let go and trust myself. By forgiving myself I was able to find *my* path and do what I *love*. Forgiving allowed me to see all the opportunities in the world, the yumminess, and the goodness the Universe provides.

Now I'm a resident in General Medicine, I've finished the first year of my master's degree in Chinese Medicine, I'm a trainer for The Infinity Life™, an energy healer, and most importantly, now I know I'm loved by my family even though I made my own choices. Letting go of my perfect life, which in the eyes of many would be seen as totally foolish, crazy, and selfish, was one of the hardest things I've ever done. I went through so many hardships this year, and my parents were by my side, facing all the challenges with me, even from afar. I visit them, and they visit me. I feel so much more confident and freer because acting based on my intuition has brought many synchronicities and fun into my life. Everything has turned out beautifully. Now I'm aware of how blessed I am, and I love my family and myself more than ever before. There's still work to do, but I know there's no right way of living life and that it's impossible to plan every detail.

Chinese medicine teaches that our purpose in life is to flourish. I choose to live life to the fullest, blossom, and take one step at a time, checking in with my heart along the way; keeping it open to forgiveness. All we can do in every moment is our best, whatever that may look like to us or others. Living the life of your dreams is possible when you open your heart and decide to follow it. Enjoying every day takes time, but when you go after your goals and forgive yourself for not being "perfect," you awaken to the magic life has to offer.

IGNITE ACTION STEPS

* Are you afraid of something? Just do it!! Start with small things. You'll be proud of yourself for leaving your comfort zone, and your self-trust will grow.
* Set the intention to receive the help you need. When somebody offers you help, or if you hear about a coach or a course that gets your attention, be willing to say yes. We all need help from qualified people.
* Dance/move/shake it out of your system. If you feel off balance or low in energy, put on a song, set the intention to release and heal, and just move, unleashing yourself.
* On the day of the new moon, use its power. Get in a quiet space, light up a candle, and get some paper and a pen. On one side, write what you wish to let go of; on the other, what you want to manifest. When you're done, burn the paper in the fire of the candle with the intention to make your wishes come true in a way that's for your highest good.

Dr. Silvia Hlavenková—Slovakia
Lover of life, travel, and fun
Doctor MD., Chinese Medicine Doctor to be, Healer, Author
dr.silvia.infinity@gmail.com
The Infinity Life™ theinfinity.life
Dr-Silvia-100862935738004
dr.silvia_h

I want to forgive.

Forgiveness is a gift
Forgiveness gives me freedom
Forgiveness allows me to move
Forgiveness upgrades my self-love
Forgiveness makes it all easier
Forgiveness takes its time

I make a choice.

I choose to forgive myself
I choose to forgive the others
I choose to forgive it all.

I take this step forward.

Because I love myself
Because I welcome the bliss
Because I call in the magic
Because I let in the miracles
Because I love my life

Because I know...

I am ready
I am safe
I am patient
I am strong
I am loved
I am supported

I am worthy of greatness
I am open to forgiveness
I am creating my best life ever

Please, help me to forgive
NOW

And so it is
Blessed be
Thank you

Ash Bhadani

ASH BHADANI

"Ignite your forgiveness to master your healing."

My intention in writing this story is to share the insights I've gained from walking through my tunnel of shame and pain. I saw the light only when I embraced my feelings without labeling them. I want to make a request to parents that they really understand the impact of their actions and words on their little ones. Parents are the guardians of a child's ability to feel connected, loved, and worthy. I want all the survivors who, as children, suffered from domestic abuse to know that it was not your fault or doing in any way, and through forgiveness, they too can heal.

BIG ENOUGH

"Go to sleep before it's too late."

It's a typical night for the twelve people living in our four-story home in my hometown of Punjab, India. It may be just another night for every other home in our city; for me, however, it is a night to be confused again. I am lying on the bed with my baby brother and sister while my mama organizes something in her cupboard in our shared bedroom. The room is not big enough; the windows are occupied with a portable room cooler and the faintest light stems from a bulb above. Mama keeps repeating that we should go to sleep before it's too late, and my mind tries to understand the meaning behind these words. While lying on the bed in our shared space, the passage of night and Papa's absence built suspense in my eight-year-old mind.

As a skinny, petite girl, I was troubled with my own thoughts and living two realities side by side. One where I'd get to sleep all night and the other where I'd wake up in the middle of the night and have to immediately cover my siblings' ears with my hands and hold my breath in such a way that pressure would build up in my ears. This helped me muffle the sound of my mama's pleas as I shut my eyes as tight as possible so as not to see anything. My eyes would hurt from how tightly I closed them, but that was the only way I knew how to protect myself and my siblings.

I hated myself for not being big enough to protect my mama. Despite being in a 'home' filled with twelve people, I felt completely alone as my mama cried and her pleas went ignored. I always wondered how nobody in this big joint family ever turned their heads, knocked on the bedroom door, or gave her a shoulder to cry on. I was tormented by witnessing these nights. My pain felt small compared to that of my mama. I felt selfish for giving attention to my pain. I tried my best to please my papa to save my mama from going through any troubles because of us. I started feeling alone and small. I asked myself over and over again when I would finally be big enough to be able to protect my mama from the emotional and physical pain she withstood, big enough to protect my siblings and myself, too.

I wanted to be big, but going through all this chaos, I wanted to be invisible also. I wanted to hide, escape, and erase what I was experiencing at home. I needed a reason to belong, to validate my existence. My mind looked for ways to feel good about myself. I found that if I slept less and spent more time on my studies, I could score the feeling of being good enough despite my small, frail body. I mattered when I was at school, compared to how I lived at home denying my existence and hating myself for not being enough. I compartmentalized my life into two disconnected parts.

I started looking at the problems differently in terms of what I could do and what was under the control of my actions. As I did not control the night, all I could do was close my eyes and hold my breath until I heard my mama's hiccupping sobs cease. I referred to it as waiting for the sound of the terrors to float into the wind. That was my permission to close my eyes and let sleep come. Being a good girl, studying hard, helping mama, and pleasing people were all under my control. That was my transition from human being to human doing. All I was trying to do was to find some peace and grasp a hold of my confused reality, my two disjointed worlds.

That was a habit I kept up through my teens. I excelled in my studies to find my worth and to get validation from my teachers. I stayed on top of all the household chores and tried to do everything and anything, so my mama could have a peaceful moment for herself. After all, peaceful nights were not guaranteed for her. I played the role of being a happy and obedient girl, thinking time would heal my wounds. I tried to shush myself over and over again. I didn't speak to anyone regarding the difficult situation at home and kept it a secret. I forbade myself from talking of these cruel nights, even with my mama. I pushed my storm so low and far within me that no one could hear it, including me.

As I transitioned to adulthood, the storm kept coming back to me; the knock of my inner child's pain started pounding within my heart. The more I delayed answering it, the louder and harder it was to avoid. After the birth of my first baby boy, my weight started piling up on my body. From ages twenty-seven to forty-five, I lost thirty pounds three times. Those thirty pounds came back again and again. I started calling myself a *yo-yo*. The word described my pattern so well. I tried weightlifting, kickboxing, and dancing. I went through waves of being either fully immersed in a strict diet and exercise regimen or eating anything and everything while staying physically still. I would burn out or do things without knowing my *why*. I developed a strange relationship with eating—it was either a chore or a method to comfort myself. Looking back at my pattern, I was trying to find control in all situations because of the years I had spent feeling incapable of protecting myself or anyone else. Even when I pursued those workouts and diets, it was rooted in the desire to be someone else, someone who I didn't know.

The transition from human doing to human being came into my life with a big announcement: COVID-19 was shutting the world down. As terrible and terrifying as it was for so many, and in so many ways, it was also a nudge for my heart. Prior to that, I was so trained in being a people pleaser, helper, and peacemaker, that I found comfort in these traits and never questioned them. Then, during the pandemic, I got COVID-19 twice and was forced to spend time with myself; I was alone in a room for quarantine.

Alone—except for my computer. I started an online telegram group, "Love Without Boundaries," to support people through their loneliness. Being fully involved in my online support groups, I found mirrors of myself repeatedly. I realized that the people who gravitated toward me for help and support were also children who witnessed domestic abuse in their families. While going through that, I once again restarted my weight-loss journey. But this time, I contacted my friends and Rapid Transformation Therapy™ (RTT) therapists—Lena and Sebastian—to get their help with tapping into my body's wisdom.

During one of these RTT sessions, in which I was hypnotized, I took a trip in my mind. I could see it so vividly and I was so scared. I saw myself under that dim light, holding my sleeping brother and sister close to my body to block out the sounds. My trembling voice said, "I don't want to be in this room. I don't want to go back. I don't want to hear my mom's cries again." The therapists allowed me to leave that room, but before I left, I cried out to my mother, "I'm sorry I was not big enough and couldn't help you. But I can now. I'm big now!"

The root of my weight gain, people-pleasing, and fear was that I was ashamed I had not been able to be a protector for my mama. Because of this, I always wanted to be big. This impacted my weight, as whenever I lost thirty pounds, they would circle back to me. The extra weight became my safety net and ammunition for protection so I could serve my mama, myself, and all the troubled children. My constant desire to make everyone around me happy was my way of avoiding conflict, a defense mechanism that allowed me to feel worthy.

I was a bystander in my experience as an eight-year-old witnessing mama's pain. I was an innocent child. Protecting my siblings and muffling my mama's cries were my way of coping and surviving. It was time to forgive myself for all the things I could not do because the truth was, they were never supposed to be my burden to carry.

The lesson in front of my eyes was that I could not heal myself from the outside. I could not find peace by being in denial and resisting my pain. I had to validate my feelings. I started my healing journey by spending time with my younger self through daily letters and conversations. I began accepting my younger self with love and compassion instead of avoiding her. I embraced that eight-year-old and appreciated her courage in helping her family despite her own pain. It was time to honor the significant role she played in the life of my siblings, and how hard she worked to protect them despite her small frame. Even if her body wasn't big enough, her heart always was. I saw the truth in her existence; there was nothing she did that I needed to forgive.

The time came to then forgive my parents and my other family members. That brought me to the next phase of my life, where I started learning different techniques to help myself by bringing compassion to older beliefs. I became a certified life coach and focused on helping others adjust their belief systems to serve their life in the present, in a healthy, loving way. With that transition, I saw everyone in *their* truth and their perspective. I opened my heart (and my eyes and ears) to understand that my mama and papa did what they learned from their generations and were living life as though none of us had a choice.

My mama felt she didn't have a choice to stand up for herself. My papa felt he didn't have a choice to express his needs in any other way than to hurt her. After moving to America, my mama made a different choice. She became strong in her mind and body, so she was not afraid to stand in front of Papa and declare on multiple occasions that she would not be quiet anymore. My papa changed also. He turned from an abuser into a genie for my mama, where all her wishes were his commands. He realized he did not have to hurt anyone to show that he's a man, however, he still has work to do to truly become heart-centered. I believe he feels small when he recalls his past wrongdoings, but his ego has not grown enough to let him come and say sorry to all of us. I know in time he will get there, at his own speed, on his journey, but I have already forgiven him.

My mama is still on her journey as well. I realize that I cannot fight for my mama and I cannot forgive anyone for her. That's her choice. I honor and respect her choices, then I honor and respect my own. I had a choice not to drink the poison of shame, anger and guilt; I had a choice to live a happy life. I found my peace by forgiving myself first, which, honestly, took more time than forgiving my parents and extended family.

Now is the time to start a new chapter in my life by understanding that I no longer need to remain quiet. I don't have to be a people pleaser anymore. I want to face my emotions and trauma, and I no longer want to remove myself from my body and be small and voiceless. I want to take my place and be me —fully me — wherein I can give myself permission to be the fullest expression of me.

I have given myself the courage to open up with others. I realized that I hadn't just created my online support groups to help other individuals, but I also wanted a safe community for myself. That made me start another online group to support women, "Daring Gracefully," where all the mamas who need support to be fully independent are unconditionally helped without being judged. It is a place where respect, love, compassion, empathy, and peace are not just empty buzzwords, but are fully integrated into everything we do. It is a place where we don't have to be an imposter nor someone other than ourselves to feel worthy. It is a community where we can belong and evolve by being unapologetically ourselves.

Since January, 2022, I have released fourteen pounds. I'm happy with this progress. It's an affirmation that I do not need extra pounds on my body to feel protected or to protect my mama. I forgave my papa, my mama, my joint family, and, above all, myself, to heal my body, mind, and soul. Being "big" now feels like having a big compassionate heart.

I chose to end the generational trauma cycle and not pass it on to my kids and their future children. I wish adults knew that giving birth to a child does not make them a parent. They are supposed to provide them with a safe, happy, nurturing environment which is equally as important as providing them with food, shelter, clothing, and education. My husband and I work together as a team to provide our kids with a healthy, nurturing, and safe environment for their upbringing. Our children not only get food, clothes, shelter, and education, but they also have a real, meaningful home; they have a safe place for their emotions and thoughts, so they feel seen, heard, valued, and can overcome any obstacles they may face in their lives. The home where they don't have to please or protect anyone. The home where everyone will stand with dignity and integrity.

I encourage all parents to spend quality time with their kids on a daily basis. Go out of your way to brighten your child's day. Give your attention freely, and know that a little goes a long way. Don't underestimate the power of unconditional love and guidance in a child's life. That's your contribution to creating a ripple effect, and that ripple can be positive or negative. You have a choice. Every small gesture will have a massive impact on your child's self-identity, and every day is your chance to pay it forward to their future. By impacting younger generations, you Ignite a transformation in the future of humankind.

As you nurture the children of the future, know that you have permission to also nurture the child of *your* past. I encourage you, my warriors, who supported everyone and loved everyone except yourselves, to honor your feelings. Bring empathy for your younger selves, and know that your heart, your love, your power, your presence, they are all *big enough*.

Ignite Action Steps

Find a place and time in your day, where and when every part of you is welcome. Talk or write to your younger self daily in this safe, non-judgmental place. Journal or practice self-love in any way which brings joy to your life.

- Bring compassion every day for all of your emotions. Sit with your feelings and give them enough time to pass through you by breathing deep inhales and exhaling out loud with a sound.
- Realize that it's not your fault and it wasn't ever your fault. Ask for and seek help if it's hard to handle your pain by yourself.
- Bring compassionate self-forgiveness for all the misunderstandings and beliefs which did not serve you in the past. Understand that forgiveness

and healing are ongoing processes, so give yourself grace and time.
- Recognize that, as you choose forgiveness over hatred, shame, and guilt, the change will happen inside and outside and you will radiate happiness, and it will touch everybody.
- Go create your ripples. Pass the love and start it from yourself. Give yourself permission to dare on your dreams and convert them into realities. Be a creator and create a place for yourself and others where love is nurtured, given, and received daily. This is your way of paying it forward.

Ash Bhadani—United States of America
Belief and Mindset Coach
www.dreamrealitycreators.com
ash@dreamrealitycreators.com
dreamrealitycreators

Forgiveness helped you not only to heal but to make better choices where you chose compassion over criticism, discussion over judgment, and embrace instead of avoidance.

It let you make better choices and gave you a sense of belonging inside and outside of you, where you received healing agreeably with grace and time.

My intentions for your healing rainbow through forgiveness.

Healing will come into your life like a rainbow when the rain of forgiveness is poured over the lights of your wounds.

To welcome in the rain of forgiveness you have to meet your wounds with the openness of light and compassion.

Hiding and shutting of your wounds from the light will not only keep you in the dark, but take your rainbow away too.

Say yes to yourself, and embrace all of your emotions.

Remember you have experienced them before, and now you know that holding them in the dark will not rescue you or anyone else, so meet them with acceptance and compassionate forgiveness, so that your life will give you a rainbow of experiences through healing.

Jayne Elizabeth Powell

JAYNE ELIZABETH POWELL

"Stand in your EXTRAordinary!"

There are dates and moments in our lives forever etched in our brains as life-defining and altering our existence. Some are full of love, joy, and laughter, while others contain sadness, hurt, and anger. These moments trigger emotional responses that we can either choose to hold onto or decide to forgive and heal from. We can choose which moments define us because we construct our identity through the narrative we tell about ourselves, and that which is told about us by others. Wouldn't it be great if we could experience a lifetime of love, courage, kindness, compassion, and positivity?

THE EXTRAORDINARY SIDE OF FORGIVENESS

Journal - August 7, 2016, 10:30pm

The anticipation of the trip made it difficult to sleep! But I was up and packed and ready to go! Check-in, security, and customs were straightforward at the Toronto airport. As I sat at the gate waiting to find out if I would get a seat because I traveled standby, I felt a jitter of excitement rise up from my feet all the way up my legs, through my spine, right to the top of my head. The Universe, ever loving and ever abundant, provided me with a seat; not just any seat —I was upgraded to first class! It was amazing because all 6'2" of me could sit comfortably and arrive rested. There was so much leg room and I was truly pampered and off to a good start.

I arrived in Phoenix, Arizona and disembarkation went smoothly; my luggage arrived with me and as I walked out of the terminal to get to the car rental, I knew that this trip was the right decision; this trip was the beginning of something huge in my life and I would be returning home a different woman. The rental company said they had many cars available and I could choose which one I wanted. Right away, I walked out to see all the cars available and I was excited to see a super-spacious, silver Hyundai Elantra. I loaded my suitcase and got in to begin this wild adventure that I had said "yes" to in an instant. This was an opportunity to take my first trip alone, to do something entirely for myself, and to have the space to heal and work on me. I started the car and left the lot. As I pulled out, I glanced at the clock, and it was 1:11 pm — the angels were with me!

The drive was easy and beautiful all the way to Sedona. The music playing on the car radio, combined with the scenery, gave me a sense of freedom so that I could feel joy and peace for the first time in a very long time. As I drove, two rock-n-roll songs came on that were a very clear indication that my brother, who had passed, was with me in the car, supporting my decision to go on this soul journey and heal from the pain caused by his death. Both songs created an electric energy that ran through me, and I felt as if Andrew was sitting in the seat next to me.

I just know that this trip is the right decision and that this week is going to be an incredible journey! Sedona!!! I am here, and I am ready.

Love,

Jayne XO ♥

Up until August 7th, 2016, my life was a series of dates and moments that had created a hurt and scared individual afraid of life. I had taken thirty-five years of abuse, hurt, and abandonment and made that my identity. I was a broken, tall, overweight, and lost woman. I absorbed all of the negative words and actions directed at me and took them to be my truth: 'unlovable,' 'wrong,' 'unable to fit in,' and 'abnormal.' What I would have given to be 'ordinary.'

Ordinary to me meant that I was the average height of 5'7, thin, beautiful, and able to fit in with the popular kids. I felt like I stuck out everywhere I went. At fourteen, I grew from 5'9" to 6'2." I wished I was tiny and cute like the other girls. In reality, I was taller, bigger, and stronger than all but one of the males in my school (including my teachers). I struggled to buy clothes and shoes that weren't from the men's department. I couldn't sit at desks comfortably, I couldn't share a school bus seat, I wasn't a part of the 'cool' crowd, and I found it difficult to relate to my peers. It had been this way since elementary school. I was always one of the taller and bigger kids, teased for my appearance and intelligence. Many kids were afraid to be my friend, thinking they would be subjected to the same torment.

In some cases, I was physically assaulted; tables, chairs, and other objects were thrown at me while I was the subject of ridicule. Once, while eating alone in the high school cafeteria, a group of kids started calling me a tall freak and shoved a table at me. This caused a domino effect, sending three tables into my rib cage with such force that it winded me and resulted in a permanent floating rib. My mom contacted the school and I was called into the administrator's office along with the students who assaulted me. I had to sit across from these three guys, in physical and emotional pain, as they twisted the story and told a different version. I felt alone and persecuted, wishing I had never told anyone. I was shocked as the administrator sided with the boys, suggesting it was my fault that the abuse had taken place. Like somehow being me was an issue and that, because I was me, I deserved what happened. All of this continued to feed into my belief that I wasn't lovable and I wasn't enough.

It would have been nice to come home from school to a safe haven, but I grew up in a house that was volatile. There was a lot of love, but also a lot of anger! I learned early on to read my dad's body language and words to understand when to be a 'good girl' and when to run. My mom was the nurturer, the comforter, the confidant, and the one who gave unconditional love. She always supported me, but her voice was drowned out by my father's; he was louder and meaner. From an early age, I listened and watched, learning that being helpful, being quiet, being introverted, and keeping myself occupied were important skills.

In my late teens, my dad and his friend were doing everyone's taxes in the basement on our family computer. I went down to bring them some additional paperwork that I had up in my room. The minute I walked into the room, my dad stated, "What the fuck, you disorganized idiot. I taught you better than this. This is an absolute embarrassment; you will never amount to anything." I stood there in shock, then remembered his friend was sitting next to him and looked at him. He sat there in silence with his mouth partially open. I was so hurt and embarrassed by his outburst that I responded with, "You are such an asshole." I turned on my heels, feeling heartbroken, devastated, and angry. I left the house, got in my car and drove to Niagara Falls, a forty-five-minute journey, crying and screaming in the car. The drive was my way of processing the torment. By the time I drove back, the two-hour journey had calmed me down and allowed me time to shove down those feelings of hurt and anger, burying them in my body so that I could continue living with the sense of not being enough.

I spent my adolescent years building my identity and low self-esteem from the many hurtful moments. Between home and school, I had become a human punching bag for verbal and physical assault. At nineteen I started dating and allowing men to get closer to me. I attracted broken and hurtful men. I was cheated on and told that I wasn't enough of *that* and I should be more like *this*. I spent my relationships trying to please these men the way I tried to please my father; all of it making me feel inadequate and unloved.

The one man who was different was my brother. Despite not always getting along while growing up, he was one of my biggest supporters. He suffered the same scrutiny from my father, possibly even worse than me, and we reached a place where we worked together to stop the tirades when my father became angry. My brother and I were a team and we worked together to keep the family protected and my dad at bay. I had been applying to go back to school and actualize my dream of becoming a teacher. My brother was the only one I had told at that point and he told me, "Do it, Jayne, just make your dreams a reality." We then discussed how I could help him find a new job because he wasn't happy with his current one. He was not making enough, didn't feel challenged, and felt like a failure. The last thing he ever said to me was, "We will talk about me doing something else someday."

I lost him to suicide on April 13th, 2008, and a piece of my heart was ripped out. An important part of my identity was taken away. I didn't know a loss could be so deep. I went to bed with a brother one night and woke up the next day without him. He never told anyone of his plans, he didn't leave a note explaining anything, and it was a complete shock. That created a deep sense of loss and guilt in me. I wondered: *How did I miss the signs? Could I have stopped that from happening? Who was going to help stand up to Dad? How would my parents, my sister, and I survive life without him?* The pain and hurt from the loss were unbearable for years, and I was diagnosed with PTSD and anxiety as I went further into solitude. I cut out friends. I felt guilty enjoying life. His sudden death fed into the narrative I had created about myself; *I was unlovable, especially if my own brother couldn't be around me anymore.* My fear of being alone and feeling lost increased, and it made me even less 'ordinary' because no one I knew had gone through the loss of a sibling.

As I was coming through the other side of losing my brother, my dad decided to leave my mom and move to another city. On March 21st, 2010, he got on a plane and left without telling me. I came home from a week away at school to hear the news of my parents' pending divorce and faced the fact that he had not waited the hour and a half to say goodbye to me. Although his departure was a relief because it meant no longer living with someone angry and volatile, it also meant another life-altering moment. The anger, devastation, and hurt set in as I sat in disbelief while my mother told me he had met someone else and left. Poof! Like that, the two most important men in my life were gone, abandoning me as if I wasn't worthy of their love and support. The sadness and anger fueled me to seek more counseling and therapy. I had started after my brother passed, and my father's leaving compounded the issues and made it more important for me to deal with my issues and inner trauma.

I continued to attend therapy and worked through some of those hurts. I learned to distance myself from the comments and actions of others, which were reflections of who they were and not who I am. I began to learn how to stand up for myself and have a voice. Through therapy and exploring my spirituality, I started forgiving my past. The idea that I would never amount to anything and be a failure was not true once I looked at my *many* accomplishments. I earned a bachelor's degree in French Language and Literature and spent a summer studying in France. I later graduated with honors when I earned my Early Childhood Education diploma, then with high honors when I earned my Masters Science of Education. I worked very hard to achieve the goals that I told my brother I wanted to, showing myself that I was someone and that someone was not an idiot. I also worked on cruise ships in the children's center; part of my responsibilities was also on stage. Though I hated the spotlight, that experience forced me to get out of my own head. Thirty seconds before stepping on stage, I was asked to come up with a nutty nickname. I gave myself the name "Giant Jayne," and it became an important part of my identity, one that I embrace and still treasure today. I loved learning about the development of humans, how to observe a child, and recognizing their strengths and weaknesses so I could plan experiences to help them grow. I wrote my thesis on fostering positive self-esteem during the developmental years because I never wanted another child to doubt how amazing they are. Still, throughout my life and academic achievements, I let the thought of being loved go. I stayed single. The belief that I was unlovable ran strong through my mind daily. Instead, I threw myself into teaching and being the best teacher I could be.

Then on February 19th, 2015, I was driving to work and found myself sitting at a light. I looked in the rearview mirror just in time to see a woman careening towards me in her car. Suddenly there was an impact. I hit my head on the roof of my car as I was thrown forward. At that moment, I sustained life-altering injuries that took away my health and my career. Everything came to a halt yet again.

During the last seven and a half years, I was forced to put myself first. I had to ask for help because I couldn't physically or mentally complete tasks on my own that I previously had no trouble doing. I have had to go to some uncomfortable places and deal with the past and present so that I can set up the future I want and deserve. During that time, I learned to meditate and the power of Morrnah Simeona and Dr. Ihaleakala Hew Len's forgiveness prayer, *Ho'oponopono*. This ancient Hawaiian tradition of reconciliation and forgiveness allowed me to begin healing. I said the four phrases, *"I love you, I'm sorry, Please forgive me, Thank you,"* over and over again. I used them toward my father for all the abuse and pain I had endured. Through therapy and *Ho'oponopono*, my relationship with my father has changed. I have forgiven him. I have forgiven myself for allowing it to happen and for allowing it to define my self-worth.

I have forgiven my brother for abandoning me, breaking my heart, and leaving me to continue living without his gorgeous smile, contagious laugh, and phenomenal enveloping hugs. I have forgiven the lady who drove into my car, the insurance company for their lack of support during my healing, and the legal cases that are still working their way through the court system as I write this story. I forgive the kids who tormented me and the administrators who denied me while I was growing up. I have forgiven the many hurtful events in my life and the people who have directly and indirectly shaped the past forty years.

I am human and can still be triggered today, but I realize that I may only feel that pain for a short period of time before I am able to forgive and move back to a loving space. Forgiveness, to me, is the journey of learning to process the hurt and pain, releasing the situation or person without forgetting the event, and being able to move forward lovingly. Forgiving allows me to let go of anguish so I can make more room in my body and soul for love. It allows me to let love in by loving myself and allowing others to love me. It is knowing that forgiveness does not guarantee that I won't be hurt again, but it does guarantee that I will find peace.

That brings me to the journal entry. I learned about a company that does soul healing and introspective journeys in Sedona, Arizona. As soon as I got on the phone to do my discovery call, I knew I was going to say "yes," deciding for *myself* for the first time in my life. I did it without consulting anyone because I knew it was exactly what I needed; that trip was me choosing me, *for* me, because of me. I was going to do the work and receive help to learn more about who I am and what I am here to do in this lifetime. What I didn't expect was that I would learn just how amazing I am. How divine I have always been, since birth, and as I will continue to be, for eternity. That trip began my most important forgiveness journey, the road to forgiving and healing myself.

I continue to learn just how amazing I am. It is not a mistake that I was born into a large framed six-foot-two-inch body. I am not ordinary, I am EXTRAordinary! I put myself first, making choices based on what is good for me and not apologizing for but rather embracing "Giant Jayne." In Sedona, I had a soul portrait done by a local artist. When she delivered it, I sat and took it in, crying with love and joy as I looked at myself and saw my beauty. It is beside my bed and is the first thing I look at every morning, reminding me how beautiful and amazing I am. I also got a tattoo in Sedona; it is my constant reminder of the power of forgiveness. Tattooed on my inner left wrist is a heart with the infinity symbol on my heartline. Every time I look at this tattoo, it reminds me to love myself infinitely, to let love in, and always come from a place of love. Like I said in my journal, I knew that was going to be an incredible journey, and forgiveness of myself and others has been the reason why!

Forgiveness allows you to regain your power. It has more to do with you than with the other person or situation. It enables you to let go of the hurt, as the hurt is not you, just something that happened to you. When you forgive, you allow the light to shine and show the world how amazing you truly are. Your uniqueness makes you special. Stand in your EXTRAordinary!

Ignite Action Steps

Let the world see who you are and embrace your amazingness.
1. Ask yourself: What are you doing to make yourself EXTRAordinary?
2. Now create an action: What action(s) are you willing to take to be EXTRAordinary consistently? (therapy, *Ho'oponopono*, forgiveness practice, journaling, walking in nature, talking to a friend, creating something artistic) Choose something that will bring you a sense of peace and joy!

Jayne Elizabeth Powell—Canada
Teacher, Life Coach, Energy and Soul Healer
giantjayne@gmail.com
Jayne Powell | *GiantJayne*

HEALING THROUGH FORGIVENESS

Let the pain of your past go,
Release the hurt from lifetimes ago,
This pain and hurt serve no current purpose,
Heal yourself with forgiveness.

Love the lessons for what they taught you,
Apologize for the stories you told,
Forgive the past, present, and future,
Gratitude for the clean slate.

Love those individuals involved in your strain,
Apologize for the part you played,
Forgive the people that caused you pain,
Gratitude for the clearing of negative energy.

Love yourself for being perfectly imperfect,

Apologize for the thoughts you expressed,

Forgive your higher self,

Gratitude for the awareness that you are complete.

Love from a place that is unconditional,

Apologize for the emotions you experienced,

Forgive the Universe,

Gratitude for the peace you feel.

Allow forgiveness to create,

Create the peace your soul desires,

Create the love your heart desires,

Create the joy your body desires.

Wanda Zayachkowski

Wanda Zayachkowski

"Love is found on the other side of forgiveness."

I desire that my story will help everyone discover their inner child of love, and together, through action inspired by love, we will change the world one heart at a time. Love is our true nature and the most powerful energy available to us. We can reach out to others and seek to improve life with love. Watch and enjoy the ripples of love expand as you touch the hearts of those around you, and they feel the love you intend for them.

Hear the Caged Heart Sing

As a young child, the friends that came to my tea parties were different. They were from the land of fairytales and magic, and only I could see them. I would set a place for them at the table along with my stuffed teddy bears and wait for them to appear. Often, I would find them hiding in the bushes or behind a tree. I would see a sparkle, and my beautiful, magical friends would appear. I never told anyone about what I could see. It was my special world. I created a safe place where I could live in this magical wonderland anytime I wanted. Whenever I was afraid, I would disappear to be with my friends until it was safe to return. My body was still in the physical world, so no one knew I was gone. It was like magic. It felt like love.

Years later, when I was thirteen, my mom surprised me when she defined what love meant to her. The love she described was one I could not have imagined. Love came into focus for me in a new way on an ordinary day. It was evening, and I was sitting by myself. For some reason, I could not concentrate long enough to follow the show on the television. My mind kept slipping away like I was fading in and out. Behind me was a wall that concealed the stairs that led to the second floor. The familiar sounds of my stepfather hitting my mom thundered down the stairs, and I said to myself, "*OH NO! It is happening again.*" So, I escaped to the world of my imagination where birds sang, animals came to greet me, flowers bloomed, rainbows sparkled, and the sun was always shining—my favorite place to be.

Suddenly, I heard an unfamiliar noise that caused me to feel panic, startling me and snatching me from my happy place. Something was falling down the stairs! My eyes flew open. Hearing movement, I realized "the something" was "a someone," and I waited in terror. A body began to emerge from the doorway, crawling toward me on hands and knees. It was my mom. When she raised her head to look at me, I understood how a brutal physical assault can completely change someone's face. What I saw was incomprehensible and unrecognizable. I sat motionless and unable to speak. I wondered in horror, "Where is my mom?" In disbelief, I watched wide-eyed as she crawled with tremendous anguish onto the couch beside me. She placed my hand in hers and put her other hand on top of mine. She looked directly at me and somehow managed to say these words:

"Don't worry. Everything is going to be okay. He loves me, and this is how he shows it."

I was not expecting my mom to say that. My mind was racing with questions and resistance. The same idea took different shapes as it played on repeat quietly in my mind: *How could anyone do this to someone they love? How is this love? This cannot be love! This cannot be true! I cannot accept this love. I do not want this love. If this is love, then love is not for me.*

Seeing love defined in this way was scary, horrifying, and painful. In a flash, my beautiful, wonderful imaginary world that had comforted me since I was a little girl shattered into pieces. At that moment, the birds did not come to sing, the playful animals and magical friends that gave me so much joy scurried away in fear, and the rainbows and sunshine melted into a dark and dreary sky. I was being pulled toward a place I did not know. It was darkness without an end, and I was spiraling downward fast. Then from somewhere that seemed far away, I heard my mom calling me. The urgency of her voice pulled me back into the moment, and when I looked at my mom again, I was reminded that this twisted meaning of love was being reflected to me in her face.

A few months later, I traded my imaginary family for the comfort of marijuana and traded the wonderful world of my imagination for time with new friends who introduced me to other amusements. I found solace in alcohol and drugs. Unfortunately, it just led to more trauma that attracted unwanted experiences into my life, including physically abusive relationships and rape. I became the love I saw represented in my mom's face that night on the couch. Love was conditional—being able to provide what someone else needed. Love affirmed that I was not worthy and that I was not good enough to do anything right. The trauma of defining love this way had me feeling like an alien with amnesia living in a strange land. I could not remember who I was.

Somewhere inside me, a voice was trying to right my path, saying, "Wanda, you need help." But the need to drown my pain—to not remember or relive it—was so much stronger than that voice. So, I kept using substances to numb my thoughts and feelings, taking myself to the brink of death well into my twenties. Alcohol abuse almost killed me many times, until one night, I passed out on my friends' couch and woke up the next morning to what looked like a scene from The Exorcist©. I would have died if my friends had not turned me onto my side that night while I was passed out. Seeing the contents of my stomach spread across her living room, I knew I was lucky to be alive. With great difficulty, I got up and bounced off the walls as I made my way down the hallway to the bathroom. I did not recognize the person in the mirror. The eyes being reflected back to me were void of life. Two days earlier, I had arrived back from a three-month, wilderness and white water canoe trip on the Nahanni River in the Northwest Territories of Canada. The contrast from being in nature's heaven to the brink of alcohol poisoning shook my soul. Who I saw in the mirror, I did not recognize. How did I get here from there? I knew it was time to heal, so I decided to seek help.

Eventually, pushing thirty, I achieved sobriety. The journey was intimidating, confusing, and heartbreaking. If not for AA™ (Alcoholics Anonymous), therapy sessions with a counselor, hypnotherapy, and a commitment to healing, I could still be in that addictive cycle today. When I began my walk down the path of sobriety, I couldn't remember anything. I couldn't remember who I was or who I had wanted to be. Every time I tried to remember the wonderful aspects of my childhood before I was thirteen, something would trigger emotions connected to what happened after that fateful day. The experiences were many, and the pain would overwhelm me. But with my community's support, I also began to remember the tea parties from my childhood imagination. I discovered I was gifted with a wonderfully creative mind, providing me with the ability to build a world where the love that I longed for thrived.

In the 12-Step program of Alcoholics Anonymous™, one of the necessary steps is making amends. We not only have to forgive ourselves but reach out to those we have wronged and ask for their forgiveness. This was incredibly difficult, but it also allowed me to see the way toward forgiving those who had hurt *me*.

My first genuine feeling of forgiveness occurred when I was forty-six, and my mom was diagnosed with terminal cancer. As she was dying in the hospital, I thought about our life together. I reflected on the experiences we shared that resulted from an abusive love, sometimes life-threatening, and, at times, mixed with tenderness and kindness. I wanted to do something for my mom that would somehow make things easier for her. When the idea of forgiveness came to me, I knew this was the gift she needed, and I needed in return.

The day came when I was alone with my mom in the hospital. She was legally blind now, but as I began to speak, her eyes sparkled like jewels of aqua blue, and it seemed as if she was looking directly into my eyes. Taking her hand between both of mine, I began to pour my heart out to her.

"Mom, I forgive you for everything. I am not holding onto anything. Everything is good with me. I'm completely okay."

My mom's hand trembled within mine, and I could see her eyes welling up with tears. Her lower lip quivered. She did not speak a word as I gazed at her lovingly. A delightful energy that felt like the ebb and flow of an ocean tide was swirling within me. It was blissful, and it was a part of me. *Divine* love was present that day, and it was within me.

Shortly after my mom transitioned, I was feeling consumed by hatred toward my stepfather. It occurred to me that the only person suffering was me. I declared out loud, "You will not take any more of my life." I began to think about forgiving him. But I did not know how to do this, as I believed some things are unforgivable. Yet, I had to be willing to try because the hatred I felt kept me bound and tethered to this person. Like the birds I saw in the sky, I wanted to be free to fly in a new direction, to a place where hatred transformed into love, to a place where my heart could sing again.

As I reflected, I realized that I needed to cleanse my heart of hatred to feel the love I longed for. I had to rid myself of the anguish and forced myself to have an imaginary conversation with my stepfather, and it began like this:

"I forgive you, and you are free. I hope that one day you find peace and love."

This conversation helped me not to be specific about anything and have the focus be on releasing the bond of hatred from my heart. As I continued my forgiveness ritual, I began to feel compassion. The more compassion I felt outward, the more love I felt inward. That real, genuine love eventually became the dominant emotion, and the hatred I once felt receded into the darkness where it belonged.

Then, as I progressed, I added new names to the list of those I wanted to forgive. It wasn't important for me to like anyone on the list or to see anyone in person to include them. The result was the same. It felt euphoric; to let go and to no longer hate. I was embracing forgiveness for myself; each time I completed a forgiveness message, my heart opened, and I felt the release of old trauma. That allowed me to feel better about my life and redefine my self-worth. I felt free to discover more of who I wanted to become and *know* love as love should be.

Not long ago, when sharing the story about my mom's traumatic fall down the stairs with a dear friend, to my surprise, I cried. I felt safe in the presence of my friend. She honored my courage to speak by allowing tears to flow and truly listening. She allowed me, through unspoken permission, to feel the pain of this experience without thinking. Love was present for me on that day; I realized that the person I needed to forgive the most was myself.

I would often ask myself why I didn't try to stop my stepfather when he was physically brutalizing my mom. Why did I allow myself to be taken advantage of? Why did I become involved in abusive relationships? Why, for so long, did I not feel love toward myself? The simple answer is that my early definition of love was given to me by misguided people who did not know its true meaning. They could not give me what they did not have or guide me in understanding what they did not know.

When I forgave myself, I was reignited with the love gifted to me on the day I was born. It took me decades to find it. When I discovered the preciousness of my divinity, it felt like I had found my core essence. I was always searching on the outside for something when I knew who I was born to be—a free and loving spirit. When I began loving myself, I found the little girl who had been hiding my whole life. She did not feel okay, and I had to coax her out from the dark shadows. When she floated up from the darkness, she was holding something in her hands. It was my heart. She had been taking care of it all along. As she opened her hands to show me, I could hear my caged heart sing for the first time in decades. To be reunited with such a sacred love was the most beautiful feeling I have ever known.

Recently I was at the Evergreen Brick Works in Toronto, Canada, which is a natural oasis in the center of the city. During my visit, I saw a rabbit, an oriole, a goldfinch, woodpeckers, a blue heron, koi, dragonflies, and a baby turtle. Crisp white clouds were floating above me in a brilliant blue sky. The sun smiled down on me. Suddenly I realized my magical friends from child-hood were with me. I felt a youthful elation and wanted to have a tea party again, as all the stress I was feeling flowed out of my body and away from me. It was bliss. Not the artificial bliss I'd created with drugs to keep my negative experiences out, but rather the natural bliss of letting the real and genuine experiences of joy and happiness in.

Now, whenever I feel misunderstood, frustrated, or angry towards someone or a group of people, I allow myself to be guided by the question, "What would love do?" Love knows how to respond in a way that makes me feel better and allows me to touch the lives of others in a positive and meaningful way. It is the greatest gift of all. Think about how you feel when you receive a warm hug from a loving person or when a stranger responds to you with kindness. When the intention is motivated by love, the ripple effect expands outward to touch hearts around the world. When we respond with love, we change how people perceive their world. In this way, we can Ignite the world one heart at a time.

I believe forgiveness is how you access the power of love. It can help you recognize that life's hardships and challenges lead to the discovery that love, real love, lives within. Like me, there is a little person inside of you, with a mind of pure childlike wonder, who can imagine anything, including a life full of boundless love. They see the love they want for the world and embody it, allowing it to transform all negative emotions. When you become the love you want to see you experience it more fully. You transcend hardship and adversity and welcome in forgiveness. Forgiveness releases us and is the pathway to healing that brings us to the discovery that love is who we are and that paradise is within us all.

All we must do is ask, "What would love do?"

IGNITE ACTION STEPS

- Make a list of all the people who harmed you and create your personal forgiveness message. You can start by saying, "I forgive you for anything and everything. May you find peace and love." Repeat the message daily. I found mornings to be the best time. Keeping the message simple will make it easier to get started. Including a message of love will help to nurture a feeling of compassion towards the person you are forgiving. As you continue, you will begin to feel an expansion of love from within, which will guide you in knowing when your forgiveness message is complete.

- Let love be your guide by asking, "What would love do? If your thoughts are negative toward yourself or others, before you initiate any action, sit quietly with your eyes closed and ask, "What would love do?" The simplicity of the answer will feel like bliss. You will experience an inner knowing that you have connected with something greater than yourself.
- Do things that make you feel joyful and happy. Take time to sing, dance, listen to music, create works of art, hug more people, walk in nature, buy yourself some flowers, have a tea party with your favorite friends. Find your joyfulness by trying new things. Listen to what your heart desires. By doing the things you love to do, you amplify the emotional state of joyfulness, happiness, and gratitude.

If you are experiencing alcohol or drug abuse, seek help. Asking for help is a strength, not a weakness. If you know a person who might be experiencing abuse at home, do not be afraid to talk with them. You could be the messenger of hope that inspires someone to rise above the darkness surrounding them.

Wanda Zayachkowski—Canada
Love Expansionist, Lightworker, Intuitive Transformation Coach
WandaLightsayer@gmail.com
🔲 *Wanda Zayachkowski*

THE LYRICAL WINGS OF FORGIVENESS

The wings of Forgiveness

Rise upward and forward with love

For you and me

As you think it

As you speak it

As you feel it

Into beingness

Forgiveness is boundless

Like the sky above

Like you and me

And divine love

Expand your wings of forgiveness

Far and wide

Explore new vistas

Let love be your guide

The Wings of Forgiveness

Untethers the song in our hearts

For you and me

As we think it

As we speak it

As we feel it

Into beingness

Feel the lightness of being

As your heart sings a gleeful tune

And you become the knowing

That forgiveness is the healer of our heart's ruin

Hear a symphony of hearts singing

And know this is untethered forgiveness amplified

For you and me

As we think it

As we speak it

As we feel it

Into beingness

We are the Magnum Opus

Divine Love is the creator

The joyous song within our hearts is us

Welcome home

Goran Karna

GORAN KARNA

"When you see the truth, you can forgive yourself and others."

I want everyone who reads my story to find inner strength and the inspiration to base their life decisions on love and forgiveness, instead of resentment and regret. Choosing a path of forgiveness can lead you to heal yourself and others. It can free you from any emotional restrictions and make your life full of love, gratitude, and abundance. This is my wish for you.

3 KEY FORGIVENESSES

Although it was a wonderful sunny day in Zadar, a beautiful town on the coast of the Adriatic sea, deep inside myself, I could feel something was drastically wrong. That sunny day, April 8ᵗʰ, 1988, became a day I would never forget. That spring afternoon, I was resting in my apartment reading a book when an acquaintance from my birth town appeared, knocking at my door. Ringing my bell frantically, he cried out, "He killed her!" My body went cold in shock, and a deep fear overtook me. I couldn't think clearly; my brain stopped working, but I just *knew*... I felt he was talking about my mother and father... and he was.

In my deeply stressed state, I had to travel by train for two hours to reach my birthplace of, Knin, Croatia. My father had been a troublemaker my whole life. From the first day, he had questioned whether I was actually his son and had bombarded my mother daily with his attacks, accusations, and jealousy. They fell in love when they were young, but their relationship was toxic from the start. They had many people constantly meddling in their marriage, and my father often questioned whether my mother was unfaithful and not devoted to him.

My mother was a beautiful Being who spent her whole life helping others. She worked as a seamstress in a local company, receiving the best employee award, and often helped others by offering her work for free. People would come to her for advice, and she always put their needs before her own. Though two of her five sisters had left the country seeking a better life, she was among those who stayed behind to support her father, caring for his cattle and working in his vineyard. She was a very hard worker and made many sacrifices in her life.

In the chaos of our home life, we were all suffering, and I was constantly trying to convince my mother to get a divorce. On that fatal day, my sister was only eleven and still living at home. I was twenty-three and studying at university in the city, a few hours away. I had always been trying to protect my mother and sister from the fighting, beatings, alcohol consumption, and daily scenes of violence, unhappiness, and stress.

Six months earlier, our mother had decided to leave our father and went to live with her brother nearby in his shanty, cramped one-bedroom house that was already home to four people. She felt safer, and more at peace living there. Then, one morning when she was going to work, Father was waiting for her on the street. He knew her route to work and confronted her. Mentally imbalanced, addicted to alcohol, and obsessed with my mother, he refused to sign the divorce papers. He killed her that day and was sentenced to eleven years in prison.

That event transformed my entire life. I had to return to Knin and take care of my sister. To become her legal guardian, I married my girlfriend. To graduate from school, I traveled two hours each way from Knin. Luckily, my wife got a job as a school teacher, and we all lived on a teacher's salary. We were grateful to receive a donation collected by workers at my mother's company to help us, and we were also given an apartment to live in. Although I knew nothing about parenting, overnight I became a guardian to my minor sister. I felt proud of being the one to model the protection and unconditional love our mother had taught us.

Following my mother's death, I lived with resentment, regret, and guilt. I blamed myself for being at school in Zadar on that fateful day and unable to prevent what happened. In my devastated state, I still had to keep working and took a summer job on the island of Ugljen, where my wife's parents owned a house. I was washing dishes and chopping vegetables at a restaurant so we could get by. I had a half-hour walk home each night and cried the whole way. Day after day, I was deep in sorrow, and could not ease the pain and suffering. I felt guilty that my mother had passed in such a way, and I believed I was the cause of it because I had persuaded her to get a divorce. My sister and I lost both our parents—I lost the person I loved most in my entire life—because I had convinced her to make that choice.

I sought answers and peace, trying to understand the meaning behind this new life I was living. I've been interested in religion since I was sixteen, especially Christianity and Buddhism. I was doing yoga and studied Indian philosophy. I was interested in holy places and traveled to India two years after my mother's passing. Through my exploration of these different modalities I came to understand that forgiveness, of my father, my mother, and myself, was necessary for healing.

When my father got out of prison, I was living in Australia as a refugee of war, having left Croatia, formerly Yugoslavia. I wrote to him, saying he was forgiven, and even sent money to support him up until he died of throat cancer.

Still, I struggled to practice that forgiveness completely, and my health suffered. I was diagnosed with irritable bowel syndrome, accompanied by constant pain, flatulence, and cramping. Although I sought out the greatest experts in the field of natural medicine, nobody could help me. The problem was not just within my body, it was more an issue in my essence. I had to go deeper to find what forgiveness truly meant.

Working with a Theta healing® practitioner, I made energetic contact with my parents during a healing seminar on Australia's Gold Coast. After not having seen them for so long, I could suddenly *feel* them, alive and present, connected to me in an energetic state. They told me they were proud of me, and I felt my body wrapped in joyful warmth. My soul, my heart, my whole being was touched as I connected with them and realized they had released their past and were at peace with themselves and each other. They worried I was carrying so much guilt and pain, and I realized it was my turn to make peace within myself.

I knew what had happened needed to happen, and it happened by their choices, not because of me. I realized I had nothing to do with their karma, life path, or earthly journey. As I meditated and worked on forgiving myself, I noticed my health improving, and the symptoms from my diagnoses were lessening. A year after focusing on my healing and full forgiveness of my parents, my health problems disappeared by eighty percent. I began embracing my purpose, feeling my true meaning, and understanding more about my life. I had so much to forgive and discovered that my life was indeed influenced by three great forgiveness stories: I needed to forgive my father, mother, and myself.

My father was descended from a family in which his father committed suicide after his wife had died of cancer. This genetic addiction involving a pathological relationship with a woman was passed down from my grandfather to my father. From that perspective, I finally understood that my father could not live without my mother and had a very hard time after she had left. I needed to forgive my father's transgressions. He was often under the influence of alcohol and influenced by his surroundings. As I was growing up, I did not like his behavior, and I did not respect him. Later on, I realized that he was doing what unhappy people, who were dissatisfied with themselves, their life, and their marriage do: using substances and anger to cope. This is not a justification for my father's abusive behavior, but I knew it was about the karma my parents had come to work out together. They had their karmic debts that needed to be settled in this lifetime, and I was not the one who had to do anything to change it. I worked on understanding my father on a deeper level and finding peace with him.

I also needed to forgive my mother also, because I felt that she had abandoned us and that her love had disappeared when she left us. That pain was tearing me apart, and I didn't know how to cope. I needed to think differently and recognize that every soul knows about and agrees to go through events like this. On a higher level, souls agree to such circumstances to bring forth a new awakening.

My mother made a great sacrifice; by sacrificing herself, she saved my sister's and my life. If that had not happened, we would never have had peace from our father. I realized that my mother was doing the best she could; that is why she wasn't able to leave my father earlier. If she had left sooner, the same thing would have happened. She did not leave because of the small-town, narrow-minded environment she grew up in. She believed, just as her parents had, that a wife should stay with her husband, no matter the abuse. When a woman has no support from her parents and the society she lives in, she becomes more insecure about leaving due to financial (and other) reasons. My mother was living in fear and agony and even asked her sister to take care of us in case anything happened to her. It took a lot of courage to leave that relationship and start a new life, a life which unfortunately had such a tragic end. Understanding my mother's life helped me forgive her and comprehend the greatness of her love. Mother sacrificed herself so we would be all right, and that is a quality of a great soul. I know on a deeper, more spiritual level that my mother came to this earth with the knowledge that she and my father would need to complete their karmic agreement in this way. I know now that she loves me dearly. I also know my father loves me and in his lifetime, he loved me in his own way, as much as he knew; as much as he could.

Through forgiving my father and mother, I came to forgive myself and understand myself more and more. I came to see the reasons for my own missteps. I'd gone through various crises. I'd consumed more alcohol than was good for me. I'd had so many fears and traumas going back to my childhood. I wasn't aware of how deeply I had suppressed all of that. This is because we feel worthiness from our relationships with our parents. This feeling of *being loved* is important for each child and adult because it helps us *love ourselves*. That is why one of the core lessons in life, and a path to healing, is resolving our relationship with our parents, so we can learn the lessons they could not learn and forgive them. The relationship we have with our parents mirrors the relationship our children will have with us. I've always dreamed about having a healthy and happy family. This is a dream that still hasn't come true, and I believe my time is yet to come. But through my three forgivenesses, I am closer to that dream than ever.

Today, I no longer feel like a victim. I feel no guilt, no regret, because I know it was all a higher plan that needed to happen so I could learn all these lessons; that have become blessings. Jesus says it is important to forgive others; this has been a religious norm for many centuries. Today, we see the importance of forgiving in the psychology of people and life. After forgiving myself, I was able to start living my life differently, balanced, and happy. I have learned that we are all connected and that whatever we do to others, we are doing to ourselves; by forgiving others, you are forgiving yourself. All these experiences led me to a healing and spiritual path. I have realized that so many people suffer and need help; they need love and happiness. It has been my mission for the last thirty years to help people improve their lives, relationships, finances, and their physical and emotional health, to reach the best version of themselves, and grow spiritually. I've worked with over five thousand people, healing and coaching them on how to forgive. I showed thousands of individuals how to forgive their parents and, in turn, forgive themselves. Along with studying different modalities such as Theta healing®, homeopathy, vibrational healing, and Yumeiho massage, I know from my own journey how vital and transformative forgiveness truly is.

In the last two years, I created my new healing method, Integration Technique®, which is both an energy and somatic modality working with the body.

212 / GORAN KARNA

By realizing deep, hidden, suppressed feelings using body awareness, and then transforming them into positive emotions and virtues, I am witnessing healing and transformations unfolding quickly and spontaneously. Users of the Integration Technique are getting balanced and harmonized; they are more grounded, stable, creative, and positive about their lives. I help them develop feelings of self-confidence and self-respect. All of that influences their health and overall well-being.

To forgive and to heal requires acceptance. Through our bodies we accept and realize our emotions and free ourselves from many emotional restrictions, limitations, shocks and trauma. When we truly accept our emotions and situations in our life, then they transform into higher energies and vibrations and stop holding us back. Instead of rejecting and fighting the past, emotions, and situations, we embrace and welcome them in our life; we become grateful for their existence and learn how they benefit our lives.

Our life can change within a single day and take a completely new course. No matter what kind of challenge we encounter, it is always a lesson that is waiting to be learned. Forgiving my father, my mother, and myself was my most precious lesson. The challenges I encountered led me down the path of deep healing and personal self-love. Choosing that path led me to a life-long mission of helping others walk the path of healing to transform their lives with happiness, joy, inner power, and peace.

I wish you many blessings on your path of forgiveness and know that you will find love, gratitude, and abundance at the end of it.

IGNITE ACTION STEPS

Below, you can find three exercises we use in Integration Technique® that will help you completely forgive. This will bring you to deep healing, and through these meditations, you will also help your ancestors feel better in their own lives and help your children, so they don't make the same mistakes you did. The meditations are simple and easy, and you don't need any previous knowledge to do them. All you have to do is take action.

The first step in forgiving: Write down what you resent about your mother, father, or some other person in your life. Write down everything you feel bitterness or dissatisfaction about. You can choose a situation that awoke those feelings in you, or you can imagine what you resent in general. Close your eyes and ask the Higher Consciousness within you, your Being or God, how this person felt or what was happening in their life when they did or did not do something you haven't been able to forgive. What was the reason for their behavior? You may hear or see an answer, or a thought may come to you. Once you see this truth and acknowledge that person's feelings, it will be much easier to understand and forgive that person because you will see them from a more genuine perspective.

The second step in forgiving: Choose one person, and write down which qualities you feel this person needs to be a better person. This could be understanding, courage, kindness, or something else. When you have written this down, think about which areas of your life are missing those qualities. Ask yourself what it would be like, and how you would feel if you had those qualities. When you receive an answer, ask yourself: "If I could feel these feelings in my body, in which body part would that be?" When you become aware of them in that body part, ask them to spread through your whole body. Just observe until this process is completed. Some parts will feel this quickly, in some parts more slowly; just wait until those feelings have spread throughout your entire body. If there is some part where you cannot spread the feeling, ask the Higher Consciousness in you or your Being to help spread those feelings. After that, thank God and the Universe for this healing, and imagine grounding yourself, growing roots from your body, through your feet deep down into the earth, a hundred meters down, and a hundred meters on all sides. When you have finished, think about how you feel now about the person from the beginning of the process. Check if you have understanding, forgiveness, compassion, and a new perspective on your relationship with them.

The third step in forgiving: Ask yourself: "If I forgave this person completely, how would I feel?" Perhaps you would feel complete, harmonious, happy, or relaxed. Once you find these feelings, ask yourself in which body part do you feel them in. For example, if this is your heart area, feel those feelings in your heart, and then, when you have found them, ask them to spread through your whole body and witness this process. Then ask yourself how you feel about that person you are working on forgiving. If everything is okay, thank the Universe for the healing and ground yourself as described in step two.

By completing these exercises, you will heal yourself and your genetic line and set new patterns in a new and positive way.

Goran Karna—Croatia
Founder of Integration Technique®, Healer,
Coach, Speaker, Author, Publisher
www.gorankarna.com
integrationtechnique | integrationtechnique

IGN TE
Forgiveness

LOVE AND
FORGIVENESS
are two sides
of the same coin.

Cynthia Fontaine R.SPE.P

Cynthia Fontaine
R.Spe.P

"Of all the messages you hear, let those from your heart play the loudest."

My hope in reading my story is that it inspires you to get to know and trust your own intuitive guidance. On a deeper soul level, your higher self knows what's best for you.

A Parade of Psychics

I am Psychic. I was born a psychic and grew up my entire life being told I was a psychic. That was my destiny in life. For my family being psychic was normal! When the babies were born, my dear grandmother, Anna, would pry open each of our mouths to see if we had the mark. The mark is a white horseshoe on the roof of the mouth, a trait my older brother and I share. It runs through both sides of my family.

You would think such powers would have filled me with confidence, but they didn't when I was younger. I was trained to be powerless by those whose outward expressions were enraged, damaged, and traumatized from their own upbringing. Savagely abusing me—mentally, emotionally, and physically—doing what they wished with no regard for me as a living, breathing human. Yet, I was determined to survive, and they couldn't break me. I got tough, compartmentalizing my way through the verbal assaults, bullying, rape, and even being held hostage at gunpoint. As I got older, I went to therapy and learned to meditate, beginning my path to healing. I also began studying healing and different modalities to distract myself from my abilities until I felt I could use them in a way to help people, not hurt them as I had been.

I was married to my high school sweetheart, though we had broken up my senior year and were apart for three years. His mother brought us back together when I was twenty-one and with my son, from a previous relationship, who was eighteen months old. The first year of the marriage was okay. I was a letter carrier and he was a restaurant manager. We worked opposite shifts, so we only saw each other on Sundays. But then, my husband changed jobs and began working the day shift. Suddenly I was dealing with a man coming home from work totally intoxicated... every day. At first, he said, "There was a party after work," then it was, "Oh, I just had a few beers at the end of my shift." The story was different every day, but the drinking was the same. He had five car accidents within a year, all under the influence, and two of them with my son in the car. Over the next couple of years, I begged and pleaded for him to stop, distraught and worried for him and even more for my son. But he continued. My psychic abilities had told me not to marry him, but I did anyway.

I was desperate, looking for a magic wand to fix the future I could see coming. My aunt Jessie, whom I confided in, took me to her psychic card reader, Eve, who was a short, plump woman in her forties and wheelchair-bound. Though Eve may have been limited physically, she didn't lack confidence in her readings. She predicted the future by reading regular playing cards like tarot or oracle cards, which was normal to me because my grandmother, Anna, read playing cards also. I was hoping for a miracle message; I hoped that Eve would say my husband was going to quit drinking. Instead, she told me he was going to be killed in a car accident! *What?! How could that be*? In disbelief, I went back to see her week after week for months, hoping what she predicted would change.

Then one gray, cold, rainy morning, my car was in the shop, and I had to take my husband's car to work. It was a little sports car that I loved and had driven numerous times. I pulled out of our street and onto the main road, approaching the traffic light. There were three lanes of bumper-to-bumper cars as I arrived at the intersection. The light turned green, and I began to accelerate. As I put my foot on the gas, I noticed the driver in a big SUV to my right open his window and stick his head out. I thought, "What is this guy doing in the cold and pouring rain?" as I sped off the line, I heard a thud. In a split second, a woman was on the hood of my car. As I slammed on the breaks I saw her fall to the asphalt with one shoe off and her umbrella flung across the road. Time stopped... I froze. All I could think of was my grandmother telling me that when someone loses their shoe in an accident, they're dead.

The closest fire station was only twenty blocks away, yet it took twenty-five minutes for the rescue vehicles to arrive. The man in the black SUV took me to his hair salon across the street so we could get out of the rain as the police took our statements, and the rescue crew did their work. The woman died that day with me at the wheel of my husband's car. All the witnesses said there was *nothing* I could have done, she had walked directly into traffic. The rescue workers left, and the police said I was free to go, with no charges or traffic violations. But I was wrecked! *Where were my psychic abilities to see this before it happened?*

Returning home an hour after, distraught and soaking wet, I sat on the side of the bed and woke up my husband to tell him what had happened. He never got out of bed, he never asked me if I was okay. He just went back to sleep, too hungover to care. I found myself grappling with an inability to forgive myself for what had happened, paired with an inability to forgive my husband for failing to support me. This left me in total darkness. I didn't go to work for weeks; I didn't leave the couch and I didn't get dressed. If it weren't for my boss at the time checking in on me every day, supporting me with his kindness, I would have checked myself off the planet.

As soon as I was able to get enough courage to get behind the wheel of a car again, I went straight to Eve. "This has to be what you saw! I was driving his car!" I insisted. No, she said, your husband is still going to die in a car accident. I felt panic that another horrible thing was going to happen. Jumping off a bridge sounded more and more tempting. My life spiraled, and I thought I was going to lose my mind! I couldn't drive through that intersection nor drive the sports car again, and I knew I had to get away from everything, so we built a house and moved. But my husband still kept drinking and I needed help. I found a counselor who decided all my problems were linked to my mother and my past. His solutions weren't helpful. So again, I turned to Eve.

This time, she told me that a man from my past, with a red motorcycle, was hanging around my house. I intuitively knew it was my son's absent father. Shortly afterward, I, in fact, ran into him. When I told him what had been happening in my life, he said his house was never locked and if I needed a place to get away and be alone, I could go there. And I did, for about a year, and that may have saved my life. But the conflict it created with my husband made life hell for the next eight years. Still, Eve had foreseen my ex returning to my life, so I trusted her. I had wanted to rely on my psychic powers, but I just didn't have the strength, and I didn't think I should take a chance and read the cards for myself.

My grandmother told me I had been seeing Eve too much, trusting her predictions over my own inner knowing. What I didn't realize at the time is that I was giving my power *away* to Eve, and paying for it dearly! Divorce became inevitable and my body was suffering from the hard physical work I did as a letter carrier. I was in a bad place, partly because I had relied on Eve to give me accurate guidance. In the wake of the disaster that had become my life, I made a pact with myself. If a card reader or psychic could screw up a person so much, I was *never* going to do that work, destined or not! I shut down all my abilities and decided to live a simpler life.

After the divorce, I purchased a small house in the neighboring town. Right after moving in, strange things started happening; windows broke, the water heater and septic tank failed, my daughter kept falling down the stairs, and I couldn't seem to meditate. Then, lifting a heavy mail tray caused a *severe* neck injury that had me bedridden for four weeks and taking a lot of strong pain medication.

That injury kept me from working at all for almost two years and forever ended my ability to work full-time as a letter carrier. Feeling overwhelmed and in despair, not knowing what to do, I turned to another psychic whom I had met around this time, Dana. She immediately recognized I was psychic and made it her mission to teach me. I was scared, not having confidence in myself or my abilities, but she pushed me. I knew psychic readings were something I could do to get cash to feed my kids now that I couldn't do the physically demanding work of delivering mail. Under Dana's guidance, I started doing psychic readings cautiously. But after a while, I started questioning her ethics, tactics, and accuracy, which led me to stop studying with her. My spirit guides were telling me to look elsewhere for answers.

Then, my ability to trust my guides was tested in a way that shook me to my core.

I had been single for a long time and wasn't looking when this guy often showed up at the same time where I would eat my lunch. He wasn't my type, plus he was separated and in the middle of a divorce. But he kept showing up. My spirit guides kept nudging me to go out with him. One drink led to over a year of dating. He was always kind to me, but there was evidence on the days when I wasn't with him, someone else was. Eventually, there was no doubt after I caught him with another woman; I was distraught, feeling mortally betrayed by my guides and emotionally shattered by him. The feelings were so overwhelming, and I was in complete disbelief as my guides had let me down. I also began to relive the betrayal I felt from working with Eve and Dana. I retreated from the world, work, and my family, not getting out of bed for weeks. One particular morning, my daughter came into my room asking if I was going to go to work. Looking up, seeing pain and love combined in her eyes, was like a cannonball hitting me in the heart and making it break wide open, feeling all at once the deep emotional grief, fear, and hurt *she* was experiencing. At that moment, I knew I had to get help... and fast! I knew in my heart a good psychic could help me at the speed needed to bring me out of this state. I had lost faith in myself, my own abilities, and the psychics I had worked with previously. Not knowing who I could go to, I searched, finding a woman, Colette Baron-Reid, who was touring with Sylvia Brown, a famous psychic. Reaching out, I discovered she had a six-month waiting list. "I can't wait that long!" I cried to her assistant, "I am desperate!" She offered to put me on a cancellation list, and miraculously, there was a cancellation for an appointment three days later! I now had hope... I could hold on for two more days.

On the morning of my appointment, I got up, watching the clock as the minutes ticked by until our phone meeting. The scheduled time came and went with no ring from my phone. I was pacing, filled with nerves, until I picked up the phone and called *her*, unable to wait a minute more. On the other end of the phone, I heard, "Oh, I am so glad you called 'cause I couldn't find your number," followed by hysterical laughter. I thought, *Oh god, I have picked another nutty psychic.* But through the laughter, I heard her profoundly say something that calmed my fears, "You're devastated, but this is the best thing that could have happened to you."

Colette described in detail things that had happened to me and was so accurate I was amazed. Through our reading, it became clear that the relationship with that unfaithful man whom was not meant to be my soulmate but was my catalyst for finding *her*. Once I realized that I found myself releasing him from blame... forgiving him. I forgave my spirit guides for leading me to him and putting me through the pain, and I forgave myself for trusting them because when all was said and done, *it had been the gift to get me here.*

That was the beginning of a beautiful and powerful relationship for me. I knew in my heart, gut, and intuition that this woman was different. Colette taught me how to find the power in my own psychic intuition and not to give power to anything outside of my own inner knowing. Even in that first reading, she had already affirmed the gifts within me when she showed me how my conscious choice to listen to my guides had ultimately led me on the right path. In a million years, I couldn't have predicted that the time spent on the phone that fateful day would be enough for me to not only choose life but change my whole future and march toward my destiny once and for all. I had finally found an ethical, light-bringing mentor who empowered me to open the windows to my intuition. I began to think that if forgiving one man had opened me up to all the good this woman had to offer, there must be even more joy for the taking if I continued to forgive.

Each time I forgave an aspect of my past, my future became clearer. Over time I forgave my ex-husband for being unable to change his character and forgave myself for investing in him for so long. I came to forgive Eve for being misguided and forgave myself for trusting her. Each time I forgave someone from my past who had wronged me, I paired it with a forgiveness for myself and the mistakes I had made. I even was able to forgive myself for one of the most painful events in my life—that day behind the wheel—accepting there was truly nothing I could have done.

It took becoming unblocked and unafraid to step into the power of my psychic intuitive gifts and truly gain the skills to be a clear and ethical channel of messages for myself and others. I had run from doing readings for so long, scared to repeat the patterns I had encountered previously. Instead, I had a deep longing to be like my grandmother, helping people with intuitive guidance, giving them positive reinforcement, maneuvering them through difficult times, and offering comfort and conviction on who they truly are. When my spirit guides brought this final mentor into my life, I finally came full circle, with a knowing deep inside that the work I do does help people. Today I am a #1 Best-Selling author and a highly sought-out psychic medium. Forgiveness and the lessons learned from my experiences guided me to become an excellent psychic, and I am able to have deep gratitude for those who hurt me along the way. In being let down by others, I was brought closer to truly knowing and trusting myself. I know I am a better psychic because of the lessons they taught me. They are behind the steps I take as I march forward finally at the head of my own parade.

We all have intuition built in naturally. Our inner knowing comes through our power center and is amplified from within. You may have your own psychic powers or intuitive messages guiding you. Listen to those. When you begin to amplify your physical senses, you are in fact activating your psychic abilities. Hone into those. Only you can let your divine voice be heard. You are the best person to guide yourself toward more happiness in your life. Trust yourself and you will see your future unfold beautifully.

IGNITE ACTION STEPS

1. **The chatter in our minds blocks intuition.** The quieter your mind, the more space for intuitive messages to come in. Before you go to bed at night, get the thoughts out of your head and dump them into a journal. Pay attention to your dreams, as they are often messages.

2. **Sit outside, with your barefoot feet touching the earth.** Sit quietly, breathe in and exhale slowly 3 times. Allow your body to release what does not serve you; worries, old grudges, anger, and hate.

3. **Practicing listening intently with your eyes closed.** Listen for the sounds of things that are around you; birds chirping, bees buzzing, water babbling; the lights hummings, the earth's heartbeat, and all the incredible things around you. Listening heightens your physical senses and activates your intuitive senses. Open your eyes slowly, softly gazing, and notice the colors are more vibrant and alive. This practice strengthens your ability to tune in.

4. **Sit quietly, breathe in, and scan your body.** Discover where you feel tension as well as ease. Say out loud, "My name is..." (say your name), and then scan your body, noticing what has shifted from when you first tuned into your body. Fine-tune your awareness by using someone else's name, "My name is...." (say a different name) and notice the change you feel (tension, tightening, or an ache or pain). This will help you know the difference between what is true and what is not. Our body has an inner truth meter and can guide our decisions. You will notice a change or discomfort in your body when you say an unaligned truth versus an aligned one. Use your body as a barometer to help make more aligned and joyful decisions in your life.

Cynthia Fontaine R.SPE.P—United States of America
Professional Psychic Medium, Intuitive Business Strategist, Speaker, Author,
Master Healer, Professional Clearer, CEO of Alchemy of the Earth Inc
www.cynthiafontaine.com
CynthiaFontaine.Intuitive
cynthiafontaine_psychic

IGNITE *Forgiveness*

When you forgive with all of your heart

You risk it all,

When you withhold Forgiveness,

You have lost nothing

Yet everything

For your heart never had a chance

To experience the potential

Of the most powerful

Wonderful vibration of all

The expansion of the heart

Feeling the joy of your heart leaping

Your face beaming with happiness

Wearing a smile so bright

Your body glowing with the freedom of Forgiveness

Pouring out of your every cell

Lighting the way

Guiding all those your life touches with compassion

Forgiveness holding the torch

© Cynthia Fontaine R.SPE.P

Emily Thiroux Threatt

EMILY THIROUX THREATT

"You can grieve and be happy at the same time."

I want you to know that holding on to judgment won't serve you. I was unhappy as I dealt with feeling stuck and afraid, not knowing how to move forward. I realized that I could only find happiness based on what I believed I could do. Finding the way to forgiveness allowed me to release judgment so I could finally have peace of mind. Know that you, too, can find happiness outside of judging yourself and others. You can move forward and embrace your life. Forgiveness is in your hands.

TREATING MYSELF TO FORGIVENESS

"I can't move back home." In my college's theater, I confessed to an attractive fellow theater major the traumatic reasons I had to escape my small hometown. We were young and thought we had a connection. He offered to solve my problem by marrying me so that I wouldn't have to return home. We barely knew each other, but we got married anyway.

That marriage was tougher than going to college. We realized we had made a mistake early on, but my dad told me the night before the wedding, "You made your bed. Now you have to lie in it." If only he would have told me in time to cancel the wedding. My new husband and I struggled to create a relationship and didn't communicate well, if at all. Then he changed his major, so we had even less in common. I couldn't seem to do anything right for him, even though I had accomplished much since we married. Among my proudest accomplishments and sources of joy was being a good mom to our two kids. I arranged my academic schedule and working hours as a nurse around the times my children were in school so we could have time together every day, though I did have to work some weekends. As much as I loved being a mom, I missed the opportunity of being parents together. I was happy taking my kids to their activities even though my husband didn't seem to notice us. When he was home, he didn't want to be bothered, and I felt isolated and alone. He would not communicate with me, except to say that I could have done better or done more. I found myself apologizing all the time, seeking forgiveness for things that I had not even done wrong. I found myself longing for a special connection with my husband that never came.

After two children and fifteen years of marriage, I realized that my children's lives and my life would not get any better if we stayed where we were. That led to our divorce. Though I felt like I failed in my marriage, I knew it was the best decision for all of us. I started my new life, realizing I was worthy of being loved sincerely and I now had the opportunity to live my best life.

I wasn't planning on getting married again, but then I met Jacques. He was a wonderful person, a professor, a writer, an actor, and a singer, plus, he loved my children. Most of all, we really loved and cherished our relationship. He was always amazed at what I did and called me a renaissance woman. Though he was twenty-one years older and a few inches shorter, I was thrilled to marry such a great guy.

After I married Jacques, my old habits resurfaced. I would apologize for so many little things: "Sorry dinner wasn't hot enough," "Sorry I didn't have time to finish the laundry," Sorry I was sitting down for a bit." Jacques was never one to complain and couldn't understand where these apologies were coming from. We discussed it, and I started seeing that I was seeking forgiveness when I didn't need to. Gradually, I stopped my "sorriness" unless it was warranted.

Jacques was chair of the Philosophy Department at his college and, as a bioethicist, his specialty was death and dying. He also co-facilitated a bereaved person's support group. I took Jacques's Ethics of Death and Dying class, and we had endless discussions about all aspects of what dying meant. Little did I know how valuable these conversations would be to me.

Around our fifth wedding anniversary, Jacques started to feel unwell. His blood pressure sky-rocketed, yet it was only when his good friend, who is a doctor, talked to him that he agreed to go to the hospital. He even wanted to drive himself because he was good at being in denial. An angiogram showed that he needed to have open heart surgery immediately. The doctor came to see me and said he had to sedate Jacques because he was so anxious. The doctor warned that I could not tell Jacques how much danger he was in because the shock of the news could cause him to panic and die. But I knew my husband; he would want to know the truth. When Jacques woke up, I crawled into bed with him in his hospital room and told him he needed the surgery and that he would feel much better after it was done. He relaxed and got ready to have the operation that would save his life. We knew how important integrity was to our relationship, and this experience made us even stronger together.

The surgery was life-changing for us, but we made the best of it and were happy. Jacques appreciated how much better he felt, and things were good until a few years later when he needed another heart operation. His recovery was slower. He continued to drive and then got into an accident. Fortunately, no one was hurt, but it made me decide it was time for us to move from a two-car family to just one car, and I would be the primary driver. I realized then that our relationship was changing, and I had become more of a caretaker than a wife. When we went to pick up the car from the dealership, it was well over a hundred degrees, and he collapsed unconscious in the parking lot, getting deep abrasions and second-degree burns from waiting for the ambulance on the hot asphalt. After a long stay in the hospital, he was discharged. I had to stop on the way home to get supplies to dress his wounds. When we got to the store, I told him he needed to stay in the car. At first, he agreed, but then abruptly decided to get out, fell, and broke his hip. That was the beginning of the end.

His kidneys could not handle the anesthesia for the hip replacement surgery, so he became confused and delusional, signs of kidney failure. He ended up on dialysis, which we thought was a cure. We were wrong. He was miserable being at the dialysis center for at least fifteen hours a week, seeing people die while he was there, and being so sick each time I brought him home. I felt guilty over the fact he had fallen, thinking I should have watched him more carefully. I felt guiltier when he was at the dialysis center because I treasured that small respite from the constant caretaking.

I cared for him for two more years, through many hospitalizations, until, after twenty-two years of marriage, he died. After Jacques' death, a doctor friend of ours said that not having dialysis generally allows a peaceful death from kidney failure versus what Jacques endured. When someone does not go on dialysis, within a week, their kidneys fail, allowing the patient to die peacefully in their sleep. I wished we had talked to that doctor sooner so I didn't have to witness Jacques in so much pain.

I was lost after Jacques died. I had to re-learn how to take care of myself, by myself. I sold our marital home and moved into a smaller gated community where I felt safe. The university asked me back to teach, and I took things one step at a time. I didn't like being alone, but I couldn't picture myself marrying again. Until some time passed and I met Ron. I had made a list of all the qualities a man would need to have for me to consider even a date. Ron was everything on the list and more. After our first date, I knew that he was the one. But just like I did with Jacques, I brought back my old habit of apologizing, seeking forgiveness where it wasn't needed.

Ron finally told me: "Do you think I want to be with a sorry person?" The sound of those words triggered an immediate slideshow in my mind of every time I had said I was sorry over things I didn't need to be. That woke me up as I realized I was trying to make up for all the perceived failures and shortcomings my first marriage had trained me to believe I had. I realized that the apologies I had been saying were unnecessary because, in most situations, what I apologized for was not even real. Then, in a surprising echo of days past, Ron called me his renaissance woman, a compliment I did not take lightly. He told me I was the woman he had dreamed of, and at that moment, I realized that I was much more than I had allowed myself to see and believe.

Being with Ron was magical. Our conversations were intimate, we connected on a deep level and I resonated with the words of wisdom he would share from his life. We were happy as we traveled around the world, made great friends, and focused on the beauty and magic of embracing the moment.

We decided to attend a New Year's Eve silent meditation retreat held in Joshua Tree, California, at an altitude of 2,700 feet. However, we weren't prepared for how cold it would be. The water would freeze in the fountains at night, and there was no heat in the cabin they put us in. Ron was grumpy, which was unlike him. We were trying to get the most out of the retreat, but his grumpiness and the freezing weather were distracting. In the middle of the second night, Ron woke me up and announced we were leaving. I started to ask why, but he just walked out the door. I knew something was wrong, and I asked if he wanted me to take him to the hospital, but he said, "No. Home."

A few days later, he was diagnosed with Congestive Heart Failure that the high altitude and cold had aggravated. Then, the news came that his kidney function was declining. Since he knew all about what happened to Jacques, we had both said that we didn't want to have dialysis for either of us unless it would be for a short time. We both executed a durable power of attorney for health care where we could clearly express our wishes, and we gave a copy of it to the hospital and the doctors caring for Ron. He was able to get treatment for his heart and felt somewhat better, though he became a frequent flyer at the emergency room. When he would get grumpy, I became vigilant and rushed him to the hospital just a few blocks away. Every time we went, I worried that this would be his last trip. I focused on staying strong and being there for whatever he needed.

When he was feeling well enough, we traveled to the Hawaiian island of Maui. Ron had loved Maui ever since he had lived there many years before. We honeymooned there and visited twice a year. We would frequently talk about what it would be like to live there. As we began to accept that his days were limited, we decided to make it happen. Everything unfolded quickly. We sold our Californian house and purchased a great home in Pukalani on Maui. Puka means "hole" and lani means "heaven." Ron wanted to spend his final years in this *special gateway to heaven.*

For a moment, I wondered if we would make it there. Two weeks before we were scheduled to move, Ron ended up in the ICU, close to death. The next week they surgically implanted a pacemaker so his heart would beat regularly. Though we were committed to our move, I was terrified that we had sold our home and most of our possessions to move across the ocean. What would I do if he didn't make it there or couldn't get the care he needed? I decided not to dwell on my concerns since there was so much to do, and through the support of our friends and neighbors, we were able to move as planned, thank God.

Though Ron was hospitalized frequently for his heart, we enjoyed our time together for over a year in a tropical paradise. His kidneys were failing, so he saw a nephrologist (kidney doctor), who seemed surprised by how well Ron was doing. Ron made friends with his doctor, and they always had long conversations; despite Ron's failing health, he was always happy and caring for others. We told the doctor about Jacques's experience with dialysis and our wishes for Ron's care. He said he understood. Ron and I stayed firm on our no-dialysis decision.

Months later, the doctor told Ron that he didn't need to return for his next visit since he was stable. But the next Saturday, the doctor's nurse called to say Ron's most recent lab reports indicated that he needed to go to the emergency room immediately for dialysis. Ron refused to go to the hospital and gave the phone to me to talk to the nurse. I knew it was time for me to emphasize what Ron wanted. I knew as I insisted on no dialysis, that I was assuring his impending death. That realization hit me so hard that even taking a breath was difficult.

I wondered if the labs could be wrong. She said if we came to the emergency room the lab tests could be repeated. Ron agreed to go to the emergency room, but when we got there, they didn't repeat the tests. They put him on dialysis without talking to us about it. Ron was devastated that his wishes had not been followed, and I was filled with guilt for not enforcing them though they had not given me that choice.

With the dialysis Ron regained his energy and was even able to play golf again. Although he had to go to the dialysis center three times a week and sit there for hours as his blood was cleaned, he decided to just make the best of it. Although I knew that his improvement was only temporary, I happily enjoyed every bonus minute we had together. My grief was only delayed for a short time.

After a few months, his nephrologist told him that he was doing so well that he was a candidate for peritoneal dialysis. This procedure could be done at home every night, allowing him to be free every day to do as he pleased. I was thrilled that he was feeling so much better and that he now had the opportunity for more flexibility in his life. Yet, when Ron started the regimen, he immediately started having trouble with the pain it caused. I felt so helpless as his pain increased. He began to have terrible itching constantly. Then his skin started to peel off all over his body in big pieces. We reported the symptoms but were told that no one else complained of anything similar and that it must not be related to the treatment. After months of worsening symptoms, Ron ended up in the hospital again. Acting as his advocate because of his weakness, I was desperately trying to get anyone to listen to me because I knew something was very wrong. No one would return phone calls, and when we got the doctors' attention, they would just say they had never seen anything like what Ron was experiencing. They didn't know how they could help.

Ron was hospitalized and lost thirty-five pounds in five days. He asked the doctor what he was going to do for him, but the doctor didn't know. So, Ron told him he was going home. I was grateful he could come home, although I was exhausted after spending a week helping with his care in the hospital twenty-four hours a day.

We knew what was inevitable and arranged for a hospital bed, 24-hour care, and eventually a hospice. His friends and family flew in from the mainland and he face-timed anyone who couldn't get there so he was able to say all his goodbyes. We were preparing to grieve, but we also happily celebrated the time we had left with him. He went to sleep on Thursday and transitioned Friday evening.

I was weary, overwhelmed by grief, and devastated by guilt. Before Ron died, we discussed what was happening to him and agreed that I would follow up on the lack of care and denial we had dealt with. So, I wrote letters describing everything that happened and sent them to each doctor, the hospital, the dialysis center, and the manufacturers. I did all I could think of, though I don't know if any changes were implemented due to my letters. Still, I was beating myself up for not doing better, for not doing more to prevent the dialysis. "Sorry," I felt my heart saying, knowing I should have been his advocate. I was seeking forgiveness, for real, this time. After much contemplation and meditation, I realized I had to be the one to forgive myself.

Forgiving myself wasn't easy. However, I finally realized that I was doing the best I could at the time, and I was right there with Ron for every step of his journey. We made the most of those last months we had together. Ultimately, choosing self-forgiveness allowed me to start moving forward instead of being stuck in guilt. I now devote my life to providing comfort, support, love, and happiness to others dealing with grief and loss. I am no longer a 'sorry person.' I am grateful for the growth I have experienced through all these life changes. Because of self-forgiveness, even through my grief, I have found real happiness.

Know that there is nothing for you to be sorry for, and forgive yourself for anything you have held against yourself. By releasing the guilt we sometimes carry, we allow ourselves the freedom and grace to move forward. Your self-forgiveness is the gateway to your happiness. Life is not always going to be perfect, but you can choose to live your best life. You can move beyond the grieving and find your inner happiness.

Ignite Action Steps

Execute or review your Durable Power of Attorney and your Durable Power of Attorney for Health Care to ensure that your wishes will be carried out when the time comes.

Talk to anyone mentioned in these documents and give each of them a copy of the document so there will be no surprises.

Make a list of anyone or anything you need to forgive. Actively forgive everyone and everything on that list. When this is complete, enjoy the lightness and happiness that comes to you.

Emily Thiroux Threatt—United States of America
Lecturer in Communications, California State University Bakersfield, Author
of Loving and Living Your Way Through Grief, host of Grief and Happiness
Podcast, Facilitator of the Grief and Happiness Alliance
lovingandlivingyourwaythroughgrief.com | www.griefandhappiness.com
⌾ emily_thiroux_threatt | ⤬ ThreattEmily

IGNITE
Forgiveness

I AM now living my life whole-heartedly by focusing on

COMPLETE FORGIVENESS
and
UNCONDITIONAL LOVE.

I AM happier now than I ever have been!

Holli Sollenbarger

HOLLI SOLLENBARGER

"Look through the lens of forgiveness to see a different view."

Anything is possible. You have chosen to be here, and you are important. No one else is exactly like you, so embrace your unique gifts and intuition. Center yourself in your truth; this will set you free. Love the journey that you are creating and if you don't love it, change it. It is safe to be you, and sometimes it just takes self-forgiveness.

A SECOND CHANCE

From the time I was a child, I was always sick. I had colds, influenza, rashes, aches, and pains that caused me to miss a lot of school. I rarely went to sleepovers, I was always at the doctor's, and I can't remember a time that I was outside and playing freely. My parents struggled to accept my constant sickness, often negating my illnesses and labeling me as a hypochondriac. I was given all kinds of antibiotics, and I spent many moments every year confined to my bedroom, feeling all alone. The pain had become my new normal, and it wasn't until my early twenties that I began to search for answers.

I actively sought help in the Western medical community for the next fifteen years. During that time, I went to countless doctors, underwent countless procedures, and had countless tests, most of which came back "normal." But I didn't *feel* "normal." My symptoms progressed to chronic fatigue, brain fog, and joint inflammation, with no explanation. I seemed to get sick for no reason, and I avoided gatherings and shut myself off from people. I closed my world when the brain fog became so dense that I couldn't remember enough words to form a sentence. If I could hold on to a thought long enough to remember it, I had no idea what to do next. I felt like I was going crazy because my symptoms would change daily, if not by the hour. I felt desperate as extreme pain attacked my joints, fatigue made it hard to function, and my neck mobility became non-existent. I longed for help, but it never came. I felt lost and confused, with no explanation for where all the pain was coming from.

Beyond being difficult to endure, the constant pain also affected my relationships. Once married, my husband and I operated a cattle ranch, a physically demanding lifestyle. I would muster enough strength to make it through our busy seasons of calving and haying, and then crash. This rollercoaster of symptoms and exhaustion went on for years. After having shingles and becoming really sick and unable to work, I was stuck in the house for days, feeling deeply lonely. I really wanted a companion, a buddy, for some emotional support. We settled on finding me a pet. My husband and I picked out Boomer, a little red and white corgi puppy, for company. He became my angel with fur, and would be by my side during the next stages of my healing journey.

I had given up on figuring out what was wrong with me when a friend begged me to go to a homeopathic doctor to see if they could help. It was discovered that I had Lyme Disease. After my diagnosis, I approached treatment full-on for the next three years. That journey took me 2500 miles from Colorado to Montana, to Arizona, and back to Colorado again. I was told that I was fortunate since I had forced myself to stay physically active because, in doing so, it hadn't allowed the pathogens to advance like they usually do. But there was still more physical and emotional healing to do.

When I started my treatment, my diet was the first place that the homeopath recommended I adjust. I have always enjoyed cooking and thought I was eating a healthy diet, but I learned that there were many things I could improve. I transitioned to a strict diet that cut out sugar, gluten, and processed foods. This was really hard for me because I love eating toast!

The next step was to start a treatment plan that included antibiotics and herbal supplements. But the antibiotics took a toll on my liver. I felt like I had the flu every day, fever and all, due to the Herxheimer reaction of *getting worse before getting better*. At that point, I didn't know enough to understand I needed to help my body detox. One of the herbal supplements was also giving me severe nosebleeds; I didn't know at the time that it was a blood thinner. At the end of a very taxing day, I was crying on my husband's shoulder when my nose started to bleed and I couldn't get it to stop. We could not reach my doctor, and tried hard not to panic over the amount of blood I was losing. It was Boomer, my faithful companion, who kept me distracted and gave me comfort. My tears shifted to gratitude for my little dog, who was trying to fix the situation by climbing on my lap and staring at me with eyes full of love.

My husband and I decided to look into going to a clinic for treatment because I wasn't improving at home. In July, at the start of our haying season, a friend and I flew to Arizona for two days to investigate a clinic specializing in the treatment of Lyme disease. I had blood tests to determine what (and how long) my treatment plan would be. The doctors decided I needed eight weeks of IV treatments with additional supportive therapies outside the clinic.

After we finished haying that summer, my husband, Boomer, and I headed to Arizona to start my treatment. I had an outpatient surgery to insert a medical port into my chest to allow direct access to the vein going to my heart and started IVs the next day. My husband flew home to keep our ranch running, and Boomer stayed with me. I was very fortunate to have friends in Arizona, and we found a condominium to rent a few doors down from them. Boomer would go to our friends for the day while I was getting treatment and wait by the sliding glass door for my return. My friends told me that if I was more than an hour late, Boomer would start pacing. He had a schedule he expected me to keep. It was a full-time job of treatment and detox: clinic five days a week, five to seven hours a day, with other appointments thrown in. At one point, I was taking seventy pills a day. It took a couple of hours every week to make sure I ordered what I needed and get everything divided out into little cups since the AM/PM pill box was not even close to big enough! My health seemed to improve as the treatment progressed, but my barometer had been off for so long that I didn't know what 'good health' actually felt like. I was chasing my symptoms and yet missing the key, underlying truths behind them all.

A week before we headed home, Boomer, my constant companion and support, started getting sick. We went to the veterinarian, but they had no idea what was wrong. Our veterinarian told us there was no medical explanation for Boomer's dangerously high fever, throwing up, and extreme body pain. All of his tests came back "normal," but I knew that negative test results don't mean you're not suffering. We made two emergency trips with Boomer to a University hospital three hours away. Procedure after procedure revealed nothing. We journeyed down the long quagmire of treatments and doctors' opinions, and I was struck by the fact that Boomer's symptoms were the same as mine. We had him tested for Lyme disease, Valley Fever, and other illnesses, and still no diagnosis. The hospital staff did ultrasound and scopes, but the only thing that seemed to control his symptoms was a prescription steroid and pain medicine. He was given pills to solve a sickness they didn't understand. It felt so similar to what was happening to me.

We returned to the clinic in Arizona for a follow-up in February, and I had the medical port removed, as it had become too uncomfortable to keep in. I was tired of feeling like a pincushion and a science experiment, something I knew Boomer could understand. On our way back from Arizona, Boomer became seriously ill, but this time there wasn't anything our veterinarian could do for him. The steroids had destroyed his digestive system, and amidst his valor and true loyalty, he passed on just before his second birthday. Losing him left a gaping hole in my broken heart, and I didn't know how I could continue.

I felt so lucky to have Boomer for the short time that I did, and the house was so empty and quiet without him. I still miss him so very much. His impact on our lives was life-changing, even though he wasn't with us very long. I grew to understand that his presence in my life was to help me through the pain. Reflecting back, I see that Boomer took on what my body couldn't handle. He sacrificed himself to give me a better life.

I spent another year trying supportive IV therapy at a clinic two hours away, but eventually, I just couldn't do it anymore. The physiological, physical, and financial toll that the disease had taken on my husband and me had to change. I was close to giving up when at one of my last treatments, another patient told me about a different type of help she was receiving. She shared that she was getting Body Code™ sessions from a practitioner in Germany, and the few sessions that she experienced were helping her. I thanked her for the information and left unclear about long-distance healing, yet curious.

It took me a couple of weeks of research before I booked my first Body Code session. It was difficult to find the strength to try *one more thing* knowing it may not work. But by my second Body Code session, I felt like a different person. Before finding that modality, I was reaching for something on the outside of myself to fix how I was feeling on the inside. When I released the "stuck" energy inside my body, my body responded with the gift of slowly healing itself. That 'one more thing' began the next shift in my life.

I learned from my sessions that our bodies can truly heal when we find the root cause of our issues and that trauma can physically manifest into a disease without us being aware of it. I knew it was time, and I was ready to find the 'real' cause behind my decades of suffering.

During a daily meditation, a memory of being sexually molested when I was three years old started to resurface. As I reflected, I realized the abuse went on for years and my parents and anyone else who knew about it did nothing. No one acknowledged it; no one helped me process it. No one protected me. I was not a hypochondriac. My illnesses were manifestations of my early trauma that had been silenced to the point that it took me over forty years to discover the truth. And when it was revealed, I finally began to process the trauma and heal.

Now, in my forties, a much clearer picture has developed. I can deal with the emotions of anger, fear, shame, guilt, and sorrow (to name a few) as they come up. It has been a process with a lot of tears. Tears for my three-year-old self and tears over how deeply my whole life has been affected. I've had so many realizations of why I took the actions I did throughout my life *because* of that experience. Learning about the abuse and my suppressed emotions explained why I had felt so dirty and would wash my hands until they cracked and bled. It explained why I always felt like I was an inconvenient problem and could do nothing right. It explained why I fell into a deep depression and had thoughts of taking my own life. It also explained why my mother used constant mental abuse to keep me silent and small to not reveal my abuser. That trauma explained why I wanted nothing to do with the family member who hurt me and why I avoided certain relationships.

I realized that the family dynamic that I grew up in was structured to keep everyone in chaos and divided. None of us had learned how to communicate with each other. My parents acted like a hub of a wheel, feeding information to each one of us and wanting to control what was being said, dictating who was getting along or not. We were fed information that wasn't true to keep all of us at odds with one another. Money and gifts were also used as a tool to control all of us. There were no gifts without strings attached. To those on the outside, we were supposed to look and act perfect, but behind closed doors, it was a mess. My friends only saw the nice clothes I wore, not the words that were said to me. No one got along, and this division ran so deep that we have all gone our separate ways.

The dis-ease of my childhood physically manifested into Lyme disease and the seven co-infections I battled for most of my life. Working on my physical body to begin my healing process was key because my body was violated. In the journey of healing my body, I also needed to heal my mind and spirit. The dialogue that I had going in my head was filled with words that I would have never said to anyone else. I was sabotaging myself with my own thoughts, believing anything and everything was my fault. I was in the habit of saying, "I'm sorry" when I had nothing to be sorry for, apologizing for simply being somewhere and taking up space. If I felt uncomfortable, I had the knee-jerk reaction to apologize. I realized that my negative talk was crushing my spirit. I was thinking that I was no good; therefore, my spirit was becoming less, and my health was following that belief.

The reality I was presented with as a child was so far from the truth of who I truly am. In my spiritual journey, I've found the strength to see the real essence of me because I have discovered a new perspective through a different lens. Seeing this truth took my breath away in so many positive ways and started my healing by forgiving myself. I realized that I am supposed to be here; I wasn't a mistake. I came here for a purpose. The things that have happened to me don't define me. They refine me, and the way I respond to them is what brings me peace. The choices I make every day about who I choose to be is what defines me now; wisdom with grace and knowledge with discernment. Bit by bit, I have become more comfortable with myself and found both the pieces of the puzzle and the peace within.

Forgiving myself and others has been a constant practice, and I know that the Creator has given me the tools and resources to deal with what comes next. Finding forgiveness has been the key to unlocking many doors. It has helped me write letters of forgiveness to my parents and my brother, asking for their forgiveness in return. I never sent the letters, but I read them to the Universe and let it all go. This was a huge relief, and it was me doing my part to move forward.

I am deeply grateful for my husband, who has stood by me and supported me through this challenging journey called life. I also feel so lucky that I had Boomer by my side, and I still miss him so very much. I have learned that every day is a new chance filled with limitless potential, and starting with forgiveness makes anything possible! This is my 'why' and has inspired me to help others, heal healers, and encourage powerful new belief systems as an Emotion Code™ and Body Code practitioner.

Everything you need is already inside you. Be inspired and empowered by the truth of that, as it can set you free. What we believe becomes our reality, and we can change it with new beliefs. Self-limitations dissolve when we let go of belief systems that are not our truth. Physical symptoms are an amazing map of where energy is stuck in the mind and body; listen to them. Allow your Spirit to expand. Let your emotions be your guide and the knowledge you acquire be guided by discernment. Take what resonates for you and leave the rest behind - this is your journey. Live your life to the fullest and love yourself.

Ignite Action Steps

- Listen to your self-dialogue. Talk to yourself as you would a friend; after all, you are there for yourself every day. Practice loving yourself and treating yourself with kindness. Doing this for yourself helps everyone; we are all part of the collective consciousness.
- Our body is the vessel that takes us through this life. Food is a vibration of energy that we put in our bodies multiple times a day. If we look at food as energy, what we eat is the vibration we receive. Choose to eat things that are minimally processed because your body can easily identify and utilize that energy. Do your best to eat foods that haven't been treated with chemicals and find food that your body enjoys.
- Being active always helps the body and mind. With physical activity, we are able to move and process energy as well as create energy. When we allow energy to move, we allow healing. Actively processing our emotions keeps the energy from getting stuck in our bodies. Learn how to identify and use the energy of your emotions. The next time you are angry, try cleaning, walking, or fluffing (punching) a pillow instead of taking your anger out on someone. Our emotions are our guidance system, and each one is important. If it seems overwhelming or scary to feel your emotions, find someone that you can trust to help you. This is your journey, but you don't have to do it alone.

Holli Sollenbarger—United States of America
Certified Emotion Code Practitioner (CECP),
Certified Body Code Practitioner (CBCP)
www.energybalance3.com
holli.sollenbarger
hollisollenbarger

IGNITE
Forgiveness

F ~ *Feel the Divine*

O ~ *Open your mind*

R ~ *Respectful with words*

G ~ *Grace in your heart*

I ~ *Illuminate your core essence*

V ~ *Value your creativity*

E ~ *Enjoy being safe in this moment*

N ~ *Nurture your connection with Mother Earth*

E ~ *Expand*

S ~ *Spiral up*

S ~ *Sparkling rainbow of light*

Katherine Davidson

KATHERINE DAVIDSON

"The decision to forgive is the first step toward freedom."

I want you to have a clear understanding of what forgiveness is, and what it is not. True forgiveness is powerful medicine in the odyssey of recovery from abuse and betrayal. It can lift your burdens, fill your soul with light, and bring peace into your daily journey. I know I cannot erase my past, but I believe forgiveness can soften my heart and impact my future. It is my hope you will feel inspired to join me.

SIPPING TEA

Early in my healing, during counseling, amidst a meditation, I saw an unexpected vision of myself. It was a vision of a broken Kathy, huddled in a corner in the fetal position, emaciated, alone, and surrounded by looming darkness. Seeing myself hurting so profoundly caused so much pain and emotional heartache. It brought tears to my eyes when I thought I was being so brave.

I have journeyed through trauma, heartache, and healing over the years so that I could invite that version of myself to sit beside me and rest her head on my shoulder. I lovingly put my arm around her to allow the darkness to lift and give way to light, peace, and relief. I hand her a cup of tea as I tell her, "We're going to be okay."

Forgiveness was not a process nor a word I welcomed during my early recovery from the heartbreak of divorce. As a matter of fact, the concept enraged me. How could I be asked to accept the wrongs and injustices I'd experienced?

How could anyone in their right mind tell an abused person the way to healing was through forgiveness? That had to be all wrong.

Writing my story of my husband's duplicitousness and betrayal in my first compilation book, *Ignite Wisdom* caused me to walk *toward* my fear of exposure and helped me find the courage I didn't know I had. I wanted to tell my story. I had spent years living with resentment and tears, experiencing loneliness and despair, and frequently being overcome with anger and discouragement. But, gradually, I was casting aside the burden of victimhood, and I felt the solid ground of empowerment beneath my feet. Through my writing, I wanted to connect with other women and let them know they were not alone; there was hope beyond the abyss of grief.

In my first chapter in *Ignite Wisdom*, I documented my path: the startling disclosure of the secret life of my husband of four decades, the agony of embracing my new reality, the end of my marriage, and finally, feelings of self-acceptance and love. Through my writing, I forced myself to look deep inside and see my unhealthiness. I acknowledged clinging behaviors and found the ability to let go and finally accept life on my own. As I stepped out of the quagmire of emotions that were dragging me down and shifted my perspective, I could acknowledge the gradual arrival of hope and healing. Even if it was aspirational and I came up short sometimes, there evolved a meaningful course forward. The desire to help others gave purpose to my suffering and fueled my desire for further learning. I was finding faith in myself and had a vision that I could overcome depression, pain, and the confusion of betrayal. After all the hurt and heartache of the past years, I frequently experience joy, gratitude, and peace in daily living because I engaged in hours of work toward healing and learned about forgiveness. I was confident I had insight worth sharing, so I quickly signed up when the opportunity to write a chapter in *Ignite Forgiveness* was announced.

It turns out… I had more to learn.

Early in my study of addiction, recovery, and self-compassion, I was introduced to the book *Forgive for Good* by Dr. Fred Luskin, and he made a good case for the value of forgiveness. My paradigm began to shift, and I started to see the value of forgiveness differently; it was NOT about the offender. My ability to consider its importance increased as I contemplated letting go of the pain and heartache, *my* pain and *my* heartache, inflicted on me by someone else. I wanted to believe that maybe I could free myself from the poison of bitterness and grief.

Forgiveness as a healing tool was difficult to embrace. Obsessive replays of the past kept the wounds open. Armed with the knowledge of his betrayals, situations from our history took on new meaning, and a recollection or thought from the past triggered emotional outbursts that started with an uncomfortable prickly sensation of anxiety washing over me. My heart began to pound as rage surged through me, and I slid into sobs of shame and disbelief. I began using Dr. Luskin's strategies for letting go of anger, recognizing that forgiveness is a choice and a skill that can be learned. He helped me understand that my grievance story was created by me, taking my husband's actions personally. I blamed my husband for the anger and heartache I felt, and I created a story of victimization that I repeated over and over in my mind and to others. I had to realize it was possible to restore peace to my life without excusing or forgetting the abuse, denying or minimizing the wrong. My healing did not require reconciliation with the offender or giving into the subconscious delusion; I was making my husband suffer by being mad at him.

Dr. Luskin's concepts of forgiveness all sounded reasonable, but the story of deceit and deception in my head was powerful when I first found out. Painful memories and thoughts of the past were constant companions: "How could he be two people?" "How could I have lived with him for so long and never known?" Anger surged through my mind many times a day. Triggers could come out of nowhere and hijack my emotions flooding my body with anguish, shame, and self-doubt. Eliminating negative thoughts about the offender from my thinking seemed impossible.

I tried to remember that just because something devastating occurred in my past, it does not mean that the present needs to be in ruins. I enriched my life through connections with friends and family. The love and joy of my grandchildren filled my heart. Whenever hurtful images flashed into my mind, I would think about new happy experiences until the painful memories left. Over time — a long time, I improved in "changing the channel" (as Dr. Luskin would say) when my mind went down the negative rabbit hole. Moments, when I relished my new adventures and freedom, were welcome interludes. Feelings of gratitude and joy were found in nature, awesome cloud formations, walks in the woods, spring wildflowers, sunsets, and wild storms on the lake. My strong emotional triggers subsided, even though milder triggers remained. I knew that Dr. Luskin had helped me begin my first steps on the road to forgiveness.

As I felt ready to write in *Ignite Forgiveness*, I began to ponder what forgiveness meant to me. Where was I on the continuum of letting go of the offenses and forgiving the past? Compassion for myself and the self-love I wrote about in the previous book were one thing, but letting go of the bitterness, and the crushing memories were quite another. Accepting the end of my marriage and modifying unhealthy habits that had sustained a toxic relationship was only part of my recovery. As I contemplated writing about forgiveness, I initiated forgiveness meditations. During those moments of reflection, I felt a rising resistance deep in my soul. Memories I thought I had left behind began to surface in those quiet moments. To my surprise, surges of intense resentment and anger began to surface as I relived the ache of deceit and abandonment. The monster of bitterness and rage could boil up, and I felt it still churning within me.

How was I going to write about forgiveness when I realized it had a shaky footing in my life? I desperately wanted to escape, once and for all, the barrage of memories brought on by harmless events, comments, or images. The Facebook pictures from past years of a smiling husband with his arm around me, hiding his duplicity, were the worst. Then there were the photos that documented the family fun of our forty-five years together that had been tainted and defiled by what I now understood was occurring. This was unquestionably unfair. Maybe I hadn't learned that much about forgiveness. Maybe I had just moved on, numbed by the familiarity of the past and stuffing my feelings deep into the core of my being. Thinking about forgiveness was awakening the trauma, reminding me of all the things I didn't WANT to forgive. Our family life changed forever, and my self-respect was shattered.

So, was I back at square one? Had I even changed at all?

I searched for new resources. The book *Forgiveness* by Di Risborough added a new dimension to my understanding of forgiveness, and it was NOT a welcome addition. She said, "True forgiveness can only happen when compassion is its ally. Without compassion, there is no forgiveness, just an illusion of letting go." She explained forgiveness requires compassion, not pity. Pity is based in the ego and contains contempt. Forgiveness contains love coming from the heart. If anger resides in the subconscious, forgiveness remains impossible. As I worked through the exercises in her book, the trauma resurfaced. She stated that your heart needs to be open, but my heart was aching and stinging from deception! I felt that I could never have this kind of compassion for my ex-husband. He used me, abused me, and betrayed my love. I had been left with deep scars. Just thinking about them caused tears to trickle down my cheeks, wrinkled by the years he took from me. I felt blamed by those who did not understand his addiction. I was alone, without companionship, after a life of faithfulness. I learned that these emotions were signposts of what still needed healing.

I moved on to the book, *8 Keys to Forgiveness* by Robert Enright, a psychologist, and professor at the University of Wisconsin-Madison, and founder of the International Forgiveness Institute. He characterized forgiveness as offering mercy to those who had shown disrespect, unkindness, and a lack of love toward you. I found some comfort in his statement that you may not *yet* have the strength for forgiveness. Betrayal by someone who was obligated to love you like a partner can take a long time to recover from. But when you forgive, you do not put justice aside. I learned that giving love and mercy does not deplete us; it renews us. Committing to forgive is the hardest part of the journey because it requires us to see each person as special, unique, and worthy of care. That was a leap beyond my present ability. But the following quote encouraged me. Enright says: "I have never found anything as effective as forgiveness for healing deep wounds. Forgiveness is strong medicine. Forgiveness can help you stand against the worst kind of injustice so that it does not defeat you."

I really wanted to believe that forgiveness would heal my wounds, even if it seemed impossible at the time. With a clear definition of forgiveness (and an overwhelming feeling that I would never get there), I moved on to the next step in Enright's book, developing a forgiving mind. The exercises in the book helped me create a new narrative of my husband, seeing him as a baby, born innocent, vulnerable, yet valued. As I imagined this tiny little person not receiving all the love and affection he needed, a warm, empathetic feeling enveloped me. I envisioned him as a young boy, freely roaming the prairie but carrying a heavy secret of an alcoholic father. He had his own emotional wounds in his adolescent and young adult years. Seeing him from this new viewpoint helped me understand more and eased my anger.

I believe this innocent child didn't ask for his situation, and he has inherent value and worth. However, it was difficult to let go of the hurt that arose when I remembered there were choices he made in how he dealt with his wounds. The options he chose caused heartbreak to both his children and me. Those wounds were passed on to me. I carry the scars of emotional detachment and abandonment, the unfulfilled need to be cherished and appreciated. I had to ask a question that settled heavily on me, "What will I do with these wounds?"

My wonderful counselor Jacqueline Thibideau, gave me a phrase to use through these difficult times. "The only way through hell is with radical acceptance." I had been in hell, and to move on, I knew I must face my reality, not minimize it, not look away, not use distraction to avoid it, but face it in all its ugliness. Her words encouraged me to be patient, and accept my feelings, to be kind and compassionate to myself. She reminded me that I had been deeply bruised and it would take time to find the compassion that had until then felt elusive. I resolved to embrace the idea that it was a long slow journey, one I am still on right now.

I am buoyed by Enright's reminder, "Beauty, when you let it, extends a hand to you from above the pit and beckons you to rise out of it for something better." There are times when the reality of my situation settles heavily on me. I am relocating alone, struggling with heavy boxes and stuffing them into a disorganized storage locker. My car needs repair, and I know nothing about cars. The complete responsibility of finances, retirement, and aging alone can feel overwhelming. Those times stir up resentment. Accepting my feelings as legitimate and having self-compassion calms me.

I started this chapter thinking that I would share how to forgive. My Ignite Moment came when I realized true forgiveness is much more than I imagined. For me, it is a long, hard pilgrimage with its ups and downs; doubts and fears. From the author of Radical Acceptance, Tara Brach, I learned about inviting "Mara" to tea; Mara is a personification of the mental state of doubt. Sometimes Mara appears to me as overwhelm and anxiety. Then, instead of ignoring Mara or driving it away, I must calmly acknowledge its presence, saying, "I see you, Mara." Then, I invite it for tea and serve it as an honored guest. Mara stays for a while and then goes. Sometimes when I identify negative sensations in my body, I say, "I see you, Mara." Using the breath and sitting with the feelings informs me and helps me move through my difficult emotions. Mara has become a friend.

Throughout this process, fervent, honest prayer has guided my searching and softened my heart. The words of this hymn resonate with me.

Where can I turn for peace? Where is my solace when other sources cease to make me whole? When with a wounded heart, anger, and malice, I draw myself apart, searching my soul?

He answers privately, reaches my reaching, in my Gethsemane, Savior and Friend. Gentle the peace he finds for my beseeching. Constant he is and kind, love without end.

I have realized that forgiveness requires constant reflection, reframing of thoughts, and a softening of the heart. When I step into this, I share something of the eternal with everyone, including the person who hurt me; it strengthens my mind toward forgiveness. When I experience glimpses of the joy I desire—the beauty of forgiveness—those moments are sweet and fill my soul with light. My forgiveness is in the process, and I have faith and hope that my ability to forgive will grow.

I encourage you to embrace your path to forgiveness and let it be the best medicine to free your soul and bring light and peace into your daily journey. Take the time to sip some tea, befriend your Mara, give yourself compassion, and let that quiet contemplation heal you from the inside out.

IGNITE ACTION STEPS

- Take the difficult first step, the decision to forgive.
- When bitterness and anger surface, stay with the emotions. Don't try to suppress them. Instead, use your breath, cry, and accept that emotions have lessons to teach. They are signposts to direct you toward healing. Have self-compassion because what you are trying to do is difficult and takes time.
- See the wounds that people carry and have mercy for those who offend you. Resolve to not pass on the hurt you receive.
- Practice forgiveness with the small offenses in life. See the wounds that lie behind any unkind behavior.
- Focus on all the good things in life. Spend time in nature. Long walks can restore peace, and gratitude for blessings uplifts the spirit. Reframe your thinking to see the good. Think about things that make you smile, make time for fun and laughter, create new memories, and plan new adventures. Move forward, filling your life with self-care. You deserve it.
- Remember gratitude cannot erase sadness; they must coexist.

Katherine Davidson—Canada
Teacher, BA, Education
Katherinedavidson.net

IGNITE
Forgiveness

Dear Heavenly Father,

*My heart is full of sadness and my mind is plagued
with anger*

Please lift this darkness and let me smile again

Help me to see the worth of every soul

Long walks in your beautiful world soothe me

Thank you for the souls who reach out in love

I know peace when your spirit touches me

Walk beside me as I struggle to forgive

I love you and I know that you love me

Diane Lemire

DIANE LEMIRE

"In stillness, I listen and forgive."

Embrace your stillness and listen to the Being that you are. Find a way to quiet the noise that has been following you—it distracts and deters you from your true path. I hope this story inspires you to find your way to your inner voice and forgive those who don't have the capacity to be there for you. In-kind, learn to forgive yourself for moments of weakness and anger, or misguided choices you made when you felt alone. I want you to feel that there is safety and enlightenment in embracing and uncovering your own story so that you, too, may heal and find freedom.

FALLING INTO GRACE

How do I share my story so as to make a difference?

Perhaps occasionally to a fault, but since adulthood, I have spent hours in spiritual self-help sections in many bookstores. I have benefited from the wisdom and experiences of others and seen the difference they made in my life. I truly believe that we all harbor the important purpose of genuinely helping one another; to support the succeeding generations, for our children, and for their children. But being the one to give guidance, rather than receive it, is something entirely different.

I sat on my bed, unmoving fingers poised on the keys of my laptop, contemplating how to begin sharing my story, that magical release of an igniting forgiveness epiphany. Through my contemplation, I realize I'd been craving to engage in the act of forgiveness for years. As I get older, it only seems fitting to embrace the essence of calmness, of stillness, of peace that living with a forgiving heart can offer.

This certainly wasn't a simple realization, where I suddenly walked about like a zen monk, with praying hands and a gentle grin, offering peace and love to all who had betrayed me. Quite the opposite actually. Like so many of us humans, it's been an arduous journey to welcome the essence of forgiveness into my life. Embarking on this journey meant long periods of isolation, childish pouting, moments of incessant crying, and embracing mourning. Here I was, ready to transform, and to do so meant one very important step: to delve into the darkness of what had prohibited me from forgiving the experience of betrayal by loved ones and of not believing in myself as a child of God; deserving of self-love. It was clear to me now that I had neglected and not allowed myself to seek out my true purpose and tribe. *Why did I feel so unworthy? Why wasn't I stepping up to who I truly am?*

It was the year that shook the world, a looming pandemic, and I had recently closed my business of twenty-five years. In the newfound quiet of joblessness, I began to fully feel the pain I was harboring within. I was finally so desperate to get to know forgiveness's powerful energy and commit to intimately walking in its path. It was during this time that I decided to embrace the spiritual teachings of the word of God. I searched and delved into everything titled 'forgiveness' in the Bible and in other literary works. I revisited the books of amazing authors such as Tara Brach, Rick Warren, and Marianne Williamson and became especially focused on a book that was collecting dust on my shelf, drawn to the messages of *There's a Spiritual Solution to Every Problem,* by Wayne W. Dyer.

As is wisely written in the Tao Te Ching, "*When the student is ready, the teacher will appear.*" Well, the teacher sure made a grand entrance!

It was the first evening in March. It was relatively mild weather after a light dusting of snow. I decided to walk Bear, our sweet German shepherd, before retiring for the evening. I texted my oldest daughter goodnight at half past ten, then unwisely decided to leave my phone at home to charge. Bear and I leisurely strolled around the block, then headed down the path through the park that returned us home. Then tragedy struck.

Both my feet left the ground as I slipped on black ice, suddenly airborne and with nothing around to break the fall. On the harsh descent, both my bottom and left leg landed on my right tibia, impacting and shattering it in multiple pieces. The intense and deafening pain, the crushing sense of fear, and the complete surrender are feelings that will stay with me forever. At that moment, my life completely changed.

I laid on my back, elevating my right leg straight up in hopes of easing the excruciating pain. Survival instincts kicked in, and after a few moments, I reached around myself to find broken pieces of ice to apply to the pain and swelling. Never before experiencing a bone break, I was under shock and the misguided impression that I had simply suffered a severe sprain. "Diane, just get home. All you need is ice and some pain medication," I repeated to myself. Bear, my loyal companion, roamed around me, occasionally resting beside me for the next two arduous hours.

I couldn't move. I desperately tried to stand, wanting to safely get home, but after one small hop, the crushing pain rushed through my limbs, and I collapsed back to the ground, again completely immobilized. I tried screaming out for help as I could see a custodian still at work in the school some fifty yards away. No luck. My cries for help went unheard, and minutes later, the school lights were off, and his red truck had driven away. I was truly alone in the bitter cold, lying on my back wondering how I would fend for myself and get myself home.

I remained on the hard, bumpy ice as my body started to shiver. Still, on my back, I bent my left leg and, with the help of my hands, pushed myself in the direction of safety and home. *Just get home.* Again I bent my leg, the right one still pointed vertically, and I pushed again. *Just get home.* I continued pushing the ground beneath me, slowly inching my way back toward my front steps. I was hoping the frosty air would ease the pain. I tried to bring my right leg down to create more force and get home sooner, but it was obvious there is no rushing through certain processes when in pain.

By that time, likely one hour had passed, and I was exhausted from the excruciating pain and the cold. Completely drained, and with still 100 yards to go, I suddenly felt the need to close my eyes and sleep. *How will I survive this? Should I give up? If I could just rest for a while. Perhaps someone would eventually find me.* It was at this time that the journey began, where I would learn about inner strength and forgiveness and how to truly harness both. I believe that if I had fallen asleep, I may not be here sharing this story.

As I started to pray, a newfound energy and willingness suddenly came over me. *"Oh dear God, please give me the strength to get home to safety."* I prayed and asked God to see my daughters become thriving women. And truthfully, I selfishly also prayed to one day hopefully hold my grandchildren. I promised Him that I would become stronger and to be of service wherever He needed me if He would only help.

Deep-seated in prayer, I slowly repositioned myself to my hands and knees. Then firmly clenching my jaw, I counted out loud 1, 2, 3, 4, 5…1, 2, 3, 4, 5 as a means to push through the pain as I crawled my way back home. Through the one hundred meters of rugged ice, the salted sidewalk, and driveway, then up five steps, I finally opened the front door and collapsed convulsing.

After a few moments, I pushed myself toward the kitchen and started messaging my neighbors. In my delirious state, I was still convinced it was just a sprain, and I wanted them to come over and get the pain meds from upstairs. It was after midnight, and of course, no one was responding. Not wanting to be a burden, I decided to call 911.

I repeatedly apologized to the operator, as she kindly consoled me until the paramedics arrived. They were so empathetic as they drove me to the hospital. Later, staring at the x-rays of my shattered tibia and fibula, emergency room doctors were in disbelief that I had had the ability to move myself to safety. The care I received from them was deeply heart touching and I had never felt so grateful to be in the company of such loving souls. What I didn't realize was the journey to my healing had *just* begun.

While in the hospital, occupational therapists discussed my new physical limitations and the arduous months ahead. They asked if I had anyone with the capacity to help or would I need a short-term care facility. Anguish came over me as I knew that my family wouldn't be able to give me the needed support. The pain from the accident greatly mirrored the pain that inhabited my soul and both were about to push me to heal and grow stronger. This tragic event that had arrived as a teacher had certainly reinforced the fact that I had neglected to show up for myself and this too needed forgiveness.

Being forced to sit immobile in complete solitude is when I allowed myself to search with the most vulnerable heart. I no longer had the distractions I had filled my life with and had no choice but to truly think and feel. I dove in to capture the essence behind what the authors I had studied were sharing as well as learning about some incredibly beautiful scriptures. I am ashamed to say, as a Christian, I was learning their magic for the first time and noticed how many of them cited self-care and gracious forgiveness.

Two weeks later, and with healing bones fused with pins and plates, my dear friend Denise picked me up from the hospital. Amidst the busyness of her own life, I was grateful as she brought me home and stayed with me overnight. I never wished to be a burden to my teenage daughters, one of whom was shouldering the high demands of a university student-athlete. Focusing on showing up for myself, I desperately wanted to model a mom that was a thriving survivor that would regain her strength. I messaged with friends, and by the grace of God, many did help me get organized to be self-sufficient amidst my healing journey. My heart was grateful when old friends offered weekends away from their loved ones to stay with me. I began awakening to the peaceful thought that oftentimes people do love you and that they show up in the only way that they can.

How liberating to trust, for the first time in my life, how the souls that can, do in fact show up and that those that simply don't have the capacity need to be released and forgiven. In the *Spiritual Solution to Every Problem,* author Dyer writes, "Completely emptying the mind of our agenda leads to forgiveness… ridding ourselves of all blame…we invite forgiveness into our hearts… and create a mindset of problem resolution" (Dyer, p. 13).

Everyone is truly doing the best they can with the script their life is offering them, and I was now attempting to practice releasing the pain within. I realized during those first few days in the chaotic reorganization at home that I had often neglected some necessary needs. It was time to give myself permission to be my own savior and to be a self-sufficient soul manifesting its purpose. Embracing this conviction forced me to also forgive myself, as I had unknowingly projected unrealistic expectations onto others to give me validation and to rescue me. With the help of my Pastor, I studied the Scriptures in Genesis, its guiding words that are believed to have been written more than 3000 years ago. As I learned from this book, my spiritual values deepened and further opened my heart to a healing nature of forgiveness. Genesis reads, "Please forgive, I beg you, the offense of your brothers and their sin, for they did you wrong.''' And, now, please forgive the offense of the servants of the God of your father" (Genesis 50:17) (NASB).

It takes great strength to forgive, but not doing so will detrimentally prevent us from being our most creative selves and becoming our most graceful selves. It certainly doesn't mean to invite the person to dinner, but, with God's strength, we can free them from our mind and soul and inherently invite in grace and spiritual intimacy.

In the following weeks, I embraced meditation and cultivated a newfound inner strength, even if physically I was weak. Perhaps this is typical of accident survivors, as they are given an overabundance of time to reflect. A guiding verse that touched my heart was, "Whatever is true, whatever is honorable, whatever is just, whatever is pure… think about these things" (Philippians 4:8). But training my mind to only focus on the good was more challenging than I'd expected. Even as I read words like, "the Universe has your back," deep down,

I felt that life and its burdens seemed so incredibly heavy. An abusive father, his death, unmet childhood needs, and frequent moves had laid an unstable foundation during my younger years. Then miscarriages, a failed relationship, the death of a very dear friend, and the closing of my business had often left me feeling abandoned as an adult. I had been carrying it all. Now in my midlife, it was time to accept these rich life experiences and to forgive, embrace solace, strengthen, empower, and to choose peace for my soul.

The weeks progressed, and the physio appointments that encouraged movement also confirmed that I had to embrace the journey inward, so that I could regain my strength, emotionally, spiritually, and physically. The vivid memory of that dark winter night, of the fear and pain, of having to dig deep to find the strength to survive, and of the arduous months that ensued woke in me the realization that the Savior is always with me and that it isn't anyone's role but my own to rescue myself. Here it was, the gift that I had to forgive myself and to forgive life as it was undoubtedly trying to nudge me closer to my own strength and encourage me toward God's love and self-love. I had to embrace the message of the Bible, "Be strong. Be brave. Be fearless. You are never alone" (Joshua 1:9), and realize in many ways, I had already embodied it, especially since that night.

The willingness to forgive is such a precious life lesson, as it's driven me to listen to my soul and its ultimate question: *Who am I?* This is a strength that I wish for my daughters to embrace when life gets challenging. One year has passed, and I am still healing and growing emotionally, spiritually, and physically. I have started strength training, yoga, and walking daily so as to become the strongest I've ever been and to show my daughters that thriving amidst setbacks is possible. As I continue reading the scriptures, I'm aware of a budding inner strength that is inviting me with open arms. I carry forward with thoughts of cultivating this inner strength to discover who I truly am, what my next vocation will be, and what my inner voice needs to express to the world.

I'm learning to embrace with conviction the true meaning of forgiveness, of others, and of myself. It was our dear Pastor, Wendy Payne, that introduced me to Rick Warren's book *Transformed*. It helped me realize that my inability to forgive myself and others blocks deep and necessary healing that could lead me to experience an innate and deserved sense of love and freedom. He quotes from the Bible, "Be kind and compassionate to one another, forgiving each other, just as Christ God forgave you Ephesians 4:31." With a newly found soulful connection to God, I had awakened to give myself permission to embrace a new inner power and self-respect. As you learn to also embrace forgiveness in your life, I hope that you have learned from my words and experiences.

As a spiritual being, I believe my fall was also a miraculous incident. As one, the outcome truly could have been worse, and two, it initiated the grandest healings I've ever experienced in my life. As I continue this organic journey toward authentic forgiveness, I realize that it's about releasing those who have hurt me, including myself, to establish clear boundaries and to send love so that healing comes with God's guidance. By falling into God's grace, I came to know true love and freedom reside within us all.

IGNITE ACTION STEPS

Life is about awakening to who we truly are, and only once we practice forgiveness do we actually heal the part of ourselves that feels rejected.

- Before that first cup of coffee, start your day with a scripture, an empowering thought, or a prayer to God, and in that silence, feel God's presence within you. We are truly never alone. All the moments we spend blaming are moments we are not fulfilling unmet needs inside our own hearts.
- Accept that painful moments are actually lessons that enable us to uncover the strength within our own hearts. Once we've worked on ourselves, we can work with another that can actually make a collective difference in the world.
- Meditate a couple of times per day. I connect with God and write questions and concerns I have for Him in a journal or Notes on my phone; it helps me greatly to discover and uncover my authentic self.
- Remind yourself of your inner good with simple little phrases: "I am", "Always with compassion… yes, always," and "For the benefit of all and harm to none."
- Embrace physical health with daily long walks, yoga practice, strength training, or any other exercise you can do and enjoy.

Diane Lemire—Canada
Nutritionist, Author, Speaker, Mentor, Entrepreneur
www.genesiswellnessgroup.ca
www.mynutrients.ca
My Nutrients
mynutrients.ca

IGN▪TE
Forgiveness

THE SWEET INVITATION

As we patiently await

For someone to apologize

Little do we realize

It is in the agony that lies

The truest of signs

It is a sweet invitation

A door waiting wide open

Begging you to come to embrace

The soul within

A life that's meant to awaken

Listen to the sweet invitation

And life will truly begin

Dianne Venit

Dianne Venit

"Sometimes rejection is God's protection."

My desire is for you to stay true to yourself no matter what. Whether those around you support or disappoint you, you can remain empowered when you are there for yourself. While taking care of others can be fulfilling, you must take care of yourself first and foremost because you cannot wait for another person to save you. Be still and let God into your life to help guide you. The truth gives you strength, so be open to it, and it will foster love. You will discover you are loved more than you have ever known.

Blindsided

Holiday dinners growing up were always around a table filled with delicious food, always punctuated with loud chatter, and *almost* always resulted in some argument that ended with a slamming bedroom door. Things weren't perfect in my middle-class Catholic family, but there was a lot of love. My father worked for the government, and my mother had the hardest job ever, being a homemaker and taking care of four children. My parents were married for forty-eight years until my father suddenly passed away from an aortic aneurysm. My family has stayed very tight-knit, all living close to each other and supporting one another. My mom's weekly Sunday dinners, when my siblings and our kids come together, keep us updated on each other's separate lives.

After graduating from college, I chose the life of a police officer, always wanting an exciting, exhilarating, action-packed job. I was headstrong in my younger years and often wondered if I could conform to the mentality of the job. As a female officer, I worked harder than my male counterparts to get the same respect. Yet now, looking back over my twenty-seven years of service, I know there were many valuable lessons I've learned. I am stronger mentally and physically because of what I have seen and gone through in my professional life. Those same strengths are what I needed most in my personal life.

As a female cop, finding a solid guy to go out with was difficult. There would be casual dates and short relationships, but none of them were ever long-term prospects. Then, one afternoon in late 2001, I went on a blind date. A mutual friend introduced us, and five days later, we went rock climbing and rappelling. We had an awesome time! He was cute, and I loved his quirkiness; he was polite and a perfect gentleman. The date was supposed to be a couple of hours but turned into the entire day. A goodbye hug became a long, slow kiss. By the end of the evening, I definitely wanted to see him again.

And again. And again.

We spent twenty years together, and I truly believed I'd found my soulmate. We were perfect together, and I fell in love with this man who was hard-working, strong, and confident. But when I asked about his family, he said he was "the black sheep," and I often questioned in my mind if he was telling me the truth. When my 'cop senses' would tingle though, I would tell myself there was no reason for him to lie. Plus, we had two children together, and family was everything to me. Even though we never married, I was content in our relationship and believed we would grow old together.

We both decided for me to retire so that I could stay home with the children. At the beginning of retirement, I felt like the Kindergarten Cop; my children were off the hook and refused to listen to me. Every day was a battle; I felt overwhelmed and exhausted and needed a break. Self-care was never my priority before, always taking care of everyone else, but I needed to start watching out for my own well-being. My friend, Annemarie, who introduced me to essential oils, approached me to go on a fourteen-day retreat to Cape Verde, off the west coast of Africa, with a few other women. I love a good adventure, and since I had no obligations except to my family, I decided to go with their blessings. My mom took care of my kids, and their father agreed to help her.

On the trip, I bonded with incredibly strong women and had an absolutely wonderful time. We did journaling, meditations, yoga, massages, and used biomats. We experienced Reiki, reconnective healing, long hikes, and went to mystical places. We pushed ourselves mentally, spiritually, and physically, farther than ever before. We were immersed in the culture and traveled to multiple islands. I started to discover my true self — a whole other person from the police sergeant who had to keep her opinions to herself and was responsible for so many others. For the first time in forever, I put myself first and began truly learning about self-care.

When I came home, I was lighter and felt good about myself, but the rat race of ordinary life crept back in, and once again, I placed self-care on the back burner. Things were hectic for me again, and when my friend Annemarie approached me with a new mental wellness company that she had found that used natural products to help balance the gut microbiome, I thought she was crazy; I was fine and had no issues. Everyone has sinus headaches, everyone is allergic in Spring, everyone is stressed, queasy, and has digestive problems, right? I declined politely, but she was persistent (and I'm glad).

During that time, my daughter was not verbal about school and would have temper tantrums. At my wit's end, I finally decided to try these supplements for myself and my kids. I had no idea my gut's microbiome had a trillion bacteria; when my microbiome was off balance, my energy was low, I was moody, I was short-tempered, my allergies were in full force, I was bloated, had stomach issues, and I felt crummy. Within two weeks, I felt amazing, and my symptoms diminished. My daughter's tantrums became a thing of the past. Our conversations shifted from one-sided grunts to her opening up about being bullied. She told me she hated her school and wanted to attend a Catholic school. I couldn't believe my ears and was thrilled she felt moving schools was a glimmer of hope for her.

I was changing for the better, but my soul mate seemed to be going in the opposite direction. He claimed his health was declining; he was working more hours, and he was spending little to no time at home. When he did come home, the atmosphere in the house felt negative. Three years after my Cape Verde retreat, he told me he was unhappy and needed to move out for a short while. Believing it was due to his medical condition, I agreed and supported him. He would show up once a week to see the kids for thirty minutes but their birthdays came and went without a call from Daddy. He finally showed up after their birthdays with extravagant presents. By the end of summer, we rarely saw him or had any indication that he was supporting us. I loved him so much, and he was pushing us away. I wasn't sure what was going on, but I was going to find out.

I did everything I could to keep the house running smoothly and create stability for my children, who are my life. I was physically and mentally exhausted every night and would get up and continue the process again the next day. One morning, their father called us and promised our daughter he would make it to her soccer game. But he was a no-show. This was daddy's little girl, how could he let her down? It was so out of character for him. I prayed for his well-being and sent him our love, but it was like he had disappeared from the world. So many questions went through my head. Why didn't he call? Was he hurt? Was he in the hospital? Is he dead and I wasn't notified? My police instincts kicked in, and I called all the hospitals in the area, checking for him with no luck. To calm my doubts, I kept telling myself he was in the Special Forces and he could handle himself.

I needed answers. I used my investigative skills and found a direct phone number for his boss. I told him my name and asked if he knew where my significant other was. He responded that my common-law husband had never once mentioned my name in the fifteen years they had worked together. I told him we have a twelve-year-old daughter and a nine-year-old son together. The boss said he didn't know me and couldn't give me any information. But he did say, "I know he has a girlfriend named Jamie."

Those words rattled in my head as my body went numb from the shock. I could not believe what I had just heard, and as my stomach twisted from the sucker punch, all I could say was "WOW" as he hung up. I was blindsided and dumbfounded. My entire world began spinning and came crashing down on me. The last twenty years flashed by in a blink of an eye as the questions raced through my mind. *What did I do to cause this to happen? Was he on vacation with Jamie? Who was she?* I never thought he would cheat on me in a million years. *Am I too naive? Why couldn't I see this coming?*

That new information felt surreal, and I couldn't believe it. I stood in my living room, stunned, and all I could think of was, "Oh God, please help me!"

I took some natural supplements for my mood and left my house needing to walk the neighborhood to clear my head. Later that day, my sister-in-law came to my house and gave me a big long hug; we both cried as she embraced me. She understood what I was going through because she went through something similar before meeting my brother. That day we bonded more than we ever had before. God has a funny way of protecting us and giving us strength. He also gives us people to lean on. I was very grateful.

I picked up the kids from school, put on a happy face, and never mentioned anything to them. That evening after they fell asleep, I tossed and turned in bed and kept reliving the nightmare. Then, I had a revelation. I needed to find his family, whom he never wanted me to meet. I spent the rest of the night using my investigative skills to locate his parents and siblings on the internet through different search sites.

I had no idea who this man was or where he was. My first concern was keeping my kids safe. I changed the locks and checked the house for any bugs or cameras. I went to the courthouse to get temporary full custody of the children. I had been to the courthouse hundreds of times as a police officer but not as a plaintiff. I felt dirty, exposed, and like a victim, weak and embarrassed. I couldn't believe I had given so many others this advice, and now I was in their shoes. I'd never had to fill out civil court paperwork, and to find out there was a fee? Yikes! I never thought in a million years I would be afraid of the man I thought was my soulmate. I needed to find the truth of who he was.

I mustered the courage to call his family to see if they knew where he had gone. *Was I opening a can of worms? What type of people were they?* My hands were shaking uncontrollably, and I felt sick to my stomach. I stopped, took a couple of deep breaths, and started calling the numbers listed next to the names and addresses I found during my all-night research. I quickly received a call back from an unknown number. The woman's voice on the phone was raspy, as if she smoked a pack of cigarettes every day. It was his mother. He never spoke about her, and after talking to her, I knew why—she was totally off her rocker. I told her she had two grandchildren, and she didn't seem to care. I was surprised by her lack of interest and how dismissive she was.

Later in the evening, I received a call from his father, who painted a picture of a very unhappy divorce. He regretfully shared the things his son experienced in his mother's care were things no child should ever have to go through; abuse, abandonment, and neglect. What an eye-opener! This new information revealed why he had been lying to me for the last twenty years, why he compartmentalized his life, and why he made up a different identity.

Then, his father threw me for another loop. My significant other was currently married to his high school sweetheart and had been for the last thirty-six years!! They also had a son with his surname!

Early in our relationship, I wanted to know if he was ever married or had any kids, and he denied both. *How could he hide this from me for twenty years?* It was like being a house of cards, and everything was crumbling. He had a whole other family besides ours and was married! It was unbearable, and despite my shock, I found myself moving into an investigative mode. All the excuses and not marrying me made sense. The late nights, the weekend trips, and last-minute work out of town were adding up. The more I found out, the more questions I had.

I gained some clarity after speaking with his parents. I began to understand there was trauma and instability behind his choices. I couldn't be sure of much, but one thing was for sure: he was emotionally and spiritually damaged. Learning about his tumultuous childhood helped me find compassion, and I began to see his behavior from a different viewpoint. Despite the betrayal, I leaned on my faith and kept praying for his well-being as I wondered if I would hear from him again.

Two weeks later, I got a call from him. *Where was he?* I waited to see what kind of story he would make up to cover for his sabbatical with his girlfriend. His voice sounded raspy as he said he was in the hospital. But I didn't believe him, so I had him Facetime me. He was lying in a hospital bed, unshaven, looking like hell with a scar down the middle of his chest. He said he had emergency surgery for an aortic aneurysm... the same condition my father died from! I was like, *WTF*!

Sadly, I didn't feel sorry for him; I was pissed. *I actually thought he staged a makeshift injury to make me feel guilty.* He lied to me for twenty years; I wasn't willing to believe anything he said. He told me the last thing he remembered was getting off the phone with me, and he started having a medical emergency. I had so many emotions: I was mad, upset, and confused, yet happy to know he was alive.

He mentioned to me he only had a ten percent chance of living. He started crying like a baby, saying he messed up so badly and was sorry. I told him I had forgiven him already, and that the truth would set him free. I had made peace with his actions but wanted him to come clean; he didn't.

I truly believe because I was sending him love and prayers, he lived through the many operations he went through. He spent a couple of months in the hospital and rehab, yet throughout it all, he refused to tell me which hospital he was recovering in.

It has been one year since his boss's words first echoed in my mind. We have come a long way. As he healed physically, we found common ground and a new normal for the sake of our kids. I was determined to have them meet their grandfather, and we even took a trip to Disney World™. I believe God works in mysterious ways because, despite this tumultuous event, my kids and I are thriving. It has been my daughter's best academic year yet. The house is much calmer, especially after I used sage to clear the negativity. Of course, we have our ups and downs, but we are resilient, and there is still much healing occurring. I tell my kids every day how much I love them.

Forgiveness is easy; the hard part is the journey. It's easy for your soul to forgive but much more difficult for the body because things are said or done that trigger us and affect us physically. We need to own our triggers and work through them. If I had never started this forgiveness transformation, I would be in a very dark place, blaming myself. Instead, I am more into healing myself and my children so we can help others going through similar circumstances.

There is light at the end of the tunnel, but sometimes you need to change your thought process and see that rejection can be God's protection. I am a stronger person now and I'm helping my children move into their own forgiveness journey. Forgiveness, in many ways, has brought us all together. Forgiveness has given me the strength to move on and find my happiness.

There are reasons for everything, so don't be afraid. Be still, and soon you will find your path. It is said that when one door closes, another one opens. I can't wait to see what the future holds for my kids and me as we open new doors because new experiences are how we learn, grow, and become stronger. We are like onions; we have many layers to ourselves and our personalities. We must pull back all the layers to get to the root cause of why we are who we are. Then, we need to love and forgive ourselves to truly feel loved, even when someone else falls out of love with us. Discovering the freedom that comes from self-love and self-forgiveness will blindside you in the best way.

IGNITE ACTION STEPS

I have used all of these tools at different times to keep me on the path to being the best version of myself! See which steps you feel aligned with and follow your heart. I encourage you to stay open to different modalities of self-care and make sure to put the oxygen mask on yourself before taking care of others.

Add the following to your forgiveness journey

- **Praying to God,** meditation, affirmation cards, and tarot cards can help you navigate your day, week, and life.
- **Breathwork:** take a moment and think things through.
- **Physical Care:** Mental Wellness Diet, exercise, massage, salt healing, therapy, talking to others, and getting quality sleep.
- **Mental Care:** Crystals, Theta healing®, Reiki, tapping, journaling.
- **Mental Wellness Supplements:** to support gut microbiome to increase your serotonin and GABA levels, and help with hormones, energy, stress resilience, and focus.

Dianne Venit—United States of America
Mother, Certified Mental Wellness Coach, Amare Wellness Partner,
Police Sergeant, Photographer, Fitness Instructor, Survivor
myamareglobal.com/30375
f *DianneVenit* | 📷 *diannevenit* | **in** *Dianne Venit*

IGNITE
Forgiveness

Dear God,

Allow me to
FOCUS ON FORGIVENESS

so that I can create a
GOOD & GRATEFUL FUTURE.

- Amen

©

Diana Lockett